Achieving QTS

Primary ICT:
Knowledge, Understanding and Practice

Second edition

Jane Sharp
John Potter
Jonathan Allen
Avril Loveless

Learning Matters

First published in 2000 by Learning Matters Ltd.
Reprinted in 2001.
Second edition published in 2002.
Reprinted in 2002.
Reprinted in 2003.
Reprinted in 2004 (twice).
Reprinted in 2005.

British Library Cataloguing in Publication Data
A CIP record for this book is available from the British Library.

ISBN 1 903300 59 2

Cover design by Topics – The Creative Partnership
Cover photo reproduced by permission of Educational Solutions (sales@edsol.co.uk)
Text design by Code 5 Design Associates Ltd
Project management by Deer Park Productions
Typeset by PDQ Typesetting Ltd, Newcastle under Lyme
Printed and bound in Great Britain by Bell & Bain Ltd, Glasgow

Learning Matters Ltd
33 Southernhay East
Exeter EXI INX
Tel: 01392 215560
Email: info@learningmatters.co.uk
www.learningmatters.co.uk

CONTENTS

Acknowledgements

The following screen shots have been reproduced by kind permission of the publishers (please see pages 235–7 for contact details):

Black Cat: pages 54, 55, 60. 61, 64, 65 and 82;
Granada Learning: pages 38 and 47;
Logotron (Longman): pages 74 and 83;
Research Machines (RM): pages 75, 84 and 93.

Thanks to Alan Pritchard, University of Warwick, for making valuable and detailed comments on an earlier draft of the book, and to the 'Brighton 5' for lively discussions about the nature and purpose of education and the role of digital technologies in creating spaces for learning. Thanks also to Dot Capes and Pam Maunders at King Alfred's College for their patience, enthusiasm and counsel.

- **What does it mean to be educated in the information society?**
- **What does it mean to be a teacher in the information society?**

These are challenging questions to ask people undertaking primary teacher training and embarking on their careers as newly qualified teachers. They lead us to examine our values and beliefs about the purposes of education, the contexts in which people learn and the roles that teachers might play. They also highlight the effect which information and communications technology (ICT) has on the ways in which we might describe our society and culture, raising interesting questions about how these technologies might contribute to the processes of teaching and learning. Teachers need an understanding of the ways in which they can use ICT to support and enhance their teaching across the curriculum. They also need an understanding of how children develop an ICT capability which enables them to deal with information in a rapidly changing world. When asked, 'Why use ICT in schools?', many people offer responses such as, 'Well, it's out there, isn't it? ... Everything is dot com these days ... Any young kid can use technology ... We would be failing the children if we didn't equip them for the future.' Perceptions of ICT are often related to a sense of change and need to cope with the world beyond the classroom – there are fewer discussions about the ways in which ICT supports children as they engage with learning and teachers as they develop their professional practice in fast-changing contexts.

This book in the *Learning Matters QTS Series* has been written to support primary teacher trainees and newly qualified teachers who wish to develop their knowledge and understanding of the ways in which ICT supports teaching which enables children to develop confidence, capability and competence as learners in the information society. The requirements of teachers in England are clearly identified in the National Curriculum and the Standards required for Qualified Teacher Status. This book identifies clear links with these requirements, but also addresses the wider context in which ICT has an impact on teaching and learning.

The features of this book include:

- **links with the *Qualifying to Teach: Professional Standards for Qualified Teacher Status;***
- **links with information and communications technology in the National Curriculum for Children (DfEE/QCA 2000);**
- **links with the Scheme of Work for ICT at Key Stages I and 2 (QCA, rev. 2000);**
- **links with recent and relevant research;**
- **practical tasks providing a focus for further reading, observation, practice, evaluation and reflection;**
- **a clear focus on the core subjects;**
- **further reading and references;**
- **a glossary of terms.**

This introduction will discuss the key ideas behind ICT capability and the features of ICT which make a distinctive contribution to learning and teaching. The pupils' National Curriculum for ICT will be described and related to the QCA Scheme of Work for ICT in Key Stages 1 and 2. The Professional Standards for QTS will then be considered in the light of these requirements and planning scheme. The Standards require all teachers in all subjects and phases to use ICT appropriately and effectively in their work. Although it has a broader brief than a focus on ICT capability as described in the pupils' National Curriculum, it is important to consider this in some detail in order to develop an understanding of the conceptual framework which needs to underpin a teacher's professional capability with ICT.

What is ICT capability?

Developing ICT capability is a challenging and stimulating aspect of teaching. The word 'capability' implies an understanding of the purpose and fitness of a task; a confidence and competence to undertake an activity; an ability to evaluate and reflect upon the situation and be open to further developments. It extends far beyond familiarity and facility with techniques within ICT – such as clicking on the right buttons to use a word processor, spreadsheet or the Internet – and encompasses a critical engagement with the appropriate use of ICT. It implies an understanding, not only of the features of ICT which support an activity in teaching and learning, but also of the ways in which working practices and knowledge within a subject context can be changed or developed. It encompasses a conceptual understanding of the ways in which information is organised, accessed, presented and communicated with these technologies.

When thinking about ICT capability, it is a useful exercise to imagine the children in a classroom in which you have observed or worked. Picture them using ICT – in the classroom; in the school; at home; with their peers; in their leisure and entertainment; in their interactions with the world outside. Think about the ways in which they might use digital technologies as they develop in the next five, ten, fifteen and twenty years.

How would you like to imagine them using the technology to express their ideas and opinions; to appreciate and understand the connections between themselves and the rest of the world; to celebrate their individuality and the individuality of others? How might they use ICT to be curious and to look at things from alternative perspectives? How might ICT play a role in helping them to become confident and self-motivated; to be inspired to work with spirit and imagination; to make decisions which might be collaborative and difficult? How do you envisage children being able to use digital technologies to provide opportunities for interactions between people, ideas, space and time? How might the use of ICT encourage risk-taking and explorations? How might our notions of literacy be extended by the ways of 'reading' and 'writing' we develop with ICT? What are your images of the times and places where children learn? What are your images of the roles that teachers play in learning as children develop ICT capability? If we consider ICT capability in the context of our values and beliefs about the purposes and practice of education, we can see that the technology is not a neutral collection of equipment and connections, but part of a complex interaction between people.

The National Curriculum for ICT states this broad view of capability for children in the wider context of their learning:

> ICT prepares pupils to participate in a rapidly changing world in which work and other activities are increasingly transformed by access to varied and developing technology. Pupils use ICT to find, explore, analyse, exchange and present information responsibly, creatively and with discrimination. They learn how to employ ICT to enable rapid access to ideas and experiences from a wide range of people, communities and cultures. Increased capability in the use of ICT promotes initiative and independent learning, with pupils being able to make informed judgements about when and where to use ICT to best effect and to consider its implications for home and work, both now and in the future.
>
> (DfEE/QCA, 2000, p. 96)

Enabling children to develop ICT capability is far more challenging than teaching a series of techniques in applications which will soon be redundant in a fast-changing context. We can use ICT not only as passive consumers and collectors of information, but also as people who are collaborative, creative and able to make critical choices. The ways in which we approach ICT capability can be a reflection of our own values and beliefs about what it means to learn and to teach in an information society.

What contribution does ICT make to learning and teaching?

As well as approaching the development of children's ICT capability, primary teachers also need to have knowledge, skills and understanding of the ways in which ICT supports their professional practice and be able to make informed decisions about when, and when not, to use ICT effectively in their teaching. Such effective use can range from researching information for planning and developing presentations and curriculum materials to incorporating ICT into a range of teaching strategies to meet pupils' needs and extend their learning experiences.

The Handbook of Guidance on QTS Standards for teacher training in England identifies Standards required in the use of ICT in subject teaching for the award of QTS. They provide a clear statement of the range of confidence and expertise expected of teachers in using ICT to improve the quality and standard of children's education. It is useful at this point to highlight the features of ICT which can make a distinctive contribution to teaching and learning. What makes ICT motivating to use in a variety of contexts? What are the characteristics which can be exploited in order to make a contribution as a resource, as a tool and as a catalyst for new ways of working in the curriculum? Which roles might teachers need to consider as they prepare and present learning experiences with ICT?

Interactivity can engage users at a number of levels, from the playing of a game in a child's bedroom to the monitoring of a space probe from Eutelsat. These two different activities have in common the ways in which ICT can give immediate and dynamic feedback and response to decisions and actions made by the user. Children could play an adventure game, undertake a search of the World Wide Web, display a graph of the changes detected by temperature sensors over a period of time, or create and navigate a multimedia presentation. Using ICT in each of these activities enables children to make decisions, see the consequences and act upon the feedback accordingly. Having curiosity and confidence to engage in such interactions might not be easy or comfortable for some children (or teachers!). Encouraging children to explore, to learn from dead ends and frustrations and develop perseverance in trying out ideas and learning from feedback is an important aspect of the teacher's interaction in these processes.

The **provisionality** of ICT enables users to make changes, try out alternatives and keep a 'trace' of the development of ideas. This feature can be recognised immediately in the writing of text with a word processor which enables the writer to make changes at a number of levels, while early versions can be saved for comparison or returned to for further development. Visual images can be modified and manipulated from the initial image created or captured on the screen and saved along the way as ideas change and develop. As with interactivity, teachers can promote positive attitudes to working with and exploiting the provisionality of ICT. They can model, discuss and make explicit the processes of evaluation, changing ideas and reviewing work.

ICT demonstrates **capacity and range** in the ways in which teachers and children can gain access to vast amounts of information in the form of text, visual images and sound. This information might be accessed on a CD ROM available in the classroom, on a website located on the other side of the world or by discussion with people living and working in a different time zone and geographical place. Gaining access to such a range of information does not, however, ensure that understanding of the authority and authenticity accompanies it and teachers play an important role in supporting children's critical approach to searching for and evaluating information.

The **speed and automatic functions** of ICT allow tasks of storing, changing and displaying information to be carried out by the technology, enabling users to read, observe, interrogate, interpret, analyse and synthesise information at higher levels. Many routine activities such as capturing and organising data, monitoring change, carrying out calculations, drawing graphs and presenting findings can be done using ICT, leaving the children time to ask questions and think about the meaning of the information with which they are presented.

As well as considering the ways in which these features support children's learning and a range of teaching strategies, teachers can also use ICT to improve their own professional efficiency in administrative tasks and maintaining links with their professional networks and resources for their subject and phase. Teachers who use ICT purposefully in a wide range of their work are more likely to be more confident and competent in developing the use of ICT in their teaching with children.

The National Curriculum for Information and Communications Technology

The National Curriculum for England identifies the 'programmes of study' and 'attainment targets' from which schools can develop their planning and organisation of the curriculum. The programmes of study identify the matters, skills and processes of a curriculum subject which children should be taught. The attainment targets describe the expected standards of children's performance and progression within the subject throughout the key stages.

The framework for the knowledge, skills and understanding in the ICT curriculum is presented in four aspects:

- **finding things out;**
- **developing ideas and making things happen;**
- **exchanging and sharing information;**
- **reviewing, modifying and evaluating work as it progresses.**

These aspects reflect the ways in which people work with ICT for particular purposes. They focus on the reasons for using ICT, not on a list of specific applications, software or resources. The knowledge, skills and understanding encompassed in these four aspects are taught in a broader context, or breadth of study, of working with a range of information, exploring a variety of ICT tools, working with others and investigating and comparing the different uses of ICT inside and outside school. It can be useful to think of these aspects as 'strands' which are distinctive, but can weave around each other in building ICT capability. It is worth considering this framework in some detail as it describes the basis of capability for both children and teachers (see table overleaf).

The attainment targets indicate the progression that children can make, from being aware of and able to describe the ways in which they can work with ICT, to an understanding of purpose, audience and the need for accuracy and validity in dealing with information. In Key Stage I the range of levels within which the great majority of children are expected to work is between Levels I and 3, with the majority attaining Level 2 at the end of the Key Stage. In Key Stage 2 the range of levels for the great majority of children is Levels 2 to 5, with the majority attaining Level 4 at age II.

Within and beyond the curriculum

ICT capability is not knowledge, skills and understanding in a specific subject domain; it supports learning across the curriculum — in other subject areas and in cross-curricular aspects of children's learning experiences. It can be seen as a catalyst for teamwork in a school in which teachers with a variety of subject specialisms are able to work together to identify the ways in which ICT can support the whole curriculum framework. It provides opportunities to promote spiritual, moral, social and cultural development. Key skills can be developed through the use of ICT, including communications, application of number, working with others, improving one's own learning and performance and problem-solving. It can also promote thinking skills, enterprise

Knowledge, skills and understanding	Key Stage 1 Pupils should be taught:	Key Stage 2 Pupils should be taught:
Finding things out	• How to gather information from a variety of sources. • How to enter and store information in a variety of forms. • How to retrieve information that has been stored.	• To talk about what information they need and how they can find and use it. • How to prepare information for development using ICT, including selecting suitable sources, finding information, classifying it and checking it for accuracy.
Developing ideas and making things happen	• To use text, tables, images and sound to develop their ideas. • How to select from and add to information they have retrieved for particular purposes. • To try things out and explore what happens in real and imaginary situations.	• How to develop and refine ideas by bringing together, organising and reorganising text, tables, images and sound as appropriate. • How to create, test, improve and refine sequences of instructions to make things happen and to monitor events and respond to them. • To use simulations and explore models in order to anwer 'What would happen if...?' questions, to investigate and evaluate the effect of changing values and to identify patterns and relationships.
Exchanging and sharing information	• How to share their ideas by presenting information in a variety of forms. • To present their completed work effectively.	• How to share and exchange information in a variety of forms, including email. • To be sensitive to the needs of the audience and think carefully about the content and quality when communicating information.
Reviewing, modifying and evaluating work as it progresses	• To review what they have done to help them develop their ideas. • To describe the effects of their actions. • To talk about what they might change in future work.	• To review what they and others have done to help them develop their ideas. • To describe and talk about the effectiveness of their work with ICT, comparing it with other methods and considering the effect it has on others. • To talk about how they could improve further work.
Breadth of study	• Working with a range of information to investigate the different ways it can be presented. • Exploring a variety of ICT tools. • Talking about the uses of ICT inside and outside school.	• Working with a range of information to consider its characteristics and purposes. • Working with others to explore a variety of information sources and ICT tools. • Investigating and comparing the uses of ICT inside and outside school.

Programme of Study: ICT National Curriculum

and entrepreneurial skills, work-related learning and education for sustainable development.

As in all areas of the curriculum, there are general teaching requirements for ICT. Three principles for **inclusion** to provide effective learning opportunities for all children should be incorporated in all teachers' planning, implementation, assessment and evaluation:

- **setting suitable learning challenges;**
- **responding to children's diverse learning needs;**
- **overcoming potential barriers to learning and assessment for individuals and groups of children.**

ICT has the potential to provide empowerment or limitations to learners. It can empower children with a wide range of learning needs through its adaptability and interactivity. Indeed, it could be argued that ICT has made most impact in schooling in the area of Special Educational Needs where software, hardware and peripherals can be designed to bypass a number of physical and cognitive learning difficulties and provide access to information and expression in new ways. It can, however, limit children's experiences and expectations of themselves as autonomous users of ICT if it perpetuates a restricted and dominant image of gender, language, culture and socio-economic class.

The QCA Scheme of Work for Key Stages 1 and 2

In order to plan, prepare and provide experiences which are relevant, challenging and enable children to develop their ICT capability, teachers need to consider the interaction between the NC Programmes of Study and the levels of the Attainment Target. The ICT Scheme of Work, published by the Department for Education and Employment (DfEE) and the Qualifications and Curriculum Authority (QCA), provides a useful, optional exemplar of a practical planning framework which offers opportunities to:

- **develop ICT capability in an organised, systematic and rigorous way which ensures progression;**
- **develop ICT processes, skills and techniques;**
- **develop ability to apply ICT capability to support language, communication and learning in other areas;**
- **explore perceptions, attitudes and values in relation to ICT in the wider society;**
- **build on children's previous and wider experiences of ICT;**
- **identify learning intentions and approaches to assessment within planned activities.**

The scheme provides a sequence of units, or activities, which can be used through Key Stages 1 and 2, providing a degree of flexibility and coherent progression linked to the programmes of study and the attainment levels. The units can be incorporated into the school's whole curriculum framework and the activities related closely to work in other subject areas and planned activities in the school. Although the Scheme of Work is an exemplar for medium- to long-term planning as it is addressed within a whole school, the principles of the scheme, the structure of the units and the sequencing for progression are also very helpful in developing short-term lesson or activity plans.

Each unit identifies:

- **the key ideas underpinning the activity and the links to programmes of study;**
- **where the unit fits with the knowledge and skills that the children need;**
- **technical vocabulary which may be needed;**
- **resources;**
- **expectations of the children by the end of the unit;**
- **learning objectives in terms of key ideas and techniques;**
- **suggested teaching activities, including setting the scene, short focused tasks and an integrated task;**
- **learning outcomes in terms of the children's understanding and actions;**
- **points to note relating the activity or possible misconceptions which might arise.**

A summary of the units, which indicates the progression in activities and expectations, is presented below:

Key stage 1	
Year 1 units	**Year 2 units**
1A An introduction to modelling 1B Using a word bank 1C The information around us 1D Labelling and classifying 1E Representing information graphically: pictograms 1F Understanding instructions and making things happen	2A Writing stories: communicating information using text 2B Creating pictures 2C Finding information 2D Routes: controlling a floor turtle 2E Questions and answers
Key stage 2	
Year 3 units	**Year 4 units**
3A Combining text and graphics 3B Manipulating sound 3C Introduction to databases 3D Exploring simulations 3E Email	4A Writing for different audiences 4B Developing images using repeating patterns 4C Branching databases 4D Collecting and presenting information: questionnaires and pie charts 4E Modelling effects on screen
Year 5 units	**Year 6 units**
5A Graphical modelling 5B Analysing data and asking questions: using complex searches 5C Evaluating information, checking accuracy and questioning plausibility 5D Introduction to spreadsheets 5E Controlling devices 5F Monitoring environmental conditions and changes	6A Multimedia presentation 6B Spreadsheet modelling 6C Control and modelling – What happens when…? 6D Using the internet to search large databases and to interpret information

ICT Scheme of Work: DfEE and QCA

Qualifying to teach: Professional Standards for QTS

How do the requirements and guidance for meeting the Professional Standards for QTS play a role in the development of teachers using ICT to promote children's learning across the curriculum? The expectations of the Standards for the award of QTS are identified in the DfES documents *Qualifying to Teach: Professional Standards for QTS* and the *Handbook of Guidance*. These present a view of ICT capability for teachers which encompasses not only a grounding in a personal capability appropriate to the profession but also an ability to use ICT in teaching children in the classroom.

Trainee primary teachers need to demonstrate that they have achieved the required standards for the use of ICT in their teaching through:

- **knowledge and understanding of ICT in the curriculum for the pupils in the age range in which they are trained;**
- **knowledge of how to use ICT effectively, both to teach and to support their wider professional role;**
- **teaching of the required knowledge, understanding and skills relevant to the ICT curriculum for pupils in the age range in which they are trained;**
- **effective and discriminating use of ICT in their teaching.**

The approach to ICT which underpins this book is grounded in a view of capability which supports learning in an information society where new technologies have an impact on all areas of the school's curriculum – from core subjects to citizenship; from PE to parents' evenings; from DT to the digital divide. It challenges teachers to consider how ICT can be used to support or extend a range of teaching strategies that enable children to learn and teachers to develop their practice. ICT capability – for children and teachers – is built up over time from experience, reflection and review. It is not the kind of knowledge that can be quickly 'transmitted' or 'delivered', but is developed through an open attitude to practical exploration, asking questions and sharing ideas with others, from technique tips to concepts and contexts for use. Trainees and new teachers need to seize opportunities to develop this capability through personal study, working with others, planning classroom experiences and developing networks of professional support. This will provide a strong model for the children as they develop in confident, informed and critical ways.

Further reading

Statutory and exemplary documentation

DfEE/QCA (1999) *The National Curriculum: Handbook for Primary Teachers in England*, DfEE/QCA.

QCA (1998, rev. 2000) *Information and Communications Technology: a Scheme of Work for Key Stages 1 and 2*, DfEE/QCA.

TTA/DfES (2002) *Qualifying to Teach: Professional Standards for Qualified Teacher Status and Requirements for Initial Teacher Training*, TTA.

TTA/DfES (2002b) *Guidance on the Standards for Qualified Teacher Status*, TTA

Websites

Professional Standards for QTS
http://www.canteach.gov.uk/community/itt/requirements/

National Curriculum
http://www.nc.uk.net

Scheme of Work
http://www.qca.org.uk
http://www.standards.dfee.gov.uk/schemes

Generic software is software which is considered to be content-free and consequently has a wide range of applications across the primary curriculum. This section explores key categories of generic software in some detail.

Each chapter includes:

- **a brief introduction and definition;**
- **reference to relevant sections of the National Curriculum for ICT;**
- **reference to related units of the Scheme of Work for ICT;**
- **background information as appropriate;**
- **examples of the ways in which teachers may interact with the software;**
- **details of the specific functions of the software with which teachers should be familiar;**
- **discussion of the distinguishing features of the software;**
- **examination of the contribution the software can make to teaching and learning;**
- **exploration of the capabilities and limitations of the software and associated issues;**
- **examples of ways in which the software can be utilised in the teaching and learning of each of the core subjects;**
- **further references and reading.**

The generic areas of software covered are:

- **word processing and desktop publishing;**
- **graphics software;**
- **graphing programs;**
- **databases, including spreadsheets;**
- **the Internet.**

The Internet is not in itself a generic software application, though use of its many facets requires a variety of generic software, browsers, email packages and web authoring programs. The potential of the Internet in the context of teaching and learning is so wide ranging that for the purposes of this book it is being considered as generic in nature.

It has not been possible to explore all the areas of generic software applicable to the primary classroom. Emphasis has been placed on those which are most widely used, have the greatest potential and are not explored in detail in other publications.

Professional Standards for QTS

The chapters in this section of the book on generic software and the Internet will inform your development towards meeting the ICT specific aspects of the Professional Standards for QTS.

You can find the relevant references in *Qualifying to Teach* (TTA/DfES, 2002) as follows:

For your personal and professional use of ICT, para. 2.5 says that those awarded QTS must demonstrate that they know how to use ICT effectively, both to teach their subject and to support their wider professional role. This ranges from using templates for lesson planning, through researching subject knowledge on the Internet, to contributing to online communities of teachers, such as the SENCO forum.

For ICT as a National Curriculum subject and the development of children's knowledge, skills and understanding across the primary school, para. 2.1b says that those awarded QTS must demonstrate that they have sufficient understanding of a range of work in ICT to be able to teach in the age range for which they are trained, with advice from an experienced colleague where necessary. Issues such as continuity and progression, assessment and common errors and misconceptions are particularly relevant.

For your utilisation of ICT in teaching and learning across the primary curriculum, para. 3.3.10 says that those awarded QTS must demonstrate that they use ICT effectively in their teaching. This includes knowing when and when not to use ICT.

Word processing is the medium through which we most often communicate information using ICT. It is also considered to be the most common use of ICT globally, and more specifically in our schools. Developments in technology and the ways in which we communicate are blurring the distinctions between word processing, desktop publishing and even multimedia, to the extent that many word processors now facilitate communication not only through text, but via the integration of images and sound.

This chapter explores the features and functions of this software and their contribution to teaching and learning in the primary school. The principal focus is the parameters of current word processing software. Exploration of the desktop publishing features now subsumed into most such programs is integrated throughout. Teachers' professional use of word processing software is considered in the context of administration and management as well as teaching and learning.

What is word processing?

Word processing software allows the entry, storage, retrieval and manipulation of text, and increasingly graphics and sound, in an electronic format. It facilitates a variety of processes which can support and enhance communication.

What is desktop publishing?

Desktop publishing (DTP) software is concerned with the design of documents containing text and graphics, usually for presentation purposes such as publication. Until recently the exclusive domain of graphics experts, DTP software provides access to sophisticated design and layout options. In recent years the accessibility of such software, in terms of both cost and user-interface (previously you needed a great deal of software-specific training to utilise the software effectively), has increased significantly. Similarly, the overlap between word processing and desktop publishing grows, as each application is enhanced to facilitate more of the features previously associated with the other.

What do the programmes of study for Key Stages 1 and 2 include?

At Key Stage 1 children should be taught to enter and store information (1b), to use text, tables, images and sounds to develop their ideas (2a) and to select from and add to existing information (2b). They should also be taught to share their ideas by presenting information in a variety of forms (3a) and to present their work effectively (3b).

At Key Stage 2, children should be taught how to prepare information (1b), how to organise and reorganise it (2a), how to share and exchange it (3a), as well as consider its suitability for its audience and its quality (3b).

At all stages children should be taught to review, modify and evaluate their work as it progresses (4a, 4b and 4c).

What does the ICT Scheme of Work include?

At Key Stage 1 word processing features in Unit 1A (An introduction to modelling), Unit 1B (Using a word bank), Unit 1D (Labelling and classifying) and Unit 2A (Writing stories: communicating information using text).

At Key Stage 2 word processing features specifically in Unit 3A (Combining text and graphics) and Unit 4A (Writing for different audiences). Unit 3E (Email) provides opportunities to transfer and apply relevant learning.

What do teachers need to know about word processing?

Teachers apply their knowledge, skills and understanding of word processing in two discrete ways. One is concerned with teaching and learning with and about word processing and the other relates to the use of word processing to support more general aspects of the professional role.

Teachers need to be competent and confident users of primary word processing software in order to facilitate children's learning. This does not mean that they need to know the answer to every and any particular question, rather they should have a working knowledge of the software such as to be able to plan, support and assess appropriate activities as well as predict likely difficulties and assist with problem-solving. Teachers also need to be competent and confident users of word processing software in order to utilise it efficiently and effectively to facilitate a range of profes-sional functions.

Effective use of word processing involves teachers:

- *Preparing resources* – **such as an electronic writing frame to support writing in history, a word bank to support an individual child or a trouble-shooting help sheet or interactive display to improve children's independence when using the spell-checker. Alternatively teachers may use ICT to prepare resources for activities which do not involve children utilising ICT, such as a shared text printed on acetate for use with an OHP, a range of three differentiated worksheets or number lotto cards to support a group mathematics activity. Some of these examples focus on using ICT as a tool for teaching and learning (in another curriculum area), others focus on the teaching and learning of ICT.**

- *Selecting appropriate opportunities* – in which word processing software can facilitate, enhance or extend children's learning, such as the importance of presentation in communication. In some instances the focus will be on teaching and learning in ICT (how to enlarge text, make newspaper-type columns or add a border to a poster); in others ICT will be used as a resource in the teaching and learning of another curriculum area (writing for a specific audience).
- *Making explicit links between related knowledge, skills and understanding* – word processing is closely associated with literacy and language work at all levels, and as a consequence has a contribution to make across the range of the primary curriculum.
- *Modelling appropriate use of ICT* – for instance, scribing and amending shared writing with the whole class or a group or preparing well-presented (paper) worksheets. In such an instance the primary learning outcome may not be ICT-related.
- *Demonstrating or intervening* – for example, inserting an image into a word processing document, cutting and pasting, or how and when to use the spell-checker. Explicit teaching of word processing knowledge, skills and understanding requires demonstration and intervention as with any other curriculum area. Such demonstrations and interventions may involve the whole class, groups or individuals and learning outcomes may or may not be ICT-related.
- *Administering and managing* – for example, correspondence with parents, amending schemes of work or school policies, using templates to prepare weekly planning, recording children's progress and producing banners for display boards.

The list below attempts to identify the knowledge, skills and understanding of primary word processing software teachers need in order to teach effectively with and about word processing:

- creating, opening, saving, closing, deleting and printing documents;
- selecting font, font size, colour, style (italic, bold), line spacing and justification;
- inserting, deleting, selecting, cutting, copying, pasting and undoing;
- utilising help;
- inserting bullet points, tables, clip art, borders, shading and columns;
- altering page orientation (landscape, portrait), background colour, page size and margins;
- altering defaults;
- forcing page breaks;
- utilising tabs and indents;
- utilising spelling- and grammar-checkers (including how to switch on and off), thesaurus, print preview, highlighter and talking facilities (including how to switch on and off) and find and replace;
- connecting alternative input devices (overlay keyboards, touch screens);
- constructing and utilising on-screen word banks;
- inserting page numbers;
- inserting text, graphics, tables and documents from other applications.

The list below details additional knowledge, skills and understanding that teachers need in order to utilise word processing efficiently and effectively to support themselves as professionals (it should be read in conjunction with the list above):

- **inserting symbols, headers and footers;**
- **creating macros and templates;**
- **utilising dynamic links between documents;**
- **customising the word processor;**
- **merging documents;**
- **formatting graphics;**
- **protecting documents.**

Teachers often utilise standard software to support themselves in their professional role as it tends to offer a wider range of functions, although in many schools primary word processors are used effectively to this end. Knowledge, skills and understanding are easily transferable between primary and standard word processing software, as they are between different packages within these categories.

What are the key features of a word processor?

Word processing software is becoming ever more sophisticated in the range of features offered. It is also becoming progressively more user-friendly, or transparent, in the ways in which it works. As with any application it is important to have an understanding of the capabilities and limitations of the software in order to use it effectively. This is not to say that it is essential or even preferable to be familiar with all the possible functions of the software in order to use it effectively. It is generally accepted that most users of the world's most common word processor, Microsoft Word, utilise as little as 10% of its functionality while still using it as an effective and efficient aid to communication.

Word processors, like any generic category of software, are defined by their common features. These features could be listed, though some word processors are more sophisticated than others, offering a wider range of functions. In others the range of possibilities is deliberately restricted. This may be because the software is designed to be used by young children, not likely to wish to insert footnotes or track the modification of a document over time, or it may be for a hand-held portable computer (palm top) where functionality has to be balanced by available memory.

Each year brings new versions of many standard and primary word processing packages, modifying, usually extending, the range of features available. In general terms, however, the key features of word processing software can be categorised as follows:

- **Editing. Editing features allow the entry and manipulation of text or images, such as insertion and deletion at any point in the document, cutting, copying and pasting to reorder and reorganise.**

- **Formatting.** Formatting features allow the utilisation of a range of fonts, text sizes, text styles (emboldening, etc.), page size, page orientation (landscape, portrait), tables, boxes and other graphics capabilities.
- **Tools.** There are a range of tools which complement and enhance the editing and formatting features of word processors. These include spelling and grammar checkers, talking capability, templates and word counting.

Many word processors now have quite sophisticated desktop publishing and even multimedia authoring and/or web authoring features; for example, Textease (Softease) and Word (Microsoft). Such packages enable children and their teachers to develop and extend their ICT capabilities without the learning of new software for specific tasks, instead building on and enhancing their existing knowledge, skills and understanding.

What do word processors have to contribute to teaching and learning?

Children using word processors can utilise the features of the software in two key respects:

- **to develop their ideas and make things happen (to modify their work, try things out, compare alternatives, etc.);**
- **to exchange and share information (to edit and review, as well as design and present their work).**

Likewise teachers can use word processors to prepare and modify teaching resources, to model effective use of ICT, to demonstrate techniques as well as to facilitate some of the administrative aspects of their work.

Word processing and the writing process

The most obvious context through which to explore the contribution word processing can make to teaching and learning is writing. If the writing process is viewed as a number of elements contributing to the whole it is possible to examine the potential contribution word processors can make to each of these aspects.

The elements of the writing process can be thought of as:

- **Composing: the ideas, the facts, the emotions being communicated through the writing.**
- **Editing: the editing or drafting element of writing can be further broken down into:**
  - **the structural aspects of writing, such as sequencing and style (in National Literacy Strategy terms, text level work);**
  - **the technical or secretarial aspects: sentence construction, punctuation, grammar, spelling (word and sentence level work).**
- **Presenting: the presentation of the writing, focusing on the layout and look of the writing.**

When children (and adults) write by hand each of these elements must be addressed simultaneously. While this in itself is a valuable life skill, writers may be unnecessarily constricted by these demands.

Word processing's contribution

COMPOSING (DEVELOPING IDEAS AND MAKING THINGS HAPPEN)

Research suggests that children tend to write sentence by sentence with little overview of the text as a whole, rarely rereading previous sentences to check the progress of the narrative. Indeed many children find difficulty retaining the thread of their thoughts while they also grapple with the physical aspects of writing, be they handwriting or keyboard entry. For some the challenge of rereading their writing may prove a further distraction. Many of the word processors available for primary children now incorporate a talking facility; for example, Talking First Word (RM), Textease (Softease), Talking Write Away (BlackCat). This can be set to read each sentence as it is completed (the full stop is placed) or to reread the entire narrative as required (by clicking). The talking facility may therefore enable children to focus on the progress of their writing as a continuous whole, rather than as a series of disjointed statements.

A range of text input strategies may be utilised in association with word processing software to enable children's speed of writing to better match their thought processes. These include overlay keyboards, word banks, possibly soon even voice recognition. Clearly keyboard skills, particularly speed relative to handwriting, are also relevant. It is suggested that children engage in the writing process for longer when ICT is involved, thus producing longer and perhaps more sophisticated narratives.

The use of writing templates (electronic writing frames), an extension of the widely used non-fiction writing strategy, may assist children to produce writing which better matches the anticipated outcomes of a writing task.

EDITING (STRUCTURAL) (DEVELOPING IDEAS AND MAKING THINGS HAPPEN)

Once text has been entered into a word processor there is clearly much scope for revision and development to enhance the quality of the writing. Since making alterations will require thought and some manipulative skill, but not a lengthy rewrite by hand, children can experiment with a view to improvement. Text can be re-sequenced, rephrased, extended and enriched. Meaning can be clarified. Attention can be paid to style, structure, genre, audience and purpose. Alternatives can be explored and compared, changes can be reversed. The act of writing becomes a process rather than an end point, a temporal dimension is introduced, with the opportunity for reflection, even research to influence subsequent amendments. Print-outs can be a useful record of the stages of the process and can provide a teaching and learning opportunity in themselves. It is suggested that a text thus revised may far better reflect the writer's intentions, than an unamended first draft. There is some evidence to suggest that children consciously write more when the prospect of subsequent redrafting is not associated with the physical effort of copying out by hand.

Research also indicates that children do not automatically use the editing possibilities afforded by word processors to improve the quality of their writing in this way – they are easily distracted by the technical editing opportunities. Rather such outcomes depend on focused and explicit teaching and task-setting.

EDITING (TECHNICAL) (DEVELOPING IDEAS AND MAKING THINGS HAPPEN)

Perhaps the most obvious contribution that word processing can make to the writing process is the opportunity for children to focus in the initial stages of a writing activity (composing) on communicating ideas, safe in the knowledge that attention can be paid to grammar, spelling and punctuation (as well as structure and style) at a later stage. Word processors now incorporate functions to address each of these issues, but the built-in tools do not even have to be utilised for children to review and amend these aspects of their word processed work. Frequently a range of such secretarial adjustments can result merely from rereading the text on screen or a print-out, again safe in the knowledge that changes will not result in lengthy rewriting or untidy work. Often this rereading and the selection of items for amendment can be done away from the computer on print-outs. This serves to maximise effective use of computer resources, but equally importantly, it is widely acknowledged that it can be far easier to see typos on paper than on screen. If word processors are to provide the opportunity for children to write like adults and/or *real* writers, drafting and redrafting work, then children need access to the range of facilities word processing has to offer. This includes printing out and using drafts of writing in progress, rather than only printing when writing is judged to be finished. Pedagogic considerations should not be sacrificed to financial constraints.

PRESENTING (EXCHANGING AND SHARING INFORMATION)

Here the opportunities are almost endless and the overlap into what was formerly the province of DTP software most pronounced. Children can adjust the font and size of their text to best fit the space available, the genre of the work, the intended method of presentation (display on the wall, for instance) and/or the audience. Colour can be added, as can borders, backgrounds and bullet points. Text can be arranged in columns to replicate newspaper or magazine layout. One of the most significant developments in word processing software is the facility to incorporate images, be they clip art, children's compositions composed in drawing and painting software, digital photographs or images scanned or copied and pasted from other locations such as the World Wide Web or CD ROMs (subject to copyright). In this age of changing and evolving literacies, where children are constantly surrounded by presentation of the highest quality, it is important that they too have access to these means through which to communicate their ideas. Teachers will also need to take advantage of presentation features to provide good models as well as visually engaging resources. Care must, however, be taken to ensure that children are aware of the value that teachers place on the content of writing relative to its presentation. While good presentation can significantly enhance communication, it is usually not the primary learning outcome of a writing activity.

There is evidence that for some children being able to word process their writing, at least some of the time, makes a substantial contribution to the development of self-esteem and confidence in their own abilities, a key determinant in children's progress.

As previously discussed, the physical effort of handwriting may be at times an active deterrent. For some children the struggle to produce tidy or even legible work may seem insurmountable. Access to a word processor may allow such children to produce writing which they feel can stand alongside that of their peers. They may also be enabled to communicate what they really want to say, but may not currently be able to commit effectively to paper by hand. Small, portable, relatively inexpensive dedicated word processors have been used successfully to support individual children in this way, often with wider social aims and gains in terms of reductions in attention-seeking behaviour and/or reliance on high levels of individual attention, and improved socialisation.

Progression of knowledge, skills and understanding

By its very nature ICT is constantly evolving and reinventing itself – and the same is true of word processing. Functions which ten years ago required a detailed knowledge of software and the recall of an extensive range of keyboard commands can now be effected by the click of an icon, while many functions have only recently become available. In this context there are obvious difficulties associated with attempting to identify skills development, and particularly with attempting to link these to levels of attainment or year groups.

With this proviso in mind, the following progression broadly corresponds with the ICT Scheme of Work and may provide a useful starting point.

Reception Year 1	Children begin to enter text and graphics via keyboard, overlay keyboard and on-screen word bank.
Year 2 Year 3	Children begin to edit text using the mouse, delete or backspace keys; to use the shift key; to alter font, font size and colour; to re-size graphics.
Year 4	Children begin to edit text using cut, copy and paste; to use underlining, bold and italicising; to use search and replace; to use spell-checkers; to import text and graphics from other documents; to use tables.
Year 5 Year 6	Children begin to select and utilise the full range of features as appropriate to their requirements independently; to independently utilise on-screen help and other problem-solving strategies.

A possible progression of word processing and desk top publishing skills.

Helen Smith (1999) identifies some specific and particular knowledge young children need in order to use word processors. Some of this knowledge is quite different from that needed to write by hand, for instance:

- *that a space must be entered after each word, but not before punctuation marks such as full stops and commas;*
- *that the shift key provides access to capital letters and some punctuation;*
- *that the backspace can be used to correct errors;*
- *that text wraps around automatically onto the next line and that line breaks can be forced using the enter/ return key.*

She also details knowledge necessary for the basic editing of word-processed work:

- *that the mouse is used to position the cursor (caret) and the importance of this;*
- *that arrow keys, page up, home, etc. can be used to move around the text;*
- *the use of strip highlighting for copying and pasting, cutting, etc.*

To this should perhaps be added:

- *the value of the undo function.*

What are the capabilities and limitations of word processing?

Text entry

Currently almost all text entry into word processing (and other) software is effected by use of the standard QWERTY keyboard. Alternatives and/or supplements such as overlay keyboards, touch screens, adult scribes and word banks can be deployed to support children entering text.

Despite the increasing use of ICT in primary schools, very little attention has been paid to the development of **keyboard skills** amongst children. As we enter the twenty-first century, computer keyboards feature large in our lives. It is likely that this will be the case for some time to come, until they are overtaken by voice recognition or some as yet unknown alternative.

Developing keyboard skills which facilitate text entry and other aspects of ICT use would seem to be a worthwhile investment for the future. Teachers have expressed concern over the inefficiency of 'hunt and peck' typing and, particularly in the early stages of keyboard use, the relative time required to enter text. It has been argued that children need to learn keyboard familiarity early on in their computer use, otherwise typing will take more time and concentration than the handwriting of the equivalent text, rendering the activity inefficient, at least on this one level. Timing is crucial because once habits are learned it is very hard to change them. If children do not develop skills which make word processing accessible as an activity they will not be able to take advantage of the opportunities word processing provides to enhance commu-nication. Keyboard skills do feature increasingly in the Individual Education Plans (IEPs) of children with identified Special Educational Needs (children with statements), particularly where the IEP also provides for the use of a portable word processor or computer.

Some knowledge, skills and understanding relating to text entry have already been discussed. There is an increasingly wide range of software available dedicated to the development of children's keyboard skills. In addition there are paper-based materials which provide keyboard familiarisation exercises. These can be used with word processing software or even paper keyboards for children to practise around the classroom or at home.

Most of these strategies focus on **touch typing**, learning to use the full range of fingers to access the standard keyboard, with the aim of being able to use the keyboard without looking first to locate letters. When compared with the commitment required to gain some mastery of a musical instrument, touch typing may not appear such an unattainable goal, indeed some children may benefit from the hand-eye co-ordination practice. There are, however, a range of alternative or partial strategies which may also be beneficial. These include:

- **knowledge and use of the 'home' keys (*asdf* for the left hand and *jkl* for the right, with *f* and *j* often having some sort of relief dot or line to facilitate the fingers in locating them by touch rather than sight);**
- **encouraging the use of at least two fingers on each hand, the thumb for the space bar and the little fingers for the shift key;**
- **the use of the number pad at the extreme right-hand side of most keyboards for the entry of numbers.**

When schools are devising their schemes of work for ICT, consideration should be given to the enhancement of children's keyboard skills and the identification of progression. Clearly there is an important role for teachers in the diagnosis and remediation of inefficient or ineffective keyboard techniques.

The physical demands that handwriting places on children and the consequent contribution word processors can make to writing when some of these are removed has already been discussed. However, it is worth remembering that some children (and adults) may prefer to write by hand or may prefer to do certain, perhaps more personal, types of writing by hand.

Practical task

Research the development of keyboard skills and potential teaching and learning strategies.

Evaluate your own keyboard skills and design a strategy to enhance them if necessary.

Evaluate some of the software and paper-based materials designed to assist the development of children's keyboard skills.

Overlay keyboards have been available in schools for many years. These can be used in conjunction with word processing as well as many other types of software. They are often referred to as Concept keyboards, reflecting the name of a popular manufacturer. The overlay keyboard is an external input device connected to the computer processor (box/tower) and can be used as an alternative to or in conjunction with a standard keyboard. They are usually rectangular, A3 or A4-sized. Overlay keyboards require space for use, particularly if they are to be used in addition to the standard keyboard.

The overlay keyboard is programmed such that, when a particular area is touched, a letter, image, word, sentence or paragraph is entered. An **overlay**, typically of paper or thin card, is placed on top of the device indicating the effect of pressing the area immediately below. For instance, a picture of a horse on the overlay could result in the input of the word 'horse' when the area is pressed. Some software comes with pre-programmed keyboard overlays; for example, to support writing activities related to talking books. You can also make your own using an editing package. This requires some investment of time the first few times, but rapidly becomes a fairly efficient process. Designing and making your own overlays enables you to customise them to the requirements of particular activities or individuals. Overlay keyboards are particularly well used in Key Stage I to support writing activities and at all stages with children with SEN.

Practical task

Find out how to:

- *connect the overlay keyboard to the computer;*
- *load the overlay you wish to use;*
- *design a range of three overlays to provide differentiated support for a science sorting activity.*

Many of these features can now be accessed through on-screen **word banks**. Word banks fall into two categories:

- **those that are a function within a word processing package;**
- **those that constitute a separate piece of software which can be used in conjunction with word processing, but may equally be utilised with other types of software – Clicker (Crick), for example.**

On-screen word banks can be quickly prepared to support specific activities; equally a graduated range can provide differentiated support. For instance, a word bank of specific vocabulary could be used in the recording and reporting of a geographic enquiry, enabling children to concentrate on articulating their understanding, rather than being diverted by the spelling of new words. Equally individual children may access personalised word banks.

Most primary word processing packages now include a word bank facility and these are generally far easier to prepare than keyboard overlays. Another advantage is that they do not require any additional space around the computer. Some of these word banks may, however, be limited to text entry. Word banks can be particularly powerful when used in conjunction with the talking feature of word processing software.

Practical task

Find out how to prepare and use a word bank to support a maths activity. Identify teaching and learning objectives with regard to:

* *numeracy;*
* *ICT.*

Note how you would organise and manage this activity:

* *in a computer suite;*
* *in a classroom with two computers.*

Clicker (Crick) and other similar software is just as straightforward. The software comes with a range of prepared word banks. Again, customised word banks can be quickly prepared. This software occupies part of the computer screen space, appearing as a separate window, and children make selections with the mouse. This is a more complete alternative to the overlay keyboard as graphic images can be used in the word bank as it appears on screen to aid selection. Similarly, the insertion of graphics is also supported.

Touch screens, while expensive and somewhat delicate, can be used in conjunction with word banks to assist text and/or graphic entry.

Adult scribes are used to assist children with emergent writing, and there is no reason why this practice cannot be transferred to the word processing arena. This can provide another strategy to assist children during the composing phase of their writing, allowing them to concentrate on the communication of ideas. Equally an adult scribe (or the teacher) could record contributions from a whole class discussion, quickly printing and distributing them to groups to facilitate a follow-up activity.

Voice recognition software has been just around the corner for a very long time. Such software provides an alternative to manual entry of text. To some extent it appears to have arrived – big-name software houses are currently marketing voice recognition products for personal and business use. The software requires the individual to spend time training it by reading prepared texts and lists of words and phrases. The computer builds up a memory of how individual words and sounds are pronounced by the particular person. If voice recognition can be effective the possibilities are wide-ranging and exciting. Voice recognition is also used as a tool to support children and adults with special needs, particularly those constrained physically.

Voice recognition software has yet to arrive in primary schools as a practical solution. Currently a number of challenges have to be overcome, the need to spend considerable time training the software being one of them, the more mundane issue of background noise being another.

Speaking or talking word processors

Most word processors designed for the primary school now incorporate a talking or speaking facility. Some even offer a range of regional accents. The quality of the sound, though, can very often be dependent on the sound card in the machine, with some older computers giving poor quality reproduction. Newer multimedia computers are likely to render more easily recognisable reading of text.

Talking word processors can be used to assist children's writing by reading back each sentence as it is completed or the entire narrative so far, reminding children of what they have written and prompting them to take the writing forward. It is suggested that the writing of children who are still emerging as readers may as a result be more coherent. Similarly, the computer will read back what children have actually written, as opposed to what they thought or wanted to write, alerting them to opportunities for revision.

RESEARCH SUMMARY

The talking facilities of word processors have been used as a strategy for spelling development, with children identifying misspelled words from the unexpected sounds as the computer tries to make sense of them.

Peter Sharp (1995) trained learning support assistants and SEN co-ordinators to use talking word processors to develop children's spelling. An SEN co-ordinator commented that the children were 'talking to themselves, analysing their spellings and self-correcting far more' (ibid. p. 7). The instant feedback from the talking word processor appeared to encourage a more reflective approach to their writing amongst children. Some concern has, however, been expressed about children's abilities to transfer such learning to writing in other contexts.

More recently Moseley, Higgins et al. (1999) reported on a class of Year 2 pupils. The class teacher was exploring the use of the speech facility of a word processor to develop sight vocabulary and spellings from the National Literacy Strategy lists as well as the use of full stops and capital letters. Results were mixed. Children's reading and spelling scores improved according to standard before-and-after measurements although the ranking of children in the class remained unchanged. A writing assessment showed that the quantity and quality of the children's writing using word processors improved considerably, but spelling accuracy decreased.

If used indiscriminately, talking word processors can be a distraction both for children writing electronically and for those working close by. Children need to be clear how the talking word processor can assist them to develop their writing and when and when not to use it. Choosing the appropriate settings (whole words or sentences, individual letters and sounds) is also important. Explicit communication of learning outcomes and classroom protocols is essential for such tools to be used effectively – for instance, completing a first draft and then listening to the computer read the text to assist with the identification of errors and opportunities for improvement. Headphones may also be useful.

Teachers need to know and make explicit to children the limitations of the talking facility, that it may not recognise words that are correctly spelled, resulting in an unusual pronunciation. Parallels with the limitations of spell-checkers can be drawn since some real names, scientific and other technical terms are likely to be outside the software's memory. Children will enjoy challenging the program with words it is not programmed to pronounce. It is also important that children do not become over-reliant on this feature of the software and consequently fail to develop skills associated with reading from the screen.

Practical task

Use the talking facility of a primary word processing package to: find out how to change the settings (when the word processor will speak); and listen to the individual letter sounds and blends as read by the machine. Plan for a pair or small group to reinforce or extend a stated literacy objective using a talking word processor. What are the issues surrounding the use of headphones with talking word processors?

Spell-checkers, thesauruses, grammar- and style-checkers

Spell-checkers can be useful to draw attention to possible errors (they are far from infallible), likewise grammar or style-checkers. Again these need to be treated with some caution, especially in software which originated outside the UK where syntactic conventions may be different. Concern has been expressed about over-reliance on such tools which can act as a disincentive to children to improve spelling. Additionally, used indiscriminately they may not only correct spellings which do not require correction (are merely not within the spell-checker's memory) but more importantly prove a distraction to writers in the early stages of the writing process. Much time can be wasted adjusting and readjusting spellings distracting children's attention from the ideas they are seeking to convey. Most spell-checkers allow for new words to be added and teachers should make use of this facility to ensure that the vocabulary associated with current curriculum work is recognised by the word processor. Some caution should be used in encouraging children to add new words – perhaps they should first be checked by the teacher or learning support assistant, to avoid the obvious difficulties associated with inaccurate suggestions being offered by the spell-checker.

Spell-checkers, like speech facilities, may be easily turned off. It may be appropriate for children to complete their initial writing and only then use the spell-checker. Teachers must employ discretion about when and to what extent these facilities should be used. A child in the early stages of writing development may be undermined by accusatory highlighting or underlining appearing on almost every word. The spell-checker may prove to be no use at all in decoding emergent spelling, or that of children with specific difficulties such as dyslexia. If too many words are identified as misspelled, and some of these may after all not be, there is little real opportunity for the writer to focus sufficiently to improve spelling.

A spell-checker may provide for a valuable learning experience in itself where unfamiliar words are suggested, particularly if used in association with a dictionary or thesaurus, enriching vocabulary. Likewise **thesauruses** can be used as part of a structured learning activity to promote familiarisation and independence.

Grammar- and/or style-checkers promise much, but again must be used judiciously. Many were originally designed for the business market, and the suggestions made reflect this. Additionally, they are unable to evaluate usage in context; for instance, picking up the repeated use of had in *he had had a poor night's sleep*. Some grammar-checkers can be customised so that they will pick up particular errors and overlook others and can be very useful for identifying overlong sentences or inappropriate use of apostrophes.

Portable computers

Word processing software is frequently used in conjunction with portable computers. There is a range of portable machines available, including:

- *Notebooks/laptops.* These are portable versions of desktop machines, they run standard software, can have multimedia and Internet capabilities and run from mains or rechargeable batteries. They tend to be rather more expensive than equivalent desktop models, but have the advantage of portability as well as compatibility with printers and other peripheral equipment.
- *Palmtops.* These machines are smaller (do not, for instance, incorporate a standard keyboard), run specific or cut-down versions of software and are powered by standard batteries. Many now allow downloading to standard computers and software, through wire or wireless (usually infrared) links.
- *Dedicated word processors.* There are a number of machines available which function only as word processors, such as AlphaSmart and DreamWriter. They allow the entry, storage, downloading and occasionally direct printing of text documents. They do not facilitate much in the way of text formatting, though they do incorporate a small screen usually displaying a few lines of text at a time, which will allow rereading and elementary editing. Text can be downloaded into a word processing program on a desktop computer to allow for revisions and printing. Because of the limited range of functions possible, such machines are generally inexpensive compared with other portable or desktop equipment. Many dedicated word processors are rechargeable.

Word processing using portable computers can have a range of benefits. Portable equipment by its very nature enables children to take their word processing on school trips, outside, to the hall or music room, even home. In cramped classrooms the possibility of using computer equipment on standard tables, rather than specially adapted and located furniture, can be attractive. A school with a number of portable machines can utilise them in a flexible way, sometimes distributed around a number of classrooms, sometimes all together constituting a portable computer suite. Dedicated word processors can be financially attractive – a number of such machines can be bought for the equivalent cost of a desktop computer, and these can be used for the time-consuming text entry aspects of word processing, freeing the more expensive desktop machines for more complex editing and presenting.

Portable word processors have proved effective tools for the support of struggling writers, often bringing associated gains in terms of improved behaviour and social confidence, particularly when used to provide differentiated support for children with SEN. Children gain confidence from the privacy and support provided by the technology. They have also been useful tools in encouraging parental involvement in children's writing, with children taking the machines home to continue their writing.

Explicit skills teaching

One key area for children (and teachers) is their developing understanding of the scope and range of word processing software – what is possible and what isn't. The swiftly evolving nature of such software means there is no lasting answer, but a developing appreciation of the possibilities goes hand-in-hand with a developing sophistication of use.

The nature of the ways in which we learn about the various functions of word processing (and other) software can lead to inefficient and ineffective practices. Much of the time we learn new skills by experimentation ourselves, by asking our peers or our teachers, by using built-in help, by observing others and by accident when we are trying to achieve something quite different. Some software also allows the same effect to be generated by a range of different strategies; for instance, in Word (Microsoft), highlighted text can be copied by accessing the copy command from the edit menu, by using the copy icon on the standard tool bar, by using the keyboard shortcut Ctrl and C and by using the right button to access a mini-menu of options, again including copy. There are probably other ways. Some of these may work in some other word processing packages and some may not. All are effective. Some are more efficient in terms of time and number of mouse clicks than others. Some suit some individuals and the ways in which they work better than others.

It is important sometimes to watch children working with word processing software and to note and confront inefficient and ineffective practices. For instance, many children access capital letters via the caps lock. This requires them to put on the caps lock, type the letter and take off the caps lock, a three-stage process. Very often children forget the final stage and may have typed several more words before they notice. Changing capitals to lower case letters once typed requires a quite detailed knowledge of some word processing software – it is just not feasible in others. In practice, children tend to delete the offending words and retype them. Time and continuity is lost. Use of the shift lock can be taught explicitly, either informally on a one-to-one basis or demonstrated to a whole class. This makes the capitalisation of letters a two-click process (shift and the letter) and avoids unwanted capitals.

Similarly, if children are typing in a number of figures, they may find the number key pad at the right-hand side of the keyboard easier than the numbers at the top of the keyboard. Many young children get into the habit of forcing their own line breaks via the enter key or a mouse click when they notice they are getting towards the right-hand side of the typing area and do not realise that the text will wrap around automatically. This becomes a problem when children subsequently edit their text and the line breaks are not then in the best positions.

A regular 'tips' slot where children demonstrate useful strategies to their peers or the teacher models a new idea can easily and fruitfully be incorporated into classroom practice. Explicit teaching of word processing, and other ICT knowledge, skills and understanding, is just as important in mathematics or any other subject.

Children need to be aware of the limitations of software tools: that the spell-checker is not always right (likewise the grammar- or style-checker); that some words may not be in its dictionary and that some of its suggestions may not be appropriate. Some understanding of the clues that spell-checkers use to offer alternatives may be useful to enable children to make best use of such facilities. Similarly, the talking function may mispronounce words not in its memory, potentially giving children the false impression that something is incorrect.

Document sizes and their implications

Text documents do not on the whole take considerable amounts of memory for storage. However, the inclusion of formatting features such as page borders and graphic images may considerably increase the size of a word processing document. This will result in longer saving and retrieval times (especially to and from floppy disk), and the possibility of memory space (again, particularly evident on floppy disk) being used up with relatively few documents. Printers also have limited memories (into which the document is transferred from the computer for printing) and some may find highly formatted documents or those containing a number of images too much to handle. If this happens the printer's memory (the print queue) will need to be cleared before any other document can be printed.

Word processing and the core subjects

The ideas and activities introduced below are intended to give a feel for the range of ways in which word processing can be utilised to support and enhance teaching and learning in mathematics, science and English. They are not intended to be comprehensive, merely to go some way towards illustrating the breadth of possibilities and to provide starting points for the customisation of ideas and the generation of others. Examples introduced under mathematics, for instance, may be just as applicable to one or more of the other areas. Other useful sources include professional journals (*Primary Science Review*, *Reading*, *Interactive*, *Junior Education*, *Child Education*, etc.), websites (National Grid for Learning, BECTa, etc.), Schemes of Work (Science, ICT, etc.).

Word processing and mathematics

Children can use word processing software to present the results of mathematical investigations. Writing can make a valuable contribution to the development and particularly the articulation of meaning and ideas, no less important in mathematics and science than in English language development work. The word processor allows children to import graphs from graphing or database programs and images from painting and drawing packages or a digital camera. They can add commentary, perhaps to pose questions for their peers or to produce fact sheets to contribute to a whole class reference document.

Of course, many graphing and database packages allow text to be added and amended for the recording and presentation of results. Children need to know that they can transfer their skills from one to the other, but also to recognise the potential limitations of such software so that they and/or their teachers can make the most appropriate choice; for instance, word banks or bullet points may not be available.

Word processing and science

The strategies discussed for mathematics can also be applied to the teaching and learning of science.

Children at all stages can use word processing software to assist with sequencing and sorting information. The degree of preparation and/or structuring required may vary with the development of the children. Young children may begin by using an overlay keyboard or on-screen word bank featuring images with text labels, to sort materials – into hard and soft, for instance.

An obvious extension for such an activity may be the writing of a sentence of explanation, with adult assistance as necessary. This could be achieved with the aid of the word processor, or to maximise access to limited computer resources, handwritten on a print-out.

Sequencing the stages of an investigation can be supported at a range of levels. Prepared sentences or bullet points may be ordered using an overlay keyboard or on-screen word bank, the mouse to position insertions and delete or backspace as appropriate. Later children can use cut and paste to sequence and re-sequence the elements of a prepared text. Children may enter their own text and use the facilities of the word processor to revise and reorder their work until they are satisfied. Activities such as these are appropriate for pairs or small groups, since the associated discussion and decision-making can be a fertile ground for rehearsing explanations, justifying opinions and articulating ideas.

One of the principal conventions of science is the systematic recording of investigations. Children begin early in their school careers to develop this skill and word processing can be used to support this writing in various ways. A word bank can be used to access new or difficult vocabulary, allowing children to concentrate on articulating their developing understanding. Teachers can use such tools as mechanisms to support differentiation across the primary age phase and to facilitate children struggling with literacy to communicate their scientific understanding more easily.

Electronic writing frames or templates, prepared files with headings and sometimes questions of a general nature which can be used in a variety of contexts or customised for particular activities, can be useful. The various parts of the template scaffold children in the framing of their ideas under each of the headings and help to ensure that important elements are not forgotten. Children can either use such a framework on screen or make use of a print-out to support writing by hand.

Word processors can be useful tools when children are seeking information from databases. Children can make their own notes about what they have found, supplementing these as appropriate with images and/or text copied and pasted from electronic sources. Children may then use their notes in either an electronic or paper-based format to develop their work further.

The examples given above focus predominantly on using the features of word processors to assist in the development of writing associated with science. Each of these can be taken a stage further, using the tools and facilities to improve the technical and presentational aspects of children's writing in science, though teachers must be clear about their primary learning objectives. The word processing and desktop publishing facilities of the software can be used to good advantage when children produce posters to communicate important facts such as *why we should clean our teeth* or *which foods we need for a healthy diet*. Equally information can be prepared in a word processing document with a view to linking it with the work of others to form a multimedia document, for the school's website or to make a non-fiction talking book or reference guide for younger children.

Word processing and English

Word processing has a range of features which support writing activities, many of which have already been discussed. Under a heading such as *All about me* young children can select and enter words, sentences and images from an on-screen bank or keyboard overlay. Alternatively or as an extension children could delete descriptions from a prepared text which do not apply to them. Such an activity also promotes skills in reading from the screen.

A wide range of sentence-level literacy activities can be facilitated – for instance, highlighting direct speech from a prepared text. Some children can use the word processor to complete this activity, others could use a highlighter and a print-out, thus making practical and effective use of classroom resources. Likewise a prepared text can be changed from reported to direct speech. Word-level work can involve inserting punctuation into a continuous narrative to produce sentences or using search and replace to substitute alternatives for *said*.

Shared text-level work on instructions may focus on *How we clean our teeth* with the class teacher fielding suggestions and acting as scribe as the class or group look on. A more complex instructional text such as a recipe for Easter biscuits can be supported at different levels according to need – a prepared list requiring reordering for some, a partial list or a blank sheet for others. Word processing allows children to insert, delete, reorder and present their work. It also allows the comparison of alternatives. Such activities carried out in groups and/or leading to feedback to the whole class can facilitate speaking and listening as children support and refine their ideas. Independent users of word processing can produce a help sheet on how to create a hyperlink in a multimedia document, thus combining instructional text with appropriate images to facilitate communication and formatting to enhance aesthetic appeal of the helpsheet.

Prepared texts can be turned from prose into note form, or notes turned into prose. Interesting comparisons can result if one group of children perform the inverse task on the work of others (once it has been saved or printed). A certain competitive element can be introduced as children seek to use the least number of words while still conveying meaning. Debate on what is and is not considered to be important may ensue.

There are opportunities for work focusing on the importance of layout, for instance, in the writing and presentation of poetry. The effects of inserting line break and capital letters, centring, illustrating or font selection and size can be examined. Cartoons and newspaper layouts can be supported at various stages. Teachers can prepare paper templates for planning and electronic templates to support some children with the layout of their work. Designing front and back covers and title pages for books can provide an alternative to the book review, although children can make use of a prepared electronic writing frame to support such writing.

Children of all ages can work with tables, to compile ongoing lists of synonyms for common adjectives.

Many of the activities suggested above make use of prepared word processing documents. Teachers should ensure that they manage the use of these carefully. Always have a back-up copy and agree with the children how the prepared document will be used. Clearly the first pair of children making adjustments and then saving their work over the original is to be avoided. Protect the master document so that changes cannot be saved and/or encourage children to save the document with a new name before they do anything else or to print out their work and then close the document without saving.

Practical task

Use the template facility of a word processing package to design:

- *headed notepaper for your home or school address;*
- *a lesson-planning proforma;*
- *a writing frame.*

Consider whether and how each of these could be utilised electronically or as print-outs. Compare the sizes of each of these documents (the amount of memory occupied by the saved document). What are the factors affecting their relative sizes?

Desktop publishing

Software is now available which enables the non-expert to produce high quality desktop published documents. Through the use of *wizards*, birthday cards, invitations, calendars and newsletters can be generated by following the on-screen instructions, inserting the required text or graphics as directed – the software does the rest. Publisher (Microsoft) is one example.

Many schools are now using such applications for half-termly newsletters, prospectuses, fliers, display banners and other publicity and display materials. They can also be usefully deployed in the classroom – for instance, for newspaper activities. DTP software does not allow for changes to be made easily, particularly in text. This mirrors the professional DTP process where graphics and text are comprehensively edited and considered to be *finished* before being incorporated in the layout.

Practical task

Plan a unit of work which will culminate with each pair of children in a class producing an A4 help sheet on a specific feature of word processing for a help file to be used as a reference document by a younger class. The children will peer assess each other's work. How will you prepare, support and moderate this activity?

Word processing and desktop publishing (DTP):
a summary of key points

Word processing can support, enhance, extend and enrich communication in a variety of ways, but only when:

- *it is used with a clear understanding of its potential and potential difficulties;*
- *learning outcomes are clearly defined, explicitly communicated and reflectively evaluated.*

Further reading

BECTa (1998) *Primarily IT: Using IT to Support English, Maths and Science at KS2,* BECTa.

BECTa (2001) *Keyboard skills in schools,* advice sheet, BECTa. www.becta.org.uk/technology/infosheets/

BECTa (2001) *Portable computers,* advice sheet, BECTa. www.becta.org.uk/technology/infosheets/

BECTa (2001) *Speech recognition systems*, advice sheet, BECTa. www.becta.org.uk/technology/infosheets/

Bennett, R. (1997) *Teaching IT*, Nash Pollock.

Bolton Curriculum ICT Centre (1998) *IT in Primary Literacy*, Bolton Curriculum ICT Centre.

Cook, D. and Finlayson, H. (1999) *Interactive Children, Communicative Teaching.* OUP.

DfEE/QCA (1999) *Curriculum Guidance for the Foundation Stage*, DfEE/QCA.

DfEE/QCA (1999) *The National Curriculum*, DfEE/QCA.

Dick, R. (1998) *IT Starts Here*, Newman College and MAPE.

Leask, M. and Meadows, J. (2000) *Teaching and Learning with ICT in the Primary School*, Routledge Falmer.

Loveless, A. (1995) *The Role of IT: Practical Issues for the Primary Teacher*, Cassell.

McFarlane, A. (ed) (1997) *Information Technology and Authentic Learning: Realising the*

Potential of Computers in the Primary School, Routledge, Chapter 8.

Mosely, D., Higgins, S. *et al*. (1999) *Ways Forward with ICT: Effective Pedagogy Using ICT for Literacy and Numeracy in Primary Schools*, University of Newcastle.

QCA/DfEE (1998, rev. 2000) *Information and Communications Technology: A Scheme of Work for Key Stages 1 and 2*, QCA/DfEE.

Scrimshaw, P. (ed) (1993) *Language, Classrooms and Computers*, Routledge.

Shreeve, A. (ed) (1997) *IT in English* series (Planning and Management, Case Studies and Materials, Literature Review, Resources for Learning), NCET.

Smith, H. (1999) *Opportunities for ICT in the Primary School*, Trentham Books.

Somekh, D. and Davis, N. (eds) (1997) *Using Information Technology Effectively in Teaching and Learning: Studies in Pre-service and In-service Teacher Education*, Routledge, Chapter 2.

Underwood, J. (ed) (1994) *Computer-Based Learning: Potential into Practice*, David Fulton, Chapter 3.

Wegerif, R. and Scrimshaw, P. (eds) (1997) *Computers and Talk in the Primary Classroom*, Multilingual Matters Ltd.

Images, patterns, shapes and colours are key features of children's early learning. Logos and icons are increasingly important in making sense of the world, from choosing breakfast cereal to operating computer software. Children learn to communicate and interpret visual imagery and ICT has a significant contribution to make to the development of visual literacy.

Recent advances in hardware have made computers with large memories necessary for the storage and manipulation of complex graphics readily accessible. At the same time graphics software has become more sophisticated in the range of features and functions supported. The continued move towards icons and tool bars for controlling these functions has improved accessibility for children and their teachers. Many generic software applications, such as word processors and databases, now support graphics. Associated peripheral equipment, particularly scanners and digital cameras, is increasingly available in primary schools.

This chapter explores graphics software in the context of primary education. Its application in the core subjects is explored, together with related capabilities and limitations.

What is graphics software?

Graphics software allows the entry, storage, retrieval and manipulation of images and their constituent elements, line, colour and texture, in an electronic format. Generic graphics software is considered to encompass painting and drawing software, although a range of other related software, such as clip art and digitising software for scanners and digital cameras, is becoming increasingly important.

What do the programmes of study for Key Stages I and 2 include?

At Key Stage I children should be taught to gather information (Ia), enter and store it (Ib) and retrieve it (Ic). They should be taught to use text, tables, images and sounds to develop their ideas (2a) and try things out and see what happens in real and imaginary situations (2d). They should also be taught to share their ideas by presenting information in a variety of forms (3a) and to present their work effectively (3b).

At Key Stage 2, children should be taught to talk about the information they need (Ia), how to prepare information (Ib), how to organise and reorganise it (2a), how to share and exchange it (3a), as well as consider its suitability for its audience and its quality (3b).

At all stages children should be taught to review, modify and evaluate their work as it progresses (4a, 4b and 4c).

What does the ICT Scheme of Work include?

At Key Stage I graphics software features in Unit IA (An introduction to modelling) and Unit 2B (Creating pictures).

At Key Stage 2 graphics software features in Unit 3A (Combining text and graphics), Unit 4B (Developing images using repeating patterns) and Unit 5A (Graphical modelling).

What do teachers need to know before using graphics software?

Drawing and painting software

Historically there have been two types of generic graphics software: drawing and painting packages, each having different strengths and limitations. One of the key differences is in the storage mechanism for the images created and manipulated within them.

Painting programs produce bitmap images (file extension .bmp). Bitmap images are minutely detailed, essentially recording separately every pixel (tiny dot) displayed on the screen, including blank areas. This results in very large documents. The image below saved as a bitmap image occupies 900KB of memory. Contrast this with the memory capacity of a floppy disk, 1.44MB.

Graphics documents can occupy large amounts of memory

Drawing programs, often called object-based or object-oriented drawing programs, operate a completely different method of storing information. Drawings are stored as a series of vectors (mathematical equations) denoting the point where a drawing or object originates, the length of line, direction, etc. This results in very much smaller file sizes.

Convergence and expansion

In common with other generic software, there has been considerable convergence and realignment in graphics software. Most graphics programs are now painting programs which also support drawing features, such as lines, arrows and shapes. The drawing package has essentially been subsumed into other software applications. Most word processing software supports a range of drawing functions – Textease (Softease) and Word (Microsoft) with its drawing tool bar, for instance. Many other generic applications, such as graphing programs, support at least a limited range of drawing tools to enhance presentation.

Compression

Most graphics software supports a range of file types offering different degrees of compression as alternatives to bitmaps, the two most common being gif (pronounced giff or sometimes jif) and jpeg (pronounced jay-peg). Compressing a file results in it occupying less memory. The image opposite occupies 154KB as a gif and 28.1KB as a jpeg file.

There is some consequent loss in image quality, especially when compressed images are enlarged. jpegs tend to occupy less memory, although gifs predominate on the World Wide Web. Issues of compression and resolution are discussed further later.

Practical task

Find out how to determine the size of an electronic document. Note the file size of a painting graphic, a drawing graphic and a photographic image all saved as jpeg images. Try saving each of these images as bitmaps and compare the differences in file size. Paste each image in turn into a graphics or word processing program and enlarge it significantly. What do you notice?

Acorn file types

The file types referred to above all relate to PC-based graphics. However, the situation is exactly mirrored on the Acorn platform. Acorn painting programs often now support bitmap and jpeg file types, although some older software utilises only sprites, which are Acorn image files and display similar qualities to bitmap images with regard to size. Acorn-based drawing programs, such as Draw, and some painting software, e.g. Splosh (Kudlian Soft), support a file type known as draw, which is vector-based.

What do teachers need to know about graphics software?

Teachers need to be competent and confident users of primary graphics software in order to facilitate children's learning. This does not mean that they need to know the answer to every and any particular question, but instead have a working knowledge of the software such as to be able to plan, support and assess appropriate activities as well as predict likely difficulties and assist with problem-solving.

Teaching with and about graphics software involves teachers:

- **Preparing resources** – such as a worksheet to support early mathematics work, a prepared graphics document in which children may explore and reinforce early symmetry work or illustrations to accompany a wall display. Some of these examples focus on using ICT as a tool for teaching and learning (in another curriculum area), while others focus on the teaching and learning of ICT.

Shape-based worksheet designed using the drawing features of Word (Microsoft)

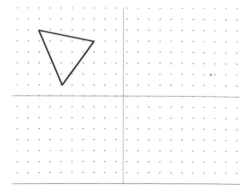

Using the grid and symmetry features of Dazzle (Granada Learning)

- *Selecting appropriate opportunities* – in which graphics software can facilitate, enhance or extend children's learning, such as the importance of presentation in communication. In some instances the focus will be on teaching and learning in ICT (how to make a border for a poem using a repeated pattern), while in others ICT will be used as a resource in the teaching and learning of another curriculum area (matching presentation to audience).
- *Making explicit links between related knowledge, skills and understanding* – graphics software has applications across the range of the primary curriculum and as a consequence may provide opportunities to make explicit links in knowledge, skills and understanding in mathematics and art, for instance.
- *Modelling appropriate use of ICT* – cropping an image from a digital camera and transferring the result into a word processor to illustrate an activity sheet.
- *Demonstrating or intervening* – for example, demonstrating a new skill such as altering the size of painting tools or intervening to assist a child to delete multiple copies of a saved image to save memory space.

The lists below attempt to identify the knowledge, skills and understanding that teachers need in order to teach effectively with and about graphics software. Many graphics programs support only a subset of these functions. This is no reflection on their usefulness – in most instances it is a strength. However, it does signal that teachers must be aware of the capabilities and limitations of any program as these will be significant in the choice of software for any teaching and learning activity.

PAINTING PROGRAMS
- creating, opening, closing, deleting and printing documents;
- selecting file type and saving documents;
- selecting page size, margins and page orientation;
- inserting, modifying and deleting background colours and textures;
- selecting, modifying and utilising tools from the tool bar (spray, round brush, draw a circle);
- utilising fill;
- utilising the pipette/choose a colour tool;
- utilising undo/redo;
- selecting, modifying and utilising the text tool (font, font size, colour);
- selecting areas (for cropping, scaling, reshaping, deletion);
- selecting, modifying, utilising and saving repeated images (stamps);
- selecting and utilising more advanced features such as tiling, flipping and rotation;
- switching grid on and off;
- utilising zoom/magnifier;
- inserting, deleting, manipulating and saving imported images;
- exporting images to other applications;
- clearing the screen;
- utilising help;
- altering defaults;
- customising set up;
- connecting alternative input devices (overlay keyboards, touch screens, graphics tablets);
- protecting documents.

DRAWING PROGRAMS

- creating, opening, saving, closing, deleting and printing documents;
- selecting page size, margins and page orientation;
- inserting, modifying and deleting background colours;
- selecting, modifying and utilising tools from the tool bar (line, arrows, shapes);
- utilising fill;
- utilising undo/redo;
- grouping and ungrouping elements;
- selecting, cutting, copying, pasting, cropping, resizing, reshaping, reordering and rotating elements and drawings;
- switching grid on and off;
- utilising zoom/magnifier;
- exporting drawings to other applications;
- utilising help;
- altering defaults;
- customising set up;
- connecting alternative input devices (overlay keyboards, touch screens, graphics tablets);
- protecting documents.

What are the key features of graphics software?

Graphics software makes use of a variety of tools, editing functions and effects for the creation and manipulation of electronic images.

Tools include brushes, lines, shapes and colour filling among many others. The variety of tools supported varies between software. Much painting software includes a selection of drawing features, although these cannot be manipulated in the same way as is possible in drawing programs or other software which supports a range of drawing features.

The distinguishing feature of drawing software is that drawings are composed of a series of layered elements (shapes, for instance) and these may be reordered as required. Similarly the elements may be grouped together to be edited. In painting software, editing functions and effects can be applied to a selected area of an image, although it is not possible to isolate the elements of the image in the same way. In this respect painting software more closely resembles traditional art media.

The image opposite (*top*) was created with the drawing tools available in Word. Objects were reordered to create the desired overlapping circle effect. Elements were grouped so that the image could be copied, the copies then being resized and rotated.

Many drawing and painting packages support a range of common editing functions, including, for example, scaling, reflecting, shearing, rotating, cropping and editing. The image opposite (*bottom*) demonstrates the effect of each of these on a simple image.

Grouping, resizing and rotating drawn objects in Word (Microsoft)

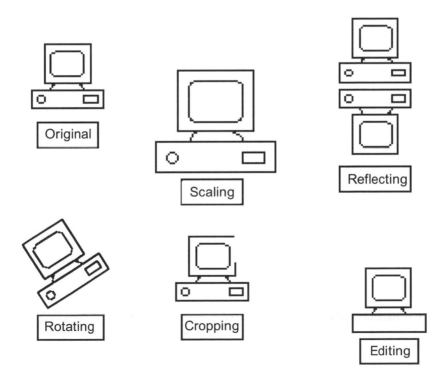

The effects of common editing functions (Microsoft Word)

Painting software provides a range of artistic effects, the variety and sophistication of these varying between packages. Common effects include a spray can, watercolour, colour blending, stamping (multiple copying), tinting and diffusing.

Practical task

Explore the tools, editing functions and effects of two common painting packages. Decide the most appropriate age range for each. If your school were purchasing a paint package which would you recommend and why? Produce an A4 help sheet to assist children in the use of a few key effects.

What does graphics software have to contribute to teaching and learning?

Finding things out

Use of graphics software provides a quite different aesthetic and kinaesthetic experience compared with traditional media. The outcomes produced are also different and there is a completely distinct physical experience associated with creating outcomes. Some children may be frustrated at the difficulties associated with using the mouse as a drawing tool, others may delight in the potential to create difficult shapes, such as curves, exactly as they wish them to look. In order to develop understanding and inform choices, children need a range of experiences on which to draw.

Drawing and painting software facilitates a range of starting points for graphic activities, from a blank screen to a photographic image to be manipulated and developed. Similarly, the sheer variety of tools, editing functions and effects available provide challenges in themselves. The range of tools, editing functions and effects can, however, be limited to promote specific learning outcomes.

Use of graphics software provides an opportunity to introduce and develop children's understanding of related technical issues such as file size and file extensions in a relevant and meaningful context.

Developing ideas and making things happen

Most graphics software allows users to undo the previous action. Many primary packages, though not all, support repeated undoing. This feature allows children to use the software to explore and experiment with effects in ways which are not possible with traditional art media. Comparisons may be made between alternatives to inform choices. Children may be encouraged to take risks. Regular saving of work can provide a similar security, allowing children to return to an earlier stage in their work and follow a different pathway.

Graphics software can provide children with access to tools, editing functions and effects which may be difficult or impossible to achieve with other arts resources commonly available in primary schools. Children may be able to develop their understanding of watercolour painting and painters by simulating watercolour effects and similarly of the potential and limitations of pop art.

Exchanging and sharing information

Graphic representation is an important area of communication. Experiencing the creation and manipulation of electronic images assists children to interpret the graphics they encounter, be they sporting goods manufacturers' logos or sophisticated film animations. Similarly the electronic nature of some graphics enables global sharing and exchange through email and the World Wide Web.

Graphics software does not in any way replace children working with the traditional range of art media, rather it increases the choices available. In certain situations the software features or even the nature of the outcome, in electronic format for instance, may make it the appropriate selection.

Progression of knowledge, skills and understanding

Graphics work will focus on the development of children's graphical communication and interpretation skills as well as software skills.

Very young children may use touch screens and concept keyboards to control the software, developing their understanding of the relationship between their actions and the effects on the screen.

A range of early language, number and science activities can be supported; for instance, using fill tools to colour in prepared drawings, the boat red, the fish orange and the seaweed green. With adult help children might draw party hats on digital photographs of themselves. With increasing independence children will be able to engage in a range of painting and drawing activities, such as producing a new label for their tray or coat hook.

As they progress children will be increasingly able to make their own choices about the creation, manipulation and presentation of images, extending their repertoire of knowledge, skills and understanding through structured activities and interventions. Older children will be able to make appropriate choices related to the task and its audience.

The improving availability of computers in primary classrooms, as well as increasing access outside school and developments in the user-interface of software, makes ordering and ascribing particular skills and techniques difficult. Consideration is more appropriately focused on the development of knowledge and understanding which underpins the use of skills.

What are the capabilities and limitations of graphics software?

Drawing with graphics software

Drawing can be both easier and more difficult with graphics software. The drawing features enable children to draw shapes and arrows, for instance, rapidly and accurately. An oval can be drawn by selecting the appropriate tool and clicking to locate the centre of the shape or edge of the shape (depending on the program), holding the mouse button down until the desired size and shape are shown. A perfect circle can be achieved by holding down Ctrl or shift (depending on the program) while moving the mouse. Drawing software also allows objects to be deleted, redrawn and resized.

Creating similar effects with painting tools is much more difficult, requiring a high degree of hand-eye co-ordination. The computer mouse is not a sensitive drawing tool and free-hand drawing can be very difficult. There are a number of strategies teachers can use to mediate this problem. Using the zoom or magnifying tool to enlarge the drawing area, drawing the required image, and then reducing may have the effect of disguising hand-wobble. It is possible to adjust the sensitivity of the mouse, but more effective is the use of a simple **graphics tablet**. A graphics tablet is made up of a small plastic board and a light pen. The light pen allows the user greater manipulative control than is possible with a mouse. Inexpensive graphics tablets are available for primary schools, such as Kids Design Pad (Genus).

Compression and resolution

Some of the more sophisticated graphics packages and digitising software that accompanies digital cameras and scanners allow the user to select the **resolution** at which an image is saved. Resolution is measured in dpi, dots (pixels) per inch. The higher the resolution the greater the detail saved, and the larger the file size.

The choice of resolution will depend on the way in which the image is to be used. Generally, images to be displayed on screen, in PowerPoint or web pages for instance, can be saved in lower resolution or compressed format unless they are to be significantly enlarged. Graphics which are to be enlarged or which require high quality print-outs such as photographs should be high resolution or uncompressed. Low resolution images which are subsequently enlarged often become pixelated (see opposite).

Conversely, despite occupying less memory, drawing images do not suffer quality reductions when they are enlarged. The vectors which describe the drawing images can be scaled to any size.

Schools without access to a network server may have difficulty in saving and storing quantities of graphics files because of their size. Teachers should ensure that children avoid saving multiple copies of large documents and that documents which are no longer needed are either deleted or saved in a way which will not occupy large amounts of memory. CD ROM writers are becoming commonplace and these allow documents

Low resolution image enlarged – pixelated result

to be quickly and permanently stored on CD ROM. Alternatives include another form of compression known as **zipping.** There is software available which will zip (com-press) electronic documents for storage or transportation, e.g. EasyZip 2000 (*http:// www.thefreesite.com/easyzipIII.htm*). Zipped documents take up smaller amounts of memory space. They are also more quickly uploaded as email attachments, for instance. Indeed some email systems are set up to refuse attachments over a certain size. Documents can be unzipped, using the same software, to be read. Similarly there are special drives and disks designed for the storage of documents in a compressed format, e.g. Zip (Iomega) and Jaz (Iomega). These are often used for long-term storage and backing up.

Sourcing graphics

In addition to drawing and painting their own graphics images, children can source prepared images from a variety of locations. Sites on the World Wide Web, CD ROMs, and scanning are common sources of images produced by others. Similarly pictures can be downloaded from digital cameras. Children often find it daunting to begin with a blank screen and the manipulation of an existing image can be a useful starting point, or a teaching and learning activity in itself where the emphasis is on exploring the features of the software. It is important to remember that any image other than clip art is likely to be subject to copyright.

Clip art

Clip art, which is widely used in primary schools, is copyright-free artwork and can be used and manipulated as required. It is usually created with drawing software in order to minimise file size. Most word processing software now comes with a range of built-in clip art and there are sites on the World Wide Web from which it can be downloaded, e.g. *http://www.clipartconnection.com*. Publishers of educational software also produce CD ROMs of clip art images, e.g. Sherston's Primary Clipart. Similarly it is possible to buy images to support specific subject areas, such as the Victorians Photobase (Longman Logotron).

Clip art may be used for a range of purposes, such as illustrating notices around the school, computer room and wet play area. Clip art images may also be a useful starting point for children to practise image-manipulation techniques in painting packages.

Digital cameras and scanners

Digital cameras are increasingly common in primary schools. This technology continues to develop and the cost, for any but the most up-to-date models, continues to fall. Essentially digital cameras focus and take images in a similar manner to conventional cameras. The difference comes in the storage of those images. Digital cameras have no film; instead the image is held as digital information in the camera's memory. Most cameras are supplied with software which enables the images to be downloaded from the camera onto a computer, manipulated if required and saved.

There are a range of camera types offering different levels of photographic features (close-up, etc.), image quality (resolution) and storage facilities (camera's memory, removable memory cards, even floppy disks). For further details see BECTa's advice sheet *http://www.becta.org.uk*. The resolution at which images are taken affects the number of images which can be stored in the memory.

A digital camera does not replace a conventional camera; each has different suitabilities. A conventional camera will be more appropriate if photographs are required of the school pond for a wall display, as the image quality from a digital camera will not be as good when printed out on paper. However, if the images are to illustrate a feature on the development of the pond for the school's website, digital images are the most appropriate as they are in electronic format and of sufficiently high quality for this medium. Once a digital camera has been purchased there are few costs associated with its use, other than batteries. Battery consumption is high, especially where the camera has an LCD display panel. The LCD display panel allows the user to view the images taken immediately, providing the opportunity to ensure that appropriate images are captured before returning to the classroom.

Images can be viewed on many cameras as described above. They can be downloaded via a computer and software and saved in a range of file types. Images can also be viewed directly on a screen. Young children may walk around the school and take images which show examples of regular shapes, e.g. door as rectangle, sand tray as circle. The children may view the images on a screen with their teacher and talk through their selections. It may not be necessary to keep the images in the long term. Alternatively, children may undertake a similar activity looking for examples of acute, right and obtuse angles. The children may download selected images and import them into a word processing document to sit alongside their notes. Images can be imported into painting software – children may paint themselves into a Viking village scene, with appropriate clothing and props, for instance. Teachers may also find digital cameras useful to provide a record of children's design and technology constructions.

Scanners allow digital images to be made of hand-drawn diagrams, existing photographs, autumn leaves and everyday (flattish) objects such as scissors. Scanners also come with software which enables images to be captured and saved in a range of file formats. Often the software will conduct a preliminary scan of the original and allow the user to select and save just the parts of the image that are required. Scanners all accommodate images, and some now have Optical Character Recognition (OCR) software which enables printed pages of text to be converted into digital format. This technology is promising, but far from infallible, so documents must be carefully checked and may require considerable alteration.

Image created with a scanned leaf and painting software effects (Dazzle, Granada Learning)

Scanners are useful for translating children's artwork, for instance, into an electronic format to allow it to be displayed on the school website. Similarly, scanned images can be the starting point for a range of activities. Children may scan leaves, import them into a graphics package and manipulate them to produce a border for a poem. Alternatively they could attempt to replicate a leaf using the drawing and painting tools in an activity designed to increase facility with these, displaying the scanned and the drawn images side by side. Due caution should be exercised to ensure that scanning does not breach copyright.

Practical task

Use a scanner or a digital camera to produce a resource to support a science activity. How will you use the resource? How will you differentiate? How will you assess the resource's effectiveness?

Printing

The large size of many graphics documents has implications for printing. Printers have memories into which documents are sent from the computer. Documents which are too large for the printer's memory will not print out. They will also prevent the printing of other documents sent subsequently to the printer until the problem document has been cleared from the print queue. Children may be disappointed to find that importing a number of graphic images into a word processing document, for instance, renders the file size too large to print. Problems with memory are usually associated with older printers.

Practical task

Find out how to delete jobs from the print queue. NB Sometimes switching the printer off and on again will not be effective.

Graphic images, particularly those which are uncompressed/high resolution and therefore contain the most detail, take a long time to print out on all but the most expensive laser printers. Waiting for printing can be frustrating and time-wasting if such eventualities are not foreseen and planned for. Further, if a backlog of print jobs accumulates in the print queue because documents are taking time to print, the printer's memory will soon be overloaded, causing it to crash.

Colour printing is expensive. Children can be encouraged to print out black and white or colour draft quality copies of drafts of their work, reserving the slower, higher quality colour print-out for finished pieces. The quality of printing is affected by the type of printer, the setting (draft, normal and best) and the type of paper used. If very high quality images are required, photographic quality paper is available, although this is very expensive.

Graphics software and the core subjects

The ideas and activities introduced below are intended to give a feel for the range of ways in which graphics software can be utilised to support and enhance teaching and learning in mathematics, science and English. They are not intended to be comprehensive, merely to go some way towards illustrating the breadth of possibilities and to provide starting points for the customisation of ideas and the generation of others. Examples introduced under mathematics, for instance, may be just as applicable to one or more of the other areas. Other useful sources include professional journals (*Primary Science Review, Reading*, etc.), websites (National Grid for Learning, BECTa, etc.) and Schemes of Work (Science, ICT, etc.).

Graphics software and science

Children may use painting software to produce images which illustrate the effects of light sources, such as street lights at night, fireworks in the sky, sunlight reflected in water. The particular qualities of graphics software, which enable light colours to be easily imposed on top of dark ones, make ICT a suitable medium for such representations, allowing children to create an artistic effect otherwise only accessible to very practised artists.

Very often science work at all levels requires illustration to aid communication. Graphics software enables Images to be created, imported and modified as required. It also supports the addition of textual labels to aid identification and explanation.

Posters may be designed to illustrate scientific understanding – the importance of a healthy breakfast or regular cleaning of teeth, for instance. Such posters can be created using traditional media, although graphics software allows revision and reorganisation to maximise presentational impact. It also enables children to incorporate images from a range of electronic sources.

Experience with graphics software in the manipulation of images, resizing or cropping for instance, is an important transferable skill relevant across the range of generic applications. These will be used in the incorporation of graphs in a word processed report, for instance.

Graphics software and mathematics

Graphics programs can be used to produce repeating patterns for wallpaper or wrapping paper. The stamping facility in many paint packages enables a design to be rapidly duplicated and arranged. The suitability of various shapes for geometric sequences can be explored.

Drawing programs may be used to support mathematical modelling activities. A teacher may prepare an electronic file containing a plan view of the classroom and the outlines of a range of furniture to be included. Children could explore possible arrangements. Extension activities might include conditions (the computer cannot be located by a south-facing window) or additions (two new children are starting on Monday, where should the extra table and chairs be located?).

Graphics software sometimes includes a grid which can be switched on and off. Grids may help children use graphics software to develop their mathematical understanding of shape. A teacher may prepare graphics files incorporating a grid, lines of symmetry and shapes in one quadrant. Children can make use of the grid to help them draw the shape reflected or rotated (see image on page 38). Similarly, a teacher may use a regular shape on a grid to rapidly and effectively demonstrate the effect of increasing perimeter on area.

Graphics software and English

The design of logos is a popular activity supporting work on interpreting methods of communication. Drawing programs in particular facilitate the production of bold, easy-to-reproduce images.

Practical task

Collect together a range of examples suitable to support a project on the design of logos. Use a drawing package to design a new logo for a common product. What are the difficulties children are likely to encounter with such a project? How can you support them?

Images are frequently used to communicate information in newspapers and magazines. Children can select and manipulate images from a wide range of sources, digital cameras, scanners, the World Wide Web, to illustrate news stories. Possible challenges include manipulating a photographic image to give a misleading or contrary impression.

The communication of information in cartoon-type format can be particularly enhanced using graphics software. A common background may be prepared and used as the basis for six or eight images telling the story of the child's journey to school or the adventures of a cat. A series of digital images may be sequenced and captioned to provide an account of the class's visit to the fire station or a record of a drama production.

Graphics software:

a summary of key points

- *Graphics can be incorporated in a wide variety of electronic documents.*
- *Sources of graphics include images composed in painting and drawing software, as well as scanned images, digital camera pictures, clip art and (copyright permitting) CD ROMs and the World Wide Web.*
- *Graphics occupy large amounts of computer memory space relative to text documents, which may cause difficulties in saving onto floppy disk and/or printing.*
- *Graphics software complements more traditional art media, it does not replace them.*
- *The functions, effects and tools incorporated in graphics software provide exciting opportunities for image creation and manipulation.*

Further reading

Ainley, J. (1996) *Enriching Primary Mathematics*, Hodder & Stoughton.

BECTa (1998) *Primarily IT: Using IT to Support English, Maths and Science at KS2*, BECTa.

BECTa (1999) *Digital Still Cameras*, advice sheet, BECTa *http://www.becta.org.uk/technology/infosheets/*

DfEE/QCA (1999) *Curriculum Guidance for the Foundation Stage*, DfEE/QCA.

DfEE/QCA (1999) *The National Curriculum*, DfEE/QCA.

Leask, M. and Meadows, J. (2000) *Teaching and Learning with ICT in the Primary School*, Routledge Falmer.

Loveless, A. (1995) *The Role of IT: Practical Issues for the Primary Teacher*, Cassell.

McFarlane, A. (ed) (1997) *Information Technology and Authentic Learning: Realising the Potential of Computers in the Primary School*, Routledge, Chapter 9.

QCA/DfEE (1998, rev. 2000) *Information and Communications Technology: A Scheme of Work for Key Stages 1 and 2*, DfEE/QCA.

Somekh, D. and Davis, N. (eds) (1997) *Using Information Technology Effectively in Teaching and Learning: Studies in Pre-service and In-service Teacher Education*, Routledge, Chapter 6.

Underwood, J. (ed) (1994) *Computer-Based Learning: Potential into Practice*, David Fulton, Chapter 3.

Graphical representations of data are everywhere, in newspapers, magazines, books, on television programmes, on websites. Children are constantly exposed to information communicated in this manner. If they are to interpret this in any meaningful way they need to develop appropriate knowledge, skills and understanding. The National Numeracy Strategy makes specific reference to the contribution graphing programs can make to the development of children's data-handling skills.

Graphing programs have been available in primary schools for many years. Recent developments, particularly the move towards the use of icons rather than keyboard commands to access common functions, have improved the accessibility of such software for children and teachers. The range of features and functions supported by many graphing programs has also been significantly enhanced.

This chapter explores the features and functions of graphing programs and their potential for the enhancement and extension of teaching and learning in the primary classroom. Cross-curricular applications are explored and links made to other generic data-handling software.

What are graphing programs?

Graphing programs facilitate the communication of information through graphical representation. Thus they allow data to be entered, stored, presented and interpreted graphically in an electronic format. Some allow the rudimentary sorting of data, into ascending or descending order of frequency, for instance. Graphing programs do not, however, support sophisticated sorting, searching or modelling. Such data-handling activity requires database software.

What do the programmes of study for Key Stages 1 and 2 include?

At Key Stage 1 children should be taught to enter and store information (1b), to use text, tables, images and sounds to develop their ideas (2a) and to try things out and explore what happens in real and imaginary situations (2d). They should also be taught to share their ideas by presenting information in a variety of forms (3a), as well as to present their work effectively (3b).

At Key Stage 2 children should be taught how to prepare information (1b), to interpret information and check its relevancy (1c), to organise and reorganise information (2a), how to share and exchange it (3a), as well as consider its suitability for its audience and its quality (3b).

At all stages children should be taught to review, modify and evaluate their work as it progresses (4a, 4b and 4c).

What does the ICT Scheme of Work include?

At Key Stage 1 graphing programs feature in Unit 1E (Representing information graphically: pictograms) and Unit 2E (Questions and answers).

At Key Stage 2 graphing programs feature alongside databases in Unit 4D (Collecting and presenting information: questionnaires and pie charts) and in the context of monitoring and sensing in Unit 5F (Monitoring environmental conditions and changes).

What do teachers need to know before using graphing programs?

In order to teach with and about graphing programs teachers need to be confident about their subject knowledge related to the handling of data. In this area there is a substantial and obvious overlap in terms of subject knowledge between science, mathematics and ICT. Relevant issues include:

- **choice of variables;**
- **types of data;**
- **grouping data;**
- **collecting and recording data;**
- **presenting data.**

Many data-handling activities begin with consideration of what data to collect. In science the choice of variables is often a key teaching and learning objective. For instance, the growth pattern of a seedling may be explored by comparing its height at 9.00am each day over a three-week period. Two variables are involved here: seedling height and time. Alternatively, the investigation could be limited to one variable by measuring the height of a number of seedlings once only three weeks after sowing. The exploration would, in this instance, focus on the distribution of heights achieved.

There are three types of data: categorical, discrete and continuous. **Categorical data** falls into distinct named categories which do not overlap and cannot be ordered. For example, children's eyes are either blue, brown, hazel, green or grey. Where **discrete data** is concerned the classes are defined by discrete whole numbers. An example might be the number of siblings class members have. **Continuous data** cannot be so easily segregated. The height of seedlings is measured on a continuous scale and each seedling's height is, potentially at least, slightly different from that of the others. The type of data collected influences how it is collected, recorded and presented.

Before data is collected and recorded decisions should be made about how to group it. In the case of categorical and discrete data the categories or classes will usually be quite obvious. Where continuous data is concerned there is a choice: either to record (and then plot) each individual item, each seedling's exact height, or to attempt to group the data into classes, effectively translating continuous data into discrete. For instance, rather than recording a seedling's height as 8cm, another at 8.5cm, another at 6cm, each of these three seedlings could be entered into the category 5.0–9.9cm, with other categories for 10.0–14.9cm, etc.

Decisions about the grouping of data will affect recording and presentation. To continue the example above, further decisions about accuracy, number of decimal places and use of rounding, for instance, will be required, and a suitable recording format must be chosen. Data may be collected and recorded in a number of ways, counting and tally charts being the most common for categorical, discrete or grouped data.

Once data has been collected and recorded, consideration can be given to presenting it graphically. It is important that the choice of graph is consistent with the data type.

Categorical and discrete data are frequently represented with bar charts, with each bar representing one discrete category or number. Bar charts can be arranged horizontally or vertically or as bar line graphs. Pie charts are also suitable for the presentation of categorical or discrete data, particularly where consideration of relative proportions is important – for instance, in comparing the ways in which members of a class travel to school. However, caution should be exercised in the use of pie charts, especially where there are two or more categories containing similar or equal amounts of data, since it may be difficult to distinguish their relative size by eye. The representation of data sets where one or more category has a value of zero is also problematic, since these will not be represented on the pie chart.

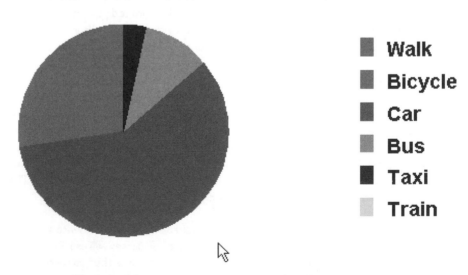

Pie chart with one category having a zero value (Counter, BlackCat)

Line graphs and scatter graphs are suitable for the presentation of continuous data. Continuous data may include two variables – for example, 12 March seedling 6.7cm, 13 March seedling 6.9cm, to be plotted on to the graph. Such graphs are sometimes called xy graphs. The seedling's height can be plotted against the date. A scatter graph represents the actual data in this instance, whereas a line graph may be used to join the individual points to give some indication of rate of growth over time. However, caution should be exercised because the joining of such plots by a line implies the existence of data which is not actually present, that is that if data had been collected at intermediate points it would necessarily fall directly on the line. Further if some data collection opportunities are missed, for instance over the weekend or half-term, graphing programs often interpret no data as having a zero-value (the line graph returns to the x-axis). Spreadsheet software, which also enables graphs to be plotted from such data, will produce a more helpful result.

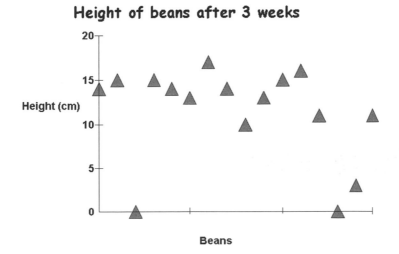

Line graph showing the effect of a break in data collection (CounterPlus, BlackCat)

Scatter plot showing distribution of seedling heights (CounterPlus, BlackCat)

Practical task

Plan a sequence of lessons to introduce the concept of tally charts for the recording of data. Choose a suitable subject context. Note how and why ICT can be used, making reference to assumptions about the availability and location of resources. Note pre-requisite knowledge, skills and understanding with respect to mathematics and ICT.

What do teachers need to know about graphing programs?

Teaching with and about graphing programs involves teachers:

- *Selecting appropriate opportunities* – in which graphing programs can facilitate, enhance or extend children's learning, such as exploring the impact of graphically representing one set of data using a range of scales. In some instances the focus will be on teaching and learning in ICT (how a graphing program can facilitate such an investigation), while in others ICT will be used as a resource in the teaching and learning of another curriculum area (the effect of choice of scale).
- *Exploring the full range of data-handling activities* – it is important that data-handling work does not always end with the production of a graph. In many instances data-handling work will begin with a graphical representation and learning will be focused on interpretation and analysis.
- *Making explicit links between related knowledge, skills and understanding* – data-handling has applications in many areas of the primary curriculum; teachers thus have opportunities to make explicit and reinforce the links between children's previous experiences and new learning across the range of contexts.
- *Modelling appropriate use of ICT* – for instance, the joining of individual plots of data by a line graph to assist in the analysis of the pattern or trend the data represents.
- *Demonstrating and intervening* – for instance, intervening to assist a child to export a graph to the appropriate place in a word-processed record of a science experiment; similarly, demonstrating and discussing the potential difficulties of interpreting data represented in a pie chart.

The list below attempts to identify the knowledge, skills and understanding of graphing software teachers need in order to teach effectively with and about graphing programs. Many graphing programs support only a subset of these functions. This is no reflection on their usefulness – in most instances it is a strength. However, it does signal that teachers must be aware of the capabilities and limitations of any program as these will be significant in the choice of software for any teaching and learning activity.

Graphing program knowledge, skills and understanding:

- **creating, opening, saving, closing, deleting and printing documents;**
- **adding, modifying and deleting data;**
- **plotting and replotting graphs;**

- selecting and displaying graph types, including more than one graphical representation of the same data (e.g. tiling);
- selecting and modifying constituent elements of graphs (e.g. changing the colours of bars in a bar chart to correspond with the data represented);
- selecting, resizing, cutting, copying and pasting graphs;
- selecting and modifying graph scales and autoscaling;
- selecting two-dimensional or three-dimensional representations;
- inserting graph titles, axes labels, key and text;
- selecting font and font size for graph and axes headings;
- exporting graphs into other applications;
- importing information from other applications (e.g. clip art);
- utilising help;
- altering defaults;
- customising the graphing program (e.g. switching off functions not needed);
- utilising alternative input devices (overlay keyboards, dataloggers);
- selecting appropriate colours and/or patterns depending on printer availability (black and white or colour);
- protecting documents.

There will be occasions on which other data-handling software, such as databases or spreadsheets, will be more suitable. Teachers need to be confident in making decisions about the most appropriate application for a particular situation.

What are the key features of a graphing program?

Graphing programs:

- produce graphs directly from data entered;
- offer a range of graph types;
- usually automatically select the scale;
- provide opportunities to reinforce the relationship between numerical and graphical representation of the same data;
- allow children to focus on using the information contained in a graph rather than the process of construction;
- do not replace children constructing graphs manually – this is an important developmental stage in the process of understanding;
- facilitate a range of learning outcomes – for instance, emphasis may be on data collection (planning, organising, recording, entering), or on interpretation, effect of scale, etc.;
- facilitate work on equivalence and differences between graph types (bar charts, pie charts, bar line charts, line graphs, scatter graphs, etc.);
- facilitate work on progression in graphical representation.

Graphing programs can be divided into two categories:

- pictogram programs, which support early graphing activities and usually allow for the representation of data only as pictograms or block graphs;

- **more sophisticated graphing programs, which support a range of graph types and functions.**

In order to facilitate the exploration of the features and contribution of each of these, they will be referred to as **pictogram programs** and **graphing programs** respectively.

What do graphing programs have to contribute to teaching and learning?

Finding things out

One of the key advantages of working with graphing programs to handle data is that much of the time-consuming work of planning and plotting graphs is automated, allowing the user to focus on the information contained in the graph. Which is the most frequently owned pet in Year 3, and how does this compare with pet ownership of children in Year 6? Other questions may then be raised, such as what might be the influences on choice of pet? What constitutes pet ownership where there is more than one child in a family? How is double-counting avoided? The emphasis can be investigation and analysis rather than representation.

An important aspect of work in handling data surrounds choosing the most appropriate graphical representation. Graphing programs facilitate immediate comparisons between the different graph types. Would pie charts be the most suitable method of representing the pet ownership information? What if some animals are owned by children in Year 3, but not by children in Year 6? It has been suggested that using graphing programs enables children to make independent choices of graph types, safe in the knowledge that the graph can be redrawn speedily if necessary. When hand-drawing is involved there may be a tendency for the teacher to direct children towards a shared class decision in order to avoid wasting time.

Most pictogram and graphing programs also enable data to be sorted at a simple level – for instance, into ascending or descending order of frequency. This can be a very useful facility, especially if there are a wide range of categories, or the scale is marked in intervals of two, or five, or ten. Using a sorting function does not obviate the need for children to be able to read information accurately from graphs – it can provide another opportunity for teaching or reinforcing that skill.

Developing ideas and making things happen

Graphing programs can be used to demonstrate the relationship between data, its recording in a frequency table and its representation as a graph. Most programs allow the frequency table to be shown alongside a graph. Making these connections is vital if children are to handle data in a meaningful way.

Developing children's understanding of the equivalence of information represented in different graphs can be facilitated by showing, for instance, a horizontal bar chart, a vertical bar chart and a bar line graph side by side. The tiling function of any PC-based program can assist with this.

Graphing programs have autoscaling features which choose the scale of the graph, usually depending on the highest value or frequency. Most programs replot graphs each time new data is entered, thus the development of a graph and the effect of each new piece of data can be powerfully demonstrated. Autoscaling often results in graphs where scales are marked in intervals of 2, 5 or more. The construction and interpretation of such graphs are important stages in the progression of children's understanding of data-handling. Sometimes the autoscaling feature can be disabled to enable children to make their own selections as appropriate.

Similarly the connection between choice of scale and the effectiveness or impact of a graph can be explored. There can be valuable learning associated with attempting to 'misrepresent' information, choosing a scale such as to make a small variation look large or a large variation look insignificant. Almost any newspaper, magazine, website or TV news programme will contain some graphical representation of information. Making links with real-life applications of knowledge and understanding which children could otherwise view as quite abstract in nature can be a powerful learning tool.

Exchanging and sharing information

Many of the issues discussed above, such as choice of graph type, equivalence, comparison and scale, also have relevance for the exchange and sharing of information. Further, if a group of children present the results of a science investigation for display on the classroom wall, decisions need to be taken not only about the most suitable type of graph for the data but also about its readability at a distance. The advantages of a horizontal bar chart over the more common vertical, where the labels might more obviously correspond with the data, might also be explored. There are instances where two or more graph-types may be equally appropriate and children can justify their personal selections and discuss the merits of each (see overleaf).

Copying and pasting a graph into a report or other document is a useful function and many pictogram and graphing programs support this. Graphs can usually then be moved and resized as any other image. It is important that children know that they can transfer their skills in this way within and between applications.

Progression of knowledge, skills and understanding

Early data-handling activities will relate closely to children themselves and their own experiences. 'Ourselves' is a common theme and many pictogram programs such as Counting Pictures (BlackCat) and Pictogram (Kudlian Soft) have a predetermined range of relevant topics to select from, e.g. pets, favourite foods and hair colour. Having chosen a suitable focus, such as children's eye colour, and discussed the likely alternatives, the teacher can call up a blank pictogram on screen and ask each child in turn their eye colour. The children may need to consult with a friend and the teacher (or

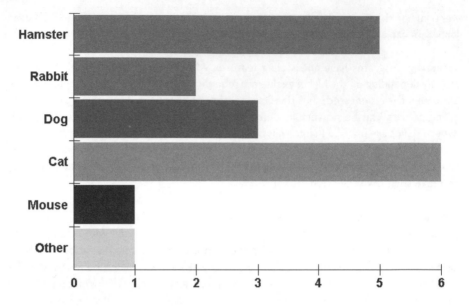

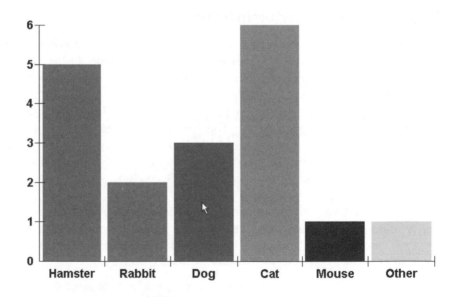

Horizontal and vertical bar charts showing the same data (CounterPlus, BlackCat)

a child) can click or drag the appropriate icon to include the information in the graph. The pictogram will be built in front of the children and the connection between each child's answer and the appearance of an icon in the relevant column made explicit. This method of data collection is appropriate for young children and the immediate building of the graph reinforces the connection between the data (the answer the child gives) and the graphical representation of that data.

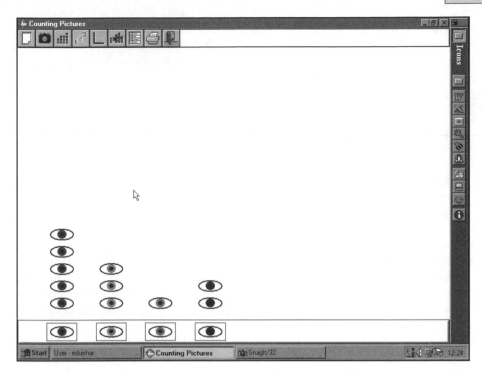

Building a pictogram (Counting Pictures, BlackCat)

At its basic level a pictogram drawn with a graphing program will consist of columns of icons indicating a one-to-one representation. The teacher can lead the children in counting to establish how many children in the class have blue eyes. There is no need for text labelling as each category is identified by an icon, although the software usually allocates a title based on the subject selected.

Pictogram programs have a variety of features which facilitate their use at various stages in supporting children's knowledge and understanding of data-handling. These might include:

- *Adding a scale.* **Reading from a scale requires a more sophisticated understanding of number than counting.**
- *Adding axes.* **The addition of x and y axes represents a stage in the development from a straightforward pictorial representation of data towards the more abstract model generally recognised as a graph.**
- *Transforming the pictogram into a block graph.* **Again, this is a development from the straightforward pictorial representation of data, towards something more abstract in nature. Each block in a block graph clearly represents an individual piece of data, which distinguishes it from a bar chart in which the divisions between the data are not distinct. Pictogram (Kudlian Soft) also supports bar charts, representing a further progression.**

Practical task

Following the compilation of a Year 1 class pictogram of favourite foods, what questions would you ask to probe and develop the children's understanding? How would you follow up the activity?

Programs such as DataPlot (Kudlian Soft) and Counter (BlackCat) facilitate more sophisticated data-handling activities. Data is entered through a frequency table and a graph is drawn and redrawn as new data is added. Text labels are transferred from the frequency table to the graph and these are necessary to identify and interpret the graph. There are a range of graph types to choose from, allowing children to experiment and select the most suitable. Scales marked at intervals greater than one can result, although such graphs can also be drawn in some pictogram packages. Options for saving, adding text, exporting to other applications, etc. are easily accessible. A further stage of sophistication (DataPlot and CounterPlus) enables each axis to be separately titled and choices to be made about colours and/or patterns. Two- and three-dimensional representations are often possible and selection can be made from a wider range of graph types. Negative and decimal numbers are usually supported.

Effective utilisation of graphing programs may facilitate the development of children's knowledge, skills and understanding of handling data independently of the motor skills required for the hand-drawing of graphs.

What are the capabilities and limitations of graphing programs?

Selecting appropriate graph types

Graphing programs do not automatically select the most suitable graph type to represent data. The choice remains with the user. Neither will the software advise against unsuitable selections. Teachers will need to ensure that children make appropriate choices based on the data. Many graphing programs automatically represent data as vertical bar charts unless another graph type is specifically selected. Again, this is no reflection on the suitability of this type of graph to the particular data but this default can serve to reinforce the use of this most common graph type and militate against exploitation of others.

Practical task

Prepare a display to demonstrate:

- *an appropriate use of each of the graph types supported by a particular graphing program;*

or
- *how to print a completed graph, including making appropriate selections to cater for the available printer;*

or
- *children's top tips for using...*

Classroom story

A student teacher had carefully prepared for an ICT lesson on graphing programs. His teaching objectives were carefully described in terms of ICT. He was familiar with the software and had selected data related to current geography work. He took the class to the ICT suite and proceeded to introduce the activity, describing the process. The children were required to access a graphing program, enter into it data related to average temperatures across a year in a distant place and the UK, and produce pie charts for comparison.

The student teacher provided each pair with a help sheet he had prepared and the lesson proceeded. After 35 minutes, each pair had produced two pie charts. These were printed out and the class returned to the classroom. Questioning the children, however, suggested that they had little understanding of the information the graphs represented. Although the data had been chosen to relate to a current geography study, the links between that and the ICT session had not been made explicit to the children. Further, there was little examination of the finished pie charts in order to interpret the data. This would in any event have been difficult using the graph type selected.

Frequency tables and tally charts

Most graphing programs allow data to be viewed through a frequency table as well as a graph. In many, the data is entered through the frequency table. This feature provides an opportunity for teachers to reinforce the correspondence of the information represented in these different ways. Counting Pictures (BlackCat) also has a tally chart function which can be used to facilitate the progression from simultaneous data collection and entry, as in the eye colour example described previously, to recording and subsequent entry, for which the tally chart is the most frequently used mechanism.

3D graphs

The more recent graphing programs have the facility to display graphs in two or three dimensions. The third dimension allows children to produce very sophisticated-looking representations which compare favourably with those they see throughout the media. However, the 3D effect can be problematic for children when reading information from scales. This is particularly pertinent where bar charts are concerned and some confusion may be experienced in deciding which lines to follow to read off information. Similarly a bar with a zero value will still contain a block of colour (see overleaf). The interpretation of 3D graphs may thus require explicit teaching.

Selecting colours

Graphing programs often allocate predetermined colours to bars in bar charts, thus the first bar may be blue, the second green, and so on. Clearly this may be problematic if the data has some link to colour – for instance, children's favourite colours, hair colour or eye colour – and there is a mismatch. A graphing program will not be an effective tool if it represents the number of people with blue eyes with a red bar. Many of the

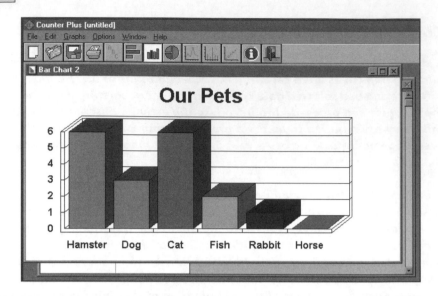

3D bar chart showing category with zero value (CounterPlus, BlackCat)

more recent, and often more sophisticated, allow colours to be changed once the initial graph has been drawn up, although there is some software in which this option is not available. Teachers need to ensure that they explore such issues when selecting software for particular tasks. The writers of the DataPlot (Kudlian Soft) software saw this as a potential difficulty and incorporated some programming that ensures that if data is identified by colour (e.g. eye colours, blue 6, green 3, brown 7) it is represented by those colours. The software also identifies hair colours such as ginger, fair and blonde and makes appropriate choices (assuming the colours have been spelt correctly).

Pictogram packages

Pictogram packages tend to have a limited range of possible graph subjects, such as pets, journeys to school, favourite colour, etc. It is entirely appropriate that young children's data-handling experiences involve data which has some relevance to them, rather than the rainfall patterns in a distant location, for instance, and most of these are catered for. Some packages provide the opportunity for this range to be extended although this involves drawing appropriate pictures using the tools provided. Within each graph subject there is also a limited range of categories; hamster, for instance, does not always appear as a pet choice, although horse often does. Again these can be customised and software houses enhance their products over time, most welcoming feedback on such issues.

Similarly there are often restrictions on the amount of data that can be entered. Counting Pictures (BlackCat), for instance, has a maximum frequency in any one category of 12, whereas Pictogram (Kudlian Soft) allows more when the block graph option is selected. With class sizes even in Key Stage I of around 30, such a limitation on numbers can be important. However, when frequencies of 10 or more are involved the use of a scale should be considered.

Printing issues

Most graphing programs make extensive use of colour. This helps children differentiate between different groups of data and aids the visual engagement with the graphic representation. However, when graphs are to be printed out this may become an issue. Colour printing is slow, expensive and not available in many classrooms. Printing a coloured graph on a black and white printer usually results in various shades of grey. These may be difficult to distinguish between and, as discussed above, if colour is a feature of data (hair colour, for instance) the use of a graphing program over hand-drawing might be questioned. There are two potential solutions available to teachers and most graphing programs should support at least one of these. Sometimes it is possible to choose to print out a graph without any colour, enabling the children to colour in by hand. DataPlot (Kudlian Soft) provides an option to switch off the colour function. Alternatively it may be possible to change the various colours to white, producing the same effect when printed out. Secondly, some programs provide a range of pattern options (stripes, dots, etc.) which can be selected instead of colours.

Links to other generic data-handling software

CounterPlus (BlackCat) allows multiple columns of numeric information to be incorporated and thus represented on the same graph, enabling comparisons to be made. This type of function is usually only possible using a spreadsheet.

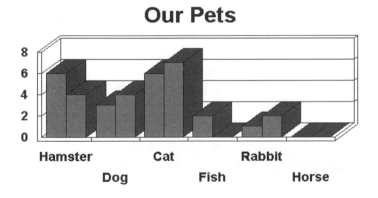

Pet	Class 1	Class 2
Hamster	6	4
Dog	3	4
Cat	6	7
Fish	2	0
Rabbit	1	2
Horse	0	0

Block graph and frequency table demonstrating comparison between two sets of data (CounterPlus, BlackCat)

Many software houses have linked ranges of data-handling programs, thus the transfer of children's skills from one to another is facilitated by familiar icons and functions. Kudlian Soft produce Pictogram and DataPlot facilitating progression from one to the other. Additionally, DataPlot is a constituent of DataSweet, which also includes the spreadsheet DataCalc as well as database software. Similarly, Counting Pictures uses the same icons as Pick a Picture, BlackCat's early database program.

Common errors and misconceptions

Although using graphing programs reduces some of the demands on children involved in graphical representation of data, it is important to ensure that value is placed on interpretation and/or understanding of the subject knowledge involved rather than on the presentation of professional-looking images. Similarly, use of a graphing package does not ensure successful teaching and learning – this will depend on appropriate task setting, differentiation, intervention, etc. as in any other teaching and learning situation.

There can be a tendency when using ICT to collect far more data than would otherwise be contemplated. On occasion this can be its advantage, for instance in the monitoring of environmental conditions. However, caution should be exercised to ensure that the volume of information does not distract from the teaching focus. It is also possible to cancel out the time saved by automatic graph plotting by requiring children to enter large quantities of data into the computer.

Autoscaling can often be disabled to allow children to select their own scale and consider the implications of differing intervals, etc.

Graphing programs have a limited range of uses, generally confined to the entry, presentation and basic manipulation of data with one or two variables. If more complex data-handling is required a spreadsheet or database program will be more appropriate.

Graphing programs and the core subjects

The ideas and activities introduced below are intended to give a feel for the range of ways in which graphing programs can be utilised to support and enhance teaching and learning in mathematics, science and English. They are not intended to be comprehensive, merely to go some way towards illustrating the breadth of possibilities and to provide starting points for the customisation of ideas and the generation of others. Examples introduced under mathematics, for instance, may be just as applicable to one or more of the other areas. Other useful sources include professional journals (*Primary Science Review, Reading, Interactive, Child Education, Junior Education*, etc.), websites (National Grid for Learning, BECTa, etc.) and Schemes of Work (Science, ICT, etc.).

There is extensive overlap between science, mathematics, English, ICT and other subject knowledge, skills and understanding in this area of data-handling. Teachers need to be clear about their primary teaching objective for any particular task or sequence of activities and maximise the opportunities for making explicit links between learning in the various curriculum contexts.

Graphing programs and science

Graphing programs have many possibilities in science for the recording and representation of experimental data. A number of possibilities have already been discussed. Most graphing programs allow text to be entered and displayed alongside graphs and graphs can usually be copied and pasted into other applications, such as word processing.

Some activities will involve the collection, entry and representation of data, while others may start with prepared data looking for patterns, causal links and evidence to test hypotheses.

Environmental monitoring and sensing

Datalogging is the process of monitoring and recording environmental data such as temperature, light, movement and sound using sensors. The data is displayed through software which can be considered to be a special application of a graphing program, having many common features and functions, such as choice of graph types and scale.

Electronic sensors are linked to a buffer box, for example LogIT, which provides an interface between the sensors and the computer. The software, such as Junior Insight (Longman Logotron), is used to set the timescale for the logging of the data, which can be very short or very long, and the intervals at which data is collected are automatically adjusted. Datalogging can take place with the interface connected to the computer enabling the results to be simultaneously displayed on screen, or remotely and subsequently downloaded.

Datalogging has a variety of uses both inside the classroom and beyond. Key Stage 1 children can hold temperature sensors in their hands and watch the screen as the sensor warms up. Similarly, they can observe the instant and dramatic effects of clapping, singing or being very quiet near a sound sensor. Recording the sound levels in a classroom over the school day can provide interesting discussion as teacher and children attempt to identify peaks and troughs and relate these to particular activities or incidents.

Older children may insert a temperature sensor into a defrosting bread roll and record data over a 24-hour period. (Temperature sensors tend to fall into two categories and not all are appropriate for contact with damp conditions.) Two temperature sensors connected to the buffer box can record the temperature inside and outside a window overnight. Similarly, away from the classroom the temperature in the school pond may be monitored night and day over a week or even longer. Another long-term project might involve placing a movement sensor in a pot with a bulb while it sprouts, flowers and dies.

Datalogging can make a valuable contribution to children's data-handling experiences. Its principal advantages are:

- *speed* – data can be recorded more quickly than by hand;
- *electronic data entry* – the data recorded is automatically entered into the

software, removing the time-consuming manual entry of data;

* *memory* – large amounts of data can be stored;
* *perseverence* – data can be logged over extended periods.

Datalogging can be used to facilitate children becoming more scientific in their experimental technique:

* enabling the realistic repetition of experiments to achieve consistency in results and appreciate the concept of experimental error;
* enabling the testing of variables over greater ranges of values and similarly wider ranges of variables to be tested.

Practical task

Find out how to:

* *connect the sensors to the datalogging interface and the interface to the computer;*
* *select the duration and/or intervals of data collection;*
* *collect data remotely and download to the computer;*
* *save and retrieve collected data.*

Briefly outline activities involving the logging of environmental data suitable for Year 1, Year 3 and Year 5 children. Relate these to the science National Curriculum.

Graphing programs and mathematics

Graphing programs can be useful tools to contribute towards the development of children's understanding of the graphical representation of data. Almost any activity involving graphs draws on children's existing mathematical knowledge and provides opportunities for reinforcement and extension work. As already discussed, graphing programs can make a substantial contribution where the speed and automatic function of the software enables teachers and learners to focus more specifically on a particular mathematical objective, be it choice of appropriate graph type or scale, the grouping of data or recording technique.

Teachers can also make use of graphing programs to provide prepared documents as starting points. Children might use print-outs for work away from the computer or complete activities involving pre-entered data. Such strategies maximise the contribution of limited ICT resources.

Graphing programs and English

All media make extensive use of the graphical representation of data to communicate information. On at least some occasions there is an element of selection, either of the data itself or of the means by which it is presented, in order to persuade the audience to reach a particular conclusion. If children are to engage with information critically they need a range of opportunities through which to explore the issues of selection and presentation of data – taking information presented in a local news story and reinterpreting it to support an alternative slant, for instance. This might involve the selective omission of data, choice of scale, even choice of graph type to accentuate or mask certain aspects.

Practical task

Find out how to switch the autoscaling facility on and off. Represent one set of data using a range of scales and comment on the selection of the most appropriate. Collect a range of graphical representations of data from the media. Plan a speaking and listening activity to explore the issues associated with the impressions conveyed.

Children can develop and apply their knowledge of genre and the classification of literature by analysing the books in the class library. A range of data-handling questions arise relating to the selection, grouping and presentation of data. Similarly children will be involved in prediction, articulating their ideas, supporting their views and decision-making. The results can be considered in the light of children's preferences. Further exploration might focus on the similarities or differences in girls' and boys' tastes.

RESEARCH SUMMARY

Children, graphs and computers

Phillips (1997) reviews three experiments conducted by others into Key Stage 2 children's abilities to interpret graphical representations of information where ICT is involved.

In the first, children were asked to interpret a car's journey on a distance/time graph. They were able to identify when the car was travelling rapidly forwards, when stationary, when going slowly backwards, although very much more difficulty was experienced with associating these movements to time. In the second study, children were readily able to distinguish and interpret datalogging sensor readings for light, sound, movements and temperature on a time graph, telling the story of the various features of the data. The last involved children investigating paper spinners to determine the optimum length of wings to maximise distance travelled. Scattergraph plots were discussed and a line of best fit used to identify the v pattern in the data and consequently the optimum wing length.

Phillips contrasts these results with data which shows poorly developed graphical interpretation skills amongst secondary children. He concludes that it takes time for children to develop graphical interpretation skills and that the increasing use of ICT for data-handling in primary schools is likely to increase the children's exposure to graphic representations with consequent positive effects. He cautions against well-presented but meaningless graphs which are all too easy to produce with ICT, highlighting informed decision-making in this respect as a key issue for intending teachers.

Graphing programs:

a summary of key points

___ *Effective teaching with graphing programs requires careful consideration of the selection, collection and recording of data.*

___ *Graphing programs enable learners to focus on the interpretation of graphical representations of data.*

___ *Graphing programs facilitate work on the equivalence and differences between graph types.*

___ *Data-logging software can be considered to be a special application of graphing.*

___ *Graphing programs have very specific features. For some data-handling activities spreadsheets or other types of databases will be more suitable.*

Further reading

Ainley, J. (1996) *Enriching Primary Mathematics*, Hodder & Stoughton.

BECTa (1998) *Primarily IT: Using IT to Support English, Maths and Science at KS2*, BECTa.

Bolton Curriculum ICT Centre (1999) *The ICT in Primary Numeracy*, Bolton Curriculum ICT Centre.

DfEE/QCA (1999) *Curriculum Guidance for the Foundation Stage*, DfEE/QCA.

DfEE/QCA (1999) *The National Curriculum*, DfEE/QCA.

Fox, B., Montague-Smith, A. and Wilkes, S. (2000) *Using ICT in Primary Mathematics: Practice and Possibilities*, David Fulton.

Frost, R. (1995) *IT in Primary Science: A Compendium of Ideas for Using Computers and Teaching*, IT in Science.

Leask, M. and Meadows, J. (2000) *Teaching and Learning with ICT in the Primary School*, Routledge Falmer, Chapter 5.

Loveless, A. (1995) *The Role of IT: Practical Issues for the Primary Teacher*, Cassell.

McFarlane, A. (ed) (1997) *Information Technology and Authentic Learning: Realising the Potential of Computers in the Primary School*, Routledge, Chapter 7.

QCA/DfEE (1998, rev. 2000) *Information and Communications Technology: A Scheme of Work for Key Stages 1 and 2*, DfEE/QCA.

Smith, H. (1999) *Opportunities for ICT in the Primary School*, Trentham Books, Chapters 4 and 12.

Somekh, D. and Davis, N. (eds) (1997) *Using Information Technology Effectively in Teaching and Learning: Studies in Pre-service and In-service Teacher Education*, Routledge, Chapter 5.

Underwood, J. (ed) (1994) *Computer Based Learning: Potential into Practice*, David Fulton, Chapter 8.

The modern world is information rich in every way. Databases as repositories of information abound, from the school library catalogue to television listings: many in electronic format. In order to access, analyse, synthesise and interpret information, children need to develop appropriate knowledge, skills and understanding. The electronic databases used in school take a variety of forms from branching tree identification keys to multimedia CD ROMs and websites.

This chapter explores the variety, features and functions of databases and their potential contribution to teaching and learning in the primary school. Clear links are made to other generic aspects of data-handling.

What are databases?

Databases are structured stores of information. They allow large amounts of data to be stored, organised, sorted, searched and retrieved quickly and easily. They facilitate more sophisticated interrogation than graphing programs. Databases enable interaction with data to explore its meaning through relationships, patterns and modelling.

Spreadsheets are data-handling software which share many of the features and functions of databases. Similarly, many databases also incorporate spreadsheet functions. As software development continues the distinctions between many generic categories blur and fade. For these reasons spreadsheets have been included in this chapter.

What do the programmes of study for Key Stages 1 and 2 include?

At Key Stage 1 children should be taught to gather information (1a), to enter and store it (1b) and to retrieve it (1c). They should be taught to use text, tables, images and sounds to develop their ideas (2a), to select from and add to information (2b) and to try things out and explore what happens in real and imaginary situations (2d). They should also be taught to share their ideas by presenting information in a variety of forms (3a), as well as to present their work effectively (3b).

At Key Stage 2 children should be taught to talk about the information they need (1a), how to prepare it (1b) and to interpret it and check its relevancy (1c). They should be taught to organise and reorganise information (2a), to evaluate the effect of changing values and to identify patterns and relationships (2c). In addition, they should be taught how to share and exchange information (3a), as well as consider its suitability for its audience and its quality (3b).

At all stages children should be taught to review, modify and evaluate their work as it progresses (4a, 4b and 4c).

What does the ICT Scheme of Work include?

At Key Stage 1 databases feature in: Unit 2C (Finding information) and Unit 2E (Questions and answers).

At Key Stage 2 databases feature in: Unit 3B (Manipulating sound), Unit 3C (Introduction to databases), Unit 4C (Branching databases), Unit 4D (Collecting and presenting information: questionnaires and pie charts), Unit 5B (Analysing data and asking questions: using complex searches), Unit 5C (Evaluating information, checking accuracy and questioning plausibility), Unit 5D (Introduction to spreadsheets), Unit 6B (Spreadsheet modelling) and Unit 6D (Using the Internet to search large databases and to interpret information).

What do teachers need to know before using databases?

Vast amounts of data are collected, from the various meanings of words, to the amount of rain that falls in a particular location, the daytime telephone numbers of families with children at a particular school and the school's annual repair budget. In order for this information to be of any use, it must be organised and stored in some way, often as an electronic database. The choice of a database is important to ensure that information can be accessed and manipulated as required.

The types of databases utilised in primary schools can appear quite separate from those employed in the world at large. As educational ICT moves ever closer to industry standards there is increasing convergence; for instance, the RM spreadsheet NumberMagic is a child-oriented version of Excel. It is important to remember, however, that database software used in schools is designed to facilitate learning about the processes and possibilities of data-handling as well as for the retrieval and manipulation of information.

A number of different types of database are commonly used in schools, including:

- **branching tree or binary databases;**
- **flatfile or tabular databases;**
- **relational databases;**
- **spreadsheets.**

Each of these is structured differently to support different functions.

Branching tree or binary databases

Branching tree or binary databases facilitate the identification of objects, people or plants, for instance, by the posing of questions relating to attributes which must be answered yes or no. The answer to any question leads to a further question to be similarly answered until only one possible outcome remains.

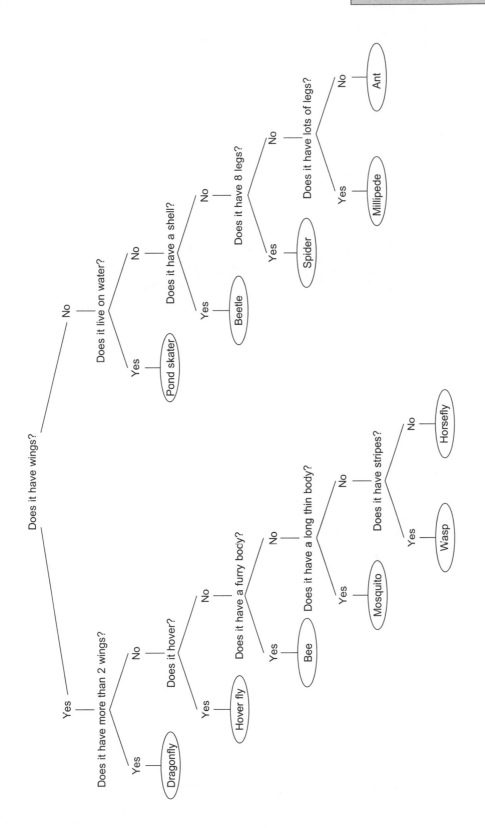

Minibeasts branching tree database

Flatfile or tabular databases

Flatfile or tabular databases are perhaps the type of database that most readily comes to mind when primary database activity is considered. A datafile comprises a number of records each containing information arranged in fields. Children will be able to relate to football cards as an analogy. The pack of cards is the datafile and each card is a record. In addition to the player's name, football cards usually include a photograph, the player's age, the name of the club they play for, the position they play, as well as dates of participation in major championships and national representation. Each of these categories is a field. Data is usually entered into a flatfile database through a form, which resembles a questionnaire and essentially prompts for data to be added to each field.

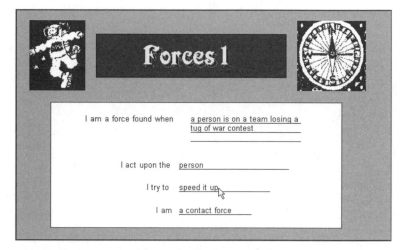

A flatfile database record (Junior PinPoint, Longman Logotron)

Situation	Object	Action	Type
a person is on a team losing a tug of war contest	person	speed it up	a contact force
hair blows in the wind	hair	keep it balanced	a contact force
using the brakes on a bicycle wheel	wheel	slow it down	a contact force
sitting on a seat	seat	change its shape	gravity
jumping from a height to the ground	person	speed it up	gravity
fridge magnets stick on a fridge	magnet	keep it balanced	a magnetic force
squeezing a sponge dry	sponge	change its shape	a contact force
stopping the wheels of a car	wheels	slow it down	a contact force
a person starts to run	person	speed him or her up	a contact force
catching a ball	ball	slow it down	a contact force
a car starts to be towed by a rope	car	speed it up	a contact force
a metal ship floats	ship	keep it balanced	a contact force
striking a match	match	slow it down	a contact force
an athlete swings a hammer around before releasing it	hammer	change its direction	a contact force
dust sticks on the screen of a television	dust	keep it balanced	an electric force

Showing: 32   sheets of: 32

Flatfile database displayed in tabular format (Junior PinPoint, Longman Logotron)

Individual records can be viewed on screen. The entire database can usually also be viewed in tabular format with each column representing a field and each row a record. Sometimes this is called a spreadsheet view.

Spreadsheets

A spreadsheet is a grid made up of cells arranged in rows and columns. Each cell is identified by an alphanumeric coordinate – A3, D4, for example. Data, often numeric, is entered into each cell by clicking and typing. This data can be searched, sorted, rearranged and presented in graphical format. More pertinently, however, individual cells can be programmed to make and display the results of calculations. In the spreadsheet below the cell B12 has been programmed with a formula which instructs it to add 17.5% VAT to the value in cell B10 and display the result.

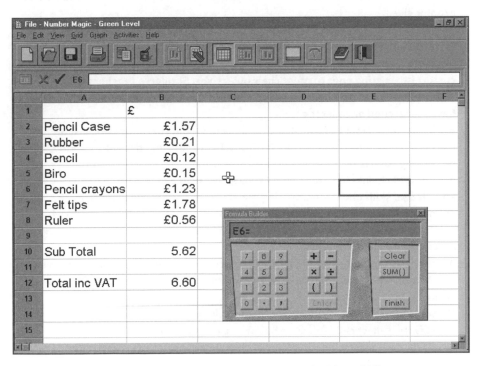

Spreadsheet showing entry of formula (NumberMagic, RM)

Relational databases

Relational databases have more complex structures than flatfile databases. Rather than information being organised as it is entered into records and fields, which then determine the types of interrogation activity the database will support, information is tagged. The tagging interrelates the information in the database. This organisational structure supports greater flexibility in interrogation. CD ROMs and World Wide Web search tools are the most relevant examples of relational databases used in primary schools. These often feature menus, indexes, keywords and hyperlinks as ways of navigating vast amounts of related information.

What do teachers need to know about databases?

Teaching with and about databases involves teachers:

- *Selecting appropriate opportunities* – in which databases can facilitate, enhance or extend children's learning, such as exploring number patterns and rules with spreadsheets. In some instances the focus will be on teaching and learning in ICT – how a database can facilitate an investigation. In others ICT will be used as a resource in the teaching and learning of another curriculum area, for instance, using a **CD ROM** to research the eating habits of minibeasts.
- *Selecting appropriate resources* – a search tool which enables safe searching of the **World Wide Web** or a **CD ROM** which supports beginning readers with audio and graphic clues.
- *Preparing suitable resources* – the majority of database activities in schools involve children interrogating prepared resources. Many are commercially available, although sometimes teachers will wish to prepare their own or customise existing ones to meet their objectives. Similarly, teachers will sometimes design databases in which children can then enter information they have researched or collected.
- *Exploring the full range of data-handling activities* – databases are not just about the retrieval of information, they facilitate hypothesising, decision-making, organising, analysing, synthesising and modelling.
- *Making explicit links between related knowledge, skills and understanding* – knowledge, skills and understanding of databases have relevance across the primary curriculum. Teachers thus have opportunities to make explicit and reinforce the links between children's previous experiences and new learning across the range of contexts.
- *Modelling appropriate use of ICT* – for instance, how producing a branching tree database in electronic format enables modifications to be made quickly and easily.
- *Demonstrating and intervening* – for instance, intervening to assist a child to identify the tallest child in a class by sorting height data in descending order. Similarly, demonstrating the effect of changing the price of sausages in a spreadsheet budget.

The list below attempts to identify the knowledge, skills and understanding of database software teachers need in order to teach effectively with and about databases. The list reflects the features of common software under each of the database categories identified. Some software packages may support only a subset of these functions. This is no reflection on their usefulness – in most instances it is a strength. However, it does signal that teachers must be aware of the capabilities and limitations of any program as these will be significant in the choice of software for any teaching and learning activity.

Branching tree or binary databases:

- creating, opening, saving, closing, deleting and printing documents;
- adding, modifying and deleting data and questions;

- plotting and replotting branching tree keys;
- inserting titles;
- selecting font and font size;
- exporting branching tree keys into other applications;
- importing information from other applications, e.g. clip art;
- utilising help;
- altering defaults;
- customising the branching tree program, e.g. switching off functions not needed;
- utilising alternative input devices, e.g. overlay keyboards;
- protecting documents.

Flatfile or tabular databases:

- opening, closing, deleting and printing existing datafiles;
- navigating through records using forwards and backwards;
- simple and complex sorting (more than one condition);
- searching to retrieve data;
- plotting and replotting graphs/reports, including:
  - adding text, title, etc.
  - selecting graph type
  - selecting and modifying colours
  - saving
  - exporting graphs to other applications;
- entering data into a prepared datafile, including:
  - selecting a new record/answer sheet
  - entering, modifying and deleting data
  - saving;
- designing a new datafile, including:
  - opening a form/questionnaire designer
  - selecting font, font size, font colour, background colour
  - inserting and modifying questions, including making appropriate selections
    for style and format of answer supported:

    words   numbers   dates
    yes/no   multiple choice
- inserting text, images, borders, arrows;
- saving.

Relational databases (e.g. CD ROMs):

- loading, including installation prior to first use;
- modifying computer display and volume settings;
- opening and closing;
- navigating using menus, hyperlinks, forwards, backwards, home;
- searching and retrieving information using menus, indexes, keywords and hyperlinks;
- playing audio and video;
- copying and pasting text, graphics, etc. into other applications;
- selecting and printing information;
- utilising help;
- critical evaluation.

Spreadsheets:

- creating, opening, saving, closing, deleting and printing documents;
- selecting worksheet and cell size;
- selecting font and font size;
- inserting, modifying and deleting row and column labels;
- inserting, modifying, moving and deleting textual and numerical data;
- inserting, modifying and deleting formulae and functions;
- inserting and deleting cells, rows and columns;
- formatting data, e.g. left alignment, centring around decimal point;
- searching and sorting data;
- adding, modifying and deleting borders and shading;
- selecting, modifying and displaying graph types;
- formatting graphs to include axes labels, key and text;
- exporting graphs and spreadsheets to other applications;
- importing information from other applications, e.g. clip art, data;
- utilising help;
- altering defaults;
- customising the spreadsheet program, e.g. switching off functions not needed;
- utilising alternative input devices, e.g. dataloggers;
- protecting cells and documents.

There will be occasions on which other data-handling software, such as graphing programs, will be more suitable. Teachers need to be confident in making decisions about the most appropriate application for a particular situation.

What are the key features of databases?

Branching tree databases:

- support sorting and classification activities at all levels;
- support data-handling activities across a range of subject areas;
- provide opportunities for developing and refining questioning techniques;
- do not replace children using paper- or book-based branching tree keys;
- facilitate the creation, revision and extension of branching tree databases;
- often support images as well as text.

Flatfile or tabular databases:

The structure of a flatfile database is determined by the choice of fields and the type of information they contain. These design issues in turn determine the ways in which the database can be used.

Flatfile databases:

- support searching to retrieve information, e.g. the names of the children in the class with blue eyes;
- support more sophisticated searching, on two variables, e.g. the names of girls whose favourite food is pizza;

- support sorting by field, e.g. to see the distribution of hair colour across the class;
- support sorting and ordering a field, e.g. into descending order to find the name of the child with the smallest feet;
- provide graphical representation of enquiry results where this is appropriate – often called a report;
- support sorting and classification activities at all levels;
- support data-handling activities across a range of subject areas;
- facilitate the development of knowledge and understanding across a range of subject areas;
- provide opportunities for developing and refining searching and sorting techniques;
- often support data held as images as well as text;
- support the rapid retrieval of information.

Relational databases:

- support searching by keyword, index and menu;
- sometimes support complex or Boolean searching (see Internet chapter);
- support data-handling activities across a range of subject areas;
- provide opportunities for developing and refining search techniques;
- do not replace children using traditional reference sources;
- facilitate the development of knowledge and understanding across a range of subject areas;
- often support video, audio and animations, as well as images and text;
- support the rapid retrieval of vast amounts of information.

RESEARCH SUMMARY

Multimedia and learning

It has been suggested that the multimedia presentation of information leads to more effective learning, the potential for interaction as well as the range of media representations used increasing the likelihood of correspondence with any one learner's preferred learning style.

Lopuck (1996) and others have drawn attention to the assumption that multimedia implies better presentation of information. Rogers and Aldrich (1996) noticed that the presence of video, animation and audio can actively distract learners from the textual and static graphic elements of CD ROMs, perhaps leading to a more fragmented understanding (Rogers and Scaife, 1998). They suggest that more understanding is needed of how children construct understanding from different information and from different representations of the same information.

Several pertinent findings have emerged from research on multimedia and learning to date. The NCET CD ROM in Schools Scheme (Steadman, Nash and Erault, 1992) and many others subsequently have focused on the need for the explicit teaching of information skills and appropriate task-setting. Aldrich, Rogers and Scaife (1998) draw attention to the design of CD ROM databases and suggest that these should promote cognitive interactivity rather than superficial interactivity at the level of button clicking.

Spreadsheets:

- support data held as text or numbers;
- display and process numerical information;
- enable automated calculations and recalculations;
- support the graphical representation of information;
- support the organisation and reorganisation of data to identify patterns, gaps and correlations;
- support the use of graphs to identify errors in data;
- provide opportunities for developing and refining searching, sorting and modelling techniques;
- support the rapid retrieval of information;
- support rapid calculations;
- sometimes support searching to retrieve information, e.g. chocolate bars available for less than 30p;
- support sorting, e.g. displaying chocolate bars in order of unit cost;
- support data-handling activities across a range of subject areas;
- sometimes support images for illustration purposes.

What do databases have to contribute to teaching and learning?

Finding things out

Databases facilitate the rapid retrieval of information. This can be a key advantage supporting a range of data-handling activities. Many of the ways in which databases can be used to support finding things out are mentioned elsewhere in this chapter.

Databases support the development of questioning skills in practical situations. Branching tree databases require very particular types of questions, to which the answer can only be yes or no, but at the same time call upon children to apply their subject knowledge as well as skills of sorting and classification. Similarly, if children are to interrogate flatfile, spreadsheet or relational databases effectively and productively they need to devise effective questions. Again, these are dependent on experience, knowledge and understanding of the data and structure of the database as well as of the subject itself.

The analysis and interpretation of information to identify patterns and explanations is facilitated by electronic databases which enable information to be rapidly searched, sorted and often presented graphically. What sorts of eyes do nocturnal animals have? If the price of every item in the tuck shop is raised by 2p, will profits increase? What is the relationship between the 3× and 9× tables?

Developing ideas and making things happen

Databases provide opportunities for children to make predictions and hypotheses and test them. For instance, is the cheapest way to buy fruit in large pre-packed bags? A spreadsheet can be used to compare the costs of different fruit bought singly, loose and pre-packed.

Decision-making is involved in all sorts of data-handling activity. Continuing the example above, decisions must be made on which to frame the investigation. Is cost per piece of fruit to be considered or cost by weight? How many different outlets are to be compared? Are the cheapest apples to be sought from each outlet, or is the focus to be Granny Smith apples only? Similarly, children may consider which is the best way to interrogate a database to retrieve information, such as details of elephants' feeding habits. Will keyword searching lead to the required information most quickly? Would using the index lead to information which may not be found by a keyword search?

Exchanging and sharing information

Many of the issues discussed above, such as display of number patterns in spreadsheets and use of multimedia to present information, also have relevance for the exchange and sharing of information.

Databases are organised stores of information. Information collected by one individual or group is only of value to others if it is accessible. The preparation of data for entry into a flatfile database requires children to order and organise and classify material around the database fields. Structuring information has many applications and is a key skill in effective communication. Children can consider the audience for their data and associated tensions, such as quality versus quantity.

Data retrieval is rarely the final outcome of data-handling activity. Often it is the start. Data retrieved from any type of database can be analysed, interpreted, synthesised and presented.

Many database programs have features which support these activities. Relational databases, such as CD ROMs, often have electronic notepad facilities in which children can make notes, perhaps copy and paste images or short extracts of text and subsequently print off or transfer to a word-processing document. Flatfile and spreadsheet databases support the presentation of data graphically. Very often these graphs can be transferred to other applications or annotated within a report section of the database software.

The presentation of data graphically is often the first stage in analysis and interpretation. It can also support the identification of relationships and potential errors and inconsistencies.

Progression of knowledge, skills and understanding

Branching tree or binary databases

Identification keys for plants and animals are the most obvious example of branching tree databases. The creation of branching tree databases which are as all-encompassing as this is a very sophisticated activity, requiring high levels of subject knowledge and understanding as well as well-developed questioning skills. It is more appropriate to use a finite set of, perhaps, minibeasts and explore questions which will progressively lead to a positive identification. Does it have six legs? Does it have a hard, shiny shell? Does it fly?

Children need to use examples of prepared branching tree databases, electronic or otherwise, before they can consider designing their own. It is useful to begin by laying out the objects, or cards representing them, on a table or the floor for children to arrange and rearrange as they select and trial questions. With only eight minibeasts to distinguish between this may take some time. Children may also need to draw upon reference material to facilitate their sorting. A considerable amount of work may be involved before using a branching tree program is appropriate.

Some of the primary packages, such as Decision Tree (Flying Fox) and FlexiTREE (Flexible) come with prepared examples. Children can test these and will soon realise that their datasets are restricted. Increasing the range of minibeasts will require more questions. An extension activity could be to try to reduce the number of questions necessary to differentiate between the minibeasts.

Flatfile or tabular databases

Early database activity often focuses on children themselves. Pick a Picture (BlackCat) has four predetermined topics: ourselves, homes, weather and minibeasts. Each topic contains a range of images and children make selections from these to build up records. Graphs can be produced in the form of pictograms or blockgraphs to display the data graphically. The contents of a datafile can also be displayed in tabular format. This software provides an accessible introduction to flatfile database activity for Early Years and Key Stage I children.

'Ourselves' record from Pick a Picture (BlackCat) which supports early database work

ALL ABOUT ME

1. What is your first name?   Daniel

2. Are you a boy or a girl?   ☒ Boy   ☐ Girl

3. What colour is your hair?   ☐ Blonde   ☐ Black   ☒ Brown   ☐ Ginger

4. What colour are your eyes?   ☐ Blue   ☐ Grey   ☐ Green   ☒ Hazel   ☐ Brown

5. How tall are you?   142 centimetres

6. How much do you weigh?   28 kilogrammes

7. What did you weigh when   4.0 kilogrammes
   you were born?

An 'ourselves' questionnaire making use of multiple choice data entry
(Junior PinPoint, Longman Logotron)

Junior PinPoint (Logotron), available for PC and Acorn, is truly generic software and can be used across the curriculum. The example above provides an appropriate model for work with younger children as the amount of information to be entered of a textual or numeric nature is minimal, with many fields requiring selections to be made from multiple choice lists by pointing and clicking.

In this example children will enter their own data, perhaps with assistance, into a prepared structure. Then, as a group or class, interrogate the data to answer questions (how many people have blue eyes?) or test hypotheses (hamsters are the most common pet).

As with graphing, it is not always necessary or appropriate for children to collect and enter their own data into a flatfile database before they interrogate it. They can also work productively with prepared databases. A number of software publishers sell prepared datafiles to support a range of curriculum areas. These have advantages which include effective design, accuracy of information, large numbers of records and saving teacher preparation time.

Children will need plenty of experience with databases before they can begin to design their own. Designing and preparing a database is a time-consuming activity and due thought should be given to long-term outcomes. A class may begin a database of plants and animals living within the school grounds, which could be monitored and expanded by subsequent classes, building into a valuable record of diversity and change over time. Trialling the design and checking the entries for errors are vital stages of the process. Such activity is generally recommended for the latter part of Key Stage 2.

Spreadsheets

Children can be introduced to spreadsheets through the functions they perform. For example, RM's NumberMagic spreadsheet software comes complete with a number of prepared examples. These will support a range of activities, mainly mathematics-focused across Key Stage 2.

Children can enter numbers into a spreadsheet set up as a function machine to determine what function the machine supports. The teacher may then draw the children's attention to the formula determining the function and encourage them to experiment with modifying the formula.

Another route into spreadsheet activity is making the link with calculators, placing emphasis on a spreadsheet's potential for supporting and facilitating calculations, especially those of a repeated nature. Children may begin by entering a number and choosing an operation to perform on that number, for instance adding 3. This process can be repeated focusing on emerging patterns, predicting and checking. At this level, spreadsheets have a number of advantages over calculators, the most pertinent being that they are easily checkable, by reviewing the formula for a calculation, or by graphing results to identify anomalies. It is important that the copying and pasting of formulae is not offered as a solution too soon, before the purpose and process of formula-writing has been understood.

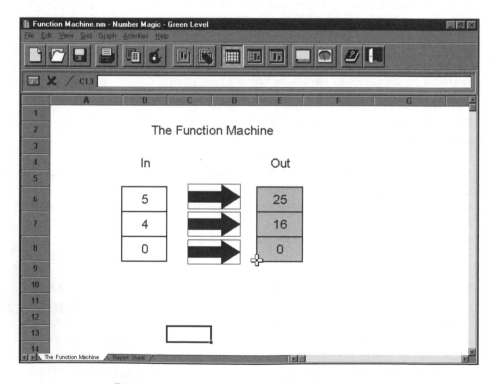

Function machine, a prepared file in RM's NumberMagic

Children will need opportunities to become familiar with the navigation of spreadsheets, the entry of numeric and textual information, the display of numeric and graphical results, saving and printing.

Spreadsheets can then be used to extend children's knowledge and understanding of number facts and arithmetic laws, supporting mental calculation as children predict and check results as well as deriving generalisations, supporting early algebra work.

Spreadsheets are ideal for modelling 'what if?' scenarios. These can be applied to mathematic and scientific situations. Budgets are a popular focus. Similarly, modelling the effect of changing variables in science work. Graphical representation of spreadsheet data can be particularly powerful in this respect.

Classroom story

A Year 6 class were applying their mathematical understanding to the comparison of data from their school weather station with national information for the same period. In order to make comparisons they needed to calculate some weekly and monthly averages from their own data recorded on a daily basis. The teacher reminded the class that, anticipating making eventual use of it, the data had been recorded in a spreadsheet as it was collected. She reminded the children how to enter a formula to calculate the arithmetical mean rainfall over one week in March. The children carefully programmed formulae into other cells to determine median and modal values. The teacher then intervened to demonstrate how formulae could be copied and applied to other cells using the fill handle. A while later the teacher was intrigued to notice that some of the children were busy checking the spreadsheet's calculations with calculators. Questioning determined that this checking regime had been a group decision to ensure that formulae copied from one location to another were actually performing the intended operation.

Relational databases

My First Amazing Incredible Dictionary (Dorling Kindersley) adds a new dimension to the traditional concept of the dictionary for young children. They can click to hear words spoken to confirm graphophonic relationships. Each word is presented through text, images and sound. Children can also follow hyperlinks to related words.

Most CD ROM databases make use of multimedia to a greater or lesser extent and whole new concepts in terms of resources have been developed. The Microsoft CD ROM *Musical Instruments* combines labelled images of orchestral and more esoteric instruments with music samples and related information. In this instance the audio aspects of the information clearly enhance the learning potential (as well as the engagement) of the resource. This database requires some quite sophisticated information-handling skills if children are to search in it independently, although the format and navigation are clear. Younger children may be directed to specific resources on the disk.

My Ultimate Human Body (Dorling Kindersley) again makes extensive and effective use

For more information on World Wide Web search tools, see page 101, Chapter 5

of multimedia and contains a wealth of information. No diagram or explanation of the heart pumping can convey meaning quite so effectively as an animation. Information on this CD ROM is accessible by category, by index, by keyword searching as well as by hyperlinking from related areas. This provides enormous flexibility for searching and retrieving information, while highlighting the need for focused task-setting.

Practical task

Design an A4 help sheet to help children navigate successfully in a specified CD ROM. What are the key features of effective help sheet design?

What are the capabilities and limitations of databases?

Selecting appropriate databases

The different types of database discussed in this chapter support different types of data-handling activity. Teachers and children will need to make informed decisions about the most appropriate tool for a particular purpose. Again, this is no reflection on the suitability of a particular piece of software as no one program supports all the features and functions discussed.

Keyword searching

For more information on advanced searching, see page 103, Chapter 5

Effective keyword searching relies on the choice of appropriate keywords. For most children such selections will require thought, discussion and practice. Some words which have a wide range of applications may not be suitable. Effective keyword selection implies some background knowledge of the search subject. Refining techniques can be used to further narrow the focus of a search.

Classroom story

A group of Year 5 girls had been charged with researching and presenting some information on the planet Earth as part of a class science study on the Earth and beyond. Two of the group decided that a CD ROM encyclopaedia might be a good place to start. They input 'earth' into the search tool and a high number of matches were found. Beginning to explore these in a systematic manner the girls became confused as the first two hits related to soil types and electrical circuits. They had not considered that, even in science, the word 'earth' can have different meanings in at least three contexts: planet Earth, electrical earth and soil.

Spelling is another issue in keyword searching. Incorrectly spelled words are unlikely to prove effective in retrieving the desired information. Some CD ROMs and websites provide support for children, to help them check their spelling before conducting a search.

One of the strengths of relational databases is that one particular item may be retrieved by searching on any one of a number of keywords. Flatfile or other databases may be more restricted in this respect.

Hypertext literacy

Reading hypertext documents requires a range of skills – many of these have parallels with those associated with traditional, linear reference texts, while some are different. Many relational databases are navigable by index as with traditional reference material. The presence of hypertext links, however, means that children's reading of these texts is not continuous – they may dart about from one narrative to another to another. Retaining a task focus throughout such a process can be demanding. Similarly, hypertext documents give no sense of geographical location within a text. Children may never know whether they have accessed everything on a particular subject.

CD ROMs

CD ROM databases should not be confused with:

- **CD ROM *talking books* – these make use of multimedia but their structure mirrors more closely the linear nature of traditional books. The subject focus of a talking book may be fiction or non-fiction. Talking books are also available on computer disk (Oxford Reading Tree, Sherston) and are being developed for the World Wide Web.**
- **CD ROM *software* – CD ROMs are used for the storage and transfer of software. Often when a school buys new software this comes in the form of a CD ROM. The software is then copied onto the school's computer or network as appropriate and used from there.**
- **CD ROM *games and resources* – some games and other resources also come in the form of CD ROMs. These are not designed to be copied onto the computer's memory – the resources they contain are used direct from the disk. Tizzy's Toybox (Sherston) and Mighty Maths Number Heros (Iona Software) are examples. Again multimedia is widely used, but the resource is subject-specific rather than generic in nature.**

Practical task

Children may bring in CD ROM resources from home. What will your response be? What are the issues involved and how will you manage them?

Relational databases, such as CD ROMs and World Wide Web sites provide access to almost unlimited quantities of information. Sometimes this can be quite daunting as making appropriate selections to satisfy the needs of the task demands that children can judge whether particular information is relevant to their enquiry as well as thinking how they might use it.

Copying

Many data-handling activities involve children retrieving information with a view to synthesising or applying it in some way. Teachers have long struggled with children copying information retrieved from reference sources, apparently without engaging with the material. One likely reason for this is that children have difficulty in making sense of the information. Often reference texts are designed with an adult audience in mind and make use of complex sentence structures and sophisticated vocabulary. Information can only be useful if children are able to read it. They also need to deploy associated higher order reading skills, such as skimming and scanning text.

Classroom story

A Year 5 teacher was encouraging her class to make use of CD ROM databases to support research across the curriculum. She was discouraged to note that many children merely copied down the text as it appeared on the screen or printed it off. She discussed this issue with the children and suggested a new strategy. Children could print entries or copy and paste them into a word processor, but must then read them through away from the computer, highlighting or underlining words that they did not fully understand and looking them up. The children then replaced these elements of the text with their own words to form a narrative that had meaning for them. Some time later she drew one child's attention to the presence of the word tectonic in his work, and was told that it was okay because he now knew what tectonic means.

Data accuracy

Effective interrogation of a database relies on accurate information. It also relies on information being entered in a format in which it can easily be searched or sorted. If a child enters information into a flatfile database on the number of brothers and sisters they have as text, it could appear as 2brothers or 2 buthrs. The data would require considerable checking and modification before it could be used. The phrasing of questions as multiple choice or yes/no wherever possible minimises the chance of such errors.

CD ROM databases are subject to editorial control by their publishers, in the same way as traditional media. No such quality monitors are exercised by the authors of most World Wide Web sites and information retrieved from these should be treated with suitable caution.

Flatfile databases and types of data

Flatfile databases can support data entered in a variety of formats, including:

- text, e.g. the name of a minibeast;
- numeric, e.g. the number of legs the minibeast has;
- dates;
- yes/no, e.g. does the minibeast live the the UK?
- multiple choice, e.g. the life expectancy of a minibeast:
  - a day
  - a week
  - a month
  - 3 months, etc.

Where textual entries are concerned it is usually possible to limit the length of answers to 20 letters, although they may be much longer – each record may contain a general paragraph of explanation about the minibeast, for instance. Numeric entries can sometimes be limited to a specific range, to reduce the chances of inaccurate data being entered in error. The use of multiple choice and yes/no answers wherever possible further reduces the risk of inaccurate entries or entries that are difficult to search or sort.

Spreadsheets and the = sign

Teachers will need to ensure that they make explicit the role of the equals sign in spreadsheet formulae. It does not balance the equation, showing that one side is equal to the other, but provides a function, effectively instructing the software to perform the calculations that follow it. This may also be explained as 'the contents of this cell are equal to'. Again this is slightly different from the use of the equals sign with calculators when the calculations are entered first and the = sign instructs the calculator to perform the functions.

> Written algorithm:
> 10 + 4 = 14 (balance, both sides of the equation are equal)
>
> Spreadsheet:
> = B3 + B7 (function, add the contents of B3 to B7 and display)
>
> Calculator:
> 10 + 4 = (function, now add 10 to 4 and display)

Professional use

Spreadsheets have great possibilities for teachers' professional use. Many teachers make a class list at the beginning of the year which they are able to use and reuse many times as mark sheets, etc. It is not suggested that teachers maintain mark sheets electronically, unless they wish to or the school requires it.

Data protection

Personal data held electronically is governed by the provisions of the Data Protection

*For more
information on
legal and
ethical issues,
see page 225,
Chapter 14*

Act 1998. Although this legislation was not formed with primary data-handling activities in mind, teachers must ensure that they comply with its requirements where applicable. The key issues are ensuring that data is secure and cannot be accessed by unauthorised individuals and that it is not held any longer than necessary.

Privacy

The collection and interpretation of personal data about children raises issues of privacy and sensitivity – children's height and weight, for instance. Teachers have devised a number of strategies in this respect. Ourselves-type data can be collected for young children's teddies, while with older children it may be appropriate to discuss some of the issues raised.

Software selection and advice

Most software and ICT-related resources, such as talking books or non-fiction CD ROMs, can be obtained from their publishers and/or software wholesalers on approval. The school usually has between 10 and 28 days to evaluate the resource and decide either to keep it and pay the account or to return it. Obtaining software on approval sometimes incurs the cost of return postage if the decision is taken not to purchase it. However, with limited budgets and an ever-increasing range of products to choose from, the costs of mistakes can be higher financially and professionally. Software should be evaluated for content and for compatibility. Some software does not sit well with particular operating systems or other software items. It is important to determine whether a piece of software will cause such problems and, if so, whether the benefits of the software outweigh the problems of overcoming compatibility issues.

*For more
information on
software
evaluation, see
page 228,
Chapter 15*

A database of CD ROMs originally generated as part of the Multimedia Portables for Teachers project and containing reviews of hundreds of titles is available via the BECTa or the NGfL websites. Similarly, TEEM are compiling an educational software database, also containing reviews and supplier information. This is available online at *www. teem. org.uk/*.

Practical task

Select a range of non-fiction CD ROMs on a specific curriculum area. Aiming to identify resources that would support the teaching and learning of that subject across a primary school, critically evaluate the resources.

Is one age range better catered for than others? Why might that be?
How might you customise and refine the evaluation criteria suggested to reflect your own:

* *subject specialism?*
* *age range specialism?*

World Wide Web

There are many high quality World Wide Web sites which provide good quality multi-media information resources. Teachers must consider, however, speed of access, cost, security, stability, consistency and accuracy when making decisions.

Navigation within CD ROM databases is often similar to that of World Wide Web browsers, although often different icons are used. Buttons to return to the home page or menu are common, similarly forwards, backwards and search.

For more information on the Internet, see page 95, Chapter 5

Printing issues

It is all too easy with some database programs, particularly spreadsheets, to accidentally print the entire database rather than the portion intended. Children may decide that it would be useful to print out the information they can see on the screen, without considering that that may be a subsection of a very large document. Often it is necessary to detail exactly what is to be printed. Sometimes copying and pasting into a word processor or other document may be useful, such as narrative or images from a CD ROM or website.

Teaching and learning

Although using database programs reduces some of the demands on children involved in the manipulation of data, it is important to ensure that value is placed on interpretation and/or understanding of the subject knowledge involved rather than on the presentation of professional-looking graphics. Similarly, use of a database does not ensure successful teaching and learning – this will depend on appropriate task-setting, differentiation, intervention, etc. as in any other teaching and learning situation.

Databases and the core subjects

The ideas and activities introduced below are intended to give a feel for the range of ways in which databases can be utilised to support and enhance teaching and learning in mathematics, science and English. They are not intended to be comprehensive, merely to go some way towards illustrating the breadth of possibilities and to provide starting points for the customisation of ideas and the generation of others. Examples introduced under mathematics, for instance, may be just as applicable to one or more of the other areas. Other useful sources include professional journals (*Primary Science Review*, *Reading*, etc.), websites (National Grid for Learning, BECTa, etc.) and Schemes of Work (Science, ICT, etc.).

There is extensive overlap between science, mathematics, English, ICT and other subject knowledge, skills and understanding in the area of data-handling. Teachers need to be clear about their primary teaching objective for any particular task or sequence of activities and maximise the opportunities for making explicit links between learning in the various curriculum contexts.

Databases and science

Databases are used extensively in primary science. 'Ourselves' is a popular focus for the collection of data. Similarly, data can be collected from children's own experimental results, entered into a spreadsheet and used to predict and explore the effect of making changes to variables – for example, recording plant growth measurements against differing quantities of water, light, warmth, etc.

Spreadsheets, and particularly graphs generated from them, can be equally valuable in highlighting errors. The concept of experimental error is often difficult to explore effectively in primary schools due to the lack of opportunity for repeated experimentation. However, data from a whole class's results entered, compared and analysed might highlight anomalies, leading to discussion and prediction of possible causes and perhaps improvements in experimental technique – the same group member operating the stopwatch each time, for instance.

The properties of materials could be a research topic for the compilation of a class datafile resource. Fields might include what they are, where they come from and what we use them for, the field structure of the database providing a structure for the children's research. Such resources can be accessed for information later and added to by other classes to build enduring resources over which children have some ownership.

CD ROMs and websites can provide access to high quality multimedia data. When the USA has a space shuttle on a mission, images are available to children in classrooms around the world as quickly as they are to NASA scientists. Such databases also provide a breadth of resources which would not be available otherwise – slow-motion video of spiders walking or animations of the way the bones or muscles in the leg move as humans walk.

Databases and mathematics

Spreadsheets can be used to generate arithmetic and geometric sequences rapidly. Teachers may generate and print these to use away from the computer. A range of problem-solving activities can be supported in this way. For instance, using a hundred square, colour in all the cells containing 7s. What do you notice? Now colour all those with numbers ending in 3. What do you notice? Many websites are effectively databases of mathematics investigations from which children can select a question to answer, again often away from the computer.

A branching tree database incorporating pictures may be used to support the sorting and classification of shapes with younger children. Does it have corners? Does it have four sides?

Mathematical investigations such as the shape of the farmer's field can be modelled using spreadsheets – creating the maximum area with the minimum fencing materials, exploring different shapes of field, working towards generalisations and early algebra.

Data-handling activities which have real relevance for children can be derived from

Using the number pattern function (NumberMagic, RM)

school sporting activities. Recording the results from the netball or football league matches week by week can provide opportunities for statistical analysis: average goals scored per match; comparison of home and away results. Children can be charged with determining the placings of athletics competitors on school sports day: calculating the overall winner based on the average of three long jumps or rounders ball throws.

Databases and English

Effective use of a range of databases in the primary school provides opportunities for the teaching and reinforcement of a range of higher order language skills, such as keyword selection and the skimming and scanning of text.

A class database of book reviews searchable by author, subject matter and reading level may be a valuable ongoing resource. In a whole-school situation children may be involved in the process at varying levels. Older children may be called upon to design and trial the structure of the resource. All children could be involved in adding records, with support varying from adult scribes to older children checking the entries for errors and inaccuracies. Similarly, all children might use the database to assist their selection of reading material.

Electronic dictionaries and thesauruses provide alternative reference sources. Some children find these easier to use than paper-based sources because of the combination of audio, images, text and hyperlinks. Most word processing packages have their own built-in dictionaries and thesaurus.

Databases, including spreadsheets:

a summary of key points

___ *Databases enable interaction with data to explore its meaning through relationships, patterns and modelling.*

___ *There are a range of types of database commonly found in primary schools. These include: binary or branching tree databases;*
> *flatfile or tabular databases;*
> *relational databases;*
> *spreadsheets.*

___ *Good database design is essential if the data contained is to be used effectively.*

Further reading

Ainley, J. (1996) *Enriching Primary Mathematics*, Hodder & Stoughton.

BECTa (1998) *Primarily IT: Using IT to Support English, Maths and Science at KS2*, BECTa.

Bolton Curriculum ICT Centre (1999) *The ICT in Primary Numeracy*, Bolton Curriculum ICT Centre.

Cook, D. and Finlayson, H. (1999) *Interactive Children, Communicative Teaching: ICT and Classroom Teaching*, Open University Press.

DfEE/QCA (1999) *Curriculum Guidance for the Foundation Stage*, DfEE/QCA.

DfEE/QCA (1999) *The National Curriculum*, DfEE/QCA.

Fox, B., Montague-Smith, A. and Wilkes, S. (2000) *Using ICT in Primary Mathematics: Practice and Possibilities*, David Fulton.

Frost, R. (1995) *IT in Primary Science: A Compendium of Ideas for Using Computers and Teaching*, IT in Science.

Loveless, A. (1995) *The Role of IT: Practical Issues for the Primary Teacher*, Cassell.

QCA/DfEE (1998, rev. 2000) *Information and Communications Technology: A Scheme of Work for Key Stages 1 and 2*, DfEE/QCA.

Smith, H. (1999) *Opportunities for ICT in the Primary School*, Trentham Books.

Somekh, D. and Davis, N. (eds) (1997) *Using Information Technology Effectively in Teaching and Learning: Studies in Pre-service and In-service Teacher Education*, Routledge, Chapter 4.

Underwood, J. (ed) (1994) *Computer Based Learning: Potential into Practice*, David Fulton, Chapter 6.

The Internet is everywhere in today's society and its influence is expanding. From its early beginnings serving special interest groups, the Internet has grown in a few short decades into a global network whose revolutionary impact is likened to that of the printing press. The British government, keen to harness this powerful tool for education, embarked on an ambitious programme in 1997 involving:

- **connecting all schools to the Internet;**
- **ensuring that all teachers and half of all children have their own email address;**
- **establishing the National Grid for Learning as a quality teaching and learning resource.**

More recently attention has shifted to:

- **increasing the ratio of computers to children;**
- **increasing the speed of school Internet connections;**
- **developing quality, interactive digital teaching and learning resources.**

While the Internet itself is not a generic software application, use of its many facets requires generic software. More importantly, the potential of the Internet in the context of teaching and learning is so wide ranging as to be effectively generic in nature.

This chapter explores the various functions of the Internet in the context of primary education. Access, navigation, communication, safety and publication are considered alongside the potential for teachers' professional use and enhancing and extending teaching and learning.

What is the Internet?

The Internet originated out of need. Sources appear to claim two different starting points, one being the US military and the other research physicists at CERN in Geneva. What is agreed, however, is that computer users realised that saving information on to disk to transfer it between machines was a slow and inefficient practice. Linking two or more machines together enabled electronic information to be transferred between them. This linking, or networking, of a group of computers is known as a Local Area Network (LAN) and many schools now have some or all of their computers linked in this way. The Internet is essentially a network of networks with LANs and individual machines being interconnected via one of a range of telephonic-type connections.

Any computer in the world can thus potentially communicate with any other computer, provided that both are connected to the Internet. In order for the various computers to be able to make sense of the information they send and receive across the Internet they use a common protocol called Transmission Control Protocol/Internet Protocol (TCP/IP) – essentially this means that they all speak the same language.

The Internet encompasses a number of communication features, including email, the World Wide Web and conferencing.

What is the World Wide Web?

The term Internet is widely misused, when often it is a part of the Internet, the World Wide Web (WWW), that is being referred to. The World Wide Web is made up of hypertext pages containing text, images, sounds and animations interconnected via hyperlinks. These pages provide information, opinion, archive material and up-to-the-moment news and images. Some provide software and games to download, while others act as portals or gateways, existing merely to provide links to a range of other pages. Anyone can publish pages on the World Wide Web. All web pages are written in the programming language hypertext mark up language (HTML).

Where do email, discussion groups and conferencing come in?

The Internet is a communications tool and much of the communication it facilitates takes place via the World Wide Web. However, it also supports two other main categories of communication: email and discussion or conferencing.

Email (electronic mail) allows a user to send electronic messages to other users. There are many parallels with letter-writing, although a range of email specific conventions, often referred to as netiquette, have grown up, such as a lack of formality, tolerance of spelling errors and a prohibition on spam (unsolicited or junk email). Messages take a basic text format, although formatted text documents, graphics or other files can be sent as attachments and increasingly as part of the email message itself. Email can facilitate rapid and sometimes low cost communication across the world or next door.

Practical task

The term 'netiquette' refers to the conventions associated with the use of email. Consult a range of sources – for example, BECTa, your email software help, a search tool home page, a school email policy – and research this. How might you introduce and develop this idea with children?

Electronic **discussion** or **conferencing** takes a variety of forms and formats. There are electronic bulletin boards or newsgroups where information or queries can be posted related to a specific subject or interest. These often lead to detailed exchanges of information and opinion between a range of contributors. Some individuals find it useful to watch the discussion without necessarily contributing themselves and they are referred to as lurkers. Access to such asynchronous discussions can be restricted – for instance, to members of a professional association – or open.

A similar function can be provided through email. In this instance it is called a **listserv** and is essentially an email distribution list with all participants automatically being circulated with each contribution. A newsgroup or listserv may be mediated by an individual who checks each contribution for relevance before it is posted.

Email and the electronic discussion possibilities described above are **asynchronous**. Users can read others' contributions and respond at a time convenient to themselves and communication is not dependent on the contributors being available at the same time.

Access to **synchronous discussion**, where the participants are online at the same time, can also be open or restricted. Electronic **conferences** can be established where specified participants meet online and contribute to a real-time discussion. Conferencing can utilise text, audio or video (video conferencing). Generally, specific software is used for each of these. Alternatively a range of open fora, often referred to as **chat rooms**, exist. These can be accessed via the World Wide Web and discussion in these is also real-time, text-based and with the focus being chosen by participants.

Participants in newsgroups, listservs or online conferences are considered to belong to **virtual communities**. A virtual community consists of individuals with common interests who communicate online. Probably the members of virtual communities will never meet face-to-face.

Practical task

Consider the similarities and differences between newsgroups and listservs. What might be the advantages of either of these?

What is an Intranet?

An Intranet is an internal network. Intranets can support a similar range of communication and information functions to the Internet, although the resources are only accessible to users of the internal network. Intranets often look and operate exactly like the World Wide Web. Schools develop Intranets to provide children and teachers with many of the benefits of the Internet while minimising the attendant costs of connection and concerns over safety.

What do the programmes of study for Key Stages 1 and 2 include?

At Key Stage 1 children should be taught to gather information from a variety of sources (1a), retrieve stored information (1c) and to use text, tables, images and sounds to develop their ideas (2a). They should also be taught to share their ideas by presenting information in a variety of forms (3a) and to present their work effectively (3b).

At Key Stage 2, children should be taught to talk about the information they need, how they can find and use it (1a), to prepare information (1b) and to interpret information and check its relevancy (1c). They should also be taught how to share and exchange information (3a) as well as consider its suitability for its audience and its quality (3b).

At all stages children should be taught to review, modify and evaluate their work as it progresses (4a, 4b and 4c).

What does the ICT Scheme of Work include?

The Internet is featured explicitly in the Key Stage 2 units: 3E (Email), 5B (Analysing data and asking questions: using complex searches) and 6D (Using the Internet to search large databases and to interpret information).

However, online resources can be used to support a variety of other units from IC (The information around us), through 3D (Exploring simulations) to 6A (Multimedia presentation).

What do teachers need to know before using the Internet?

The Internet and the World Wide Web are growing and evolving all the time, as are the ways in which they are used. Some background knowledge and understanding is essential to underpin teachers' decisions about the effective use of these resources. Relevant issues include:

- **accessing the Internet;**
- **accessing the World Wide Web;**
- **navigating the World Wide Web;**
- **searching the World Wide Web;**
- **publishing on the World Wide Web;**
- **sending and receiving email.**

Accessing the Internet

Access to the Internet requires:

- *hardware* – **a suitable computer;**
- *connection* – **a modem and telephone line, an ISDN line or broadband connection;**
- *an Internet Service Provider (ISP)* – **provides onward connection to the Internet through large servers;**
- *software* – **an email package and/or browser, for instance, enabling Internet-related activities.**

Some computers, often single machines in homes, connect to the Internet via a modem and a conventional telephone line. This is called a **dial-up connection** as the computer dials the telephone number of the ISP in order to make the connection. Modems, which are built into many PCs, translate electronic information into a signal which can be passed along the telephone line. Similarly they decode incoming signals. This is the slowest way to access the Internet.

Alternatively, connection can be via ISDN (Integrated Services Digital Network) which allows faster downloading and uploading of information. Many primary schools use ISDN and it is considered suitable for a number of machines connecting at once. Broadband connection – for example, JANET (Joint Academic NETwork), through which all Higher Education Institutions (HEIs) connect to the Internet in the UK – offers very fast access for high numbers of simultaneous users.

The speed of Internet access will also be affected by the speed of the computer and the server, as well as the level of traffic. It is accepted that access in the UK is generally slower from 2pm onwards when US users become active.

Accessing the World Wide Web

In order to access the World Wide Web of interconnecting documents, a piece of software called a **browser** is required. The browser is an interface that enables the user to view and navigate web pages. The two most common browsers are Netscape and Internet Explorer, although others are available. Acorn users, for instance, may use Fresco (ANT Ltd). Most browsers support email access, web page authoring and other activities, although alternative dedicated applications are also available for these functions.

Navigating the World Wide Web

URLs

Navigation is via pointing and clicking on hypertext links. These links (often text coloured blue, although they can be buttons or images) take the user from one hypertext document to another. The cursor will become a hand symbol when it is moved over a hypertext link. Although any website may have any number of pages linked together, each of these pages is essentially a separate document and has its own individual Uniform Resource Locator or URL. This is the web page address and it is this unique URL which enables navigation through the almost limitless range of web pages. URLs may at first appear confusing, although familiarity quickly enables the user to decode and even predict some URLs. Briefly, using as an example the URL *http:// www.wkac.ac.uk/education/*

- **http stands for hypertext transport protocol and means the document is being accessed through hypertext;**
- **www. stands for World Wide Web;**
- **wkac is the name of the server being accessed, in this case King Alfred's College, Winchester, and this is the server on which the web page being accessed is stored;**
- **.ac stands for academic – all academic institutions in the UK have this as part of their URL; *http://www.ex.ac.uk/* is Exeter University;**
- **.uk means that the site is based in the United Kingdom; similarly .es is Spain; an address without a country designation is usually based in the US;**
- **/education is the directory or pathway on the server in which the specific page is located, i.e. where the document is stored.**

On this basis, .edu stands for academic institutions in the USA, .co.uk is the suffix for UK-based companies (although increasingly businesses are opting for .com, the US business suffix), .gov indicates a government site and .org stands for a non-profit-making organisation, such as the Association of Teachers of Mathematics *http://www.atm.org.uk/*. A new suffix .sch has recently been introduced and some schools already have website addresses which incorporate this.

Browsers

When a browser is first opened it will display a home page. This may be the home page of the browser itself or of the ISP. In a university or college it will usually be the institution's home page. A home page is merely the front page of a website and usually takes the form of an index or menu providing links to other pages. The home page displayed when the browser is first opened can easily be changed as required. In school it may be the front page of the school's website, or it could be another page specifically designed to facilitate children's use of the web, providing links to safe searching environments or sites relevant to current topics.

Practical task

Find out how to change your home page (the page opened automatically by your browser when you first open the browser).

Accessing web pages

The URL of a particular web page can be entered directly into the browser in order to take the user directly to that page. Click in the space where the current web page address is displayed (usually towards the top of the screen), carefully type in the address and press return. Accuracy in terms of the case of letters, absence of spaces and direction of slashes (obliques) is vital – any variation will result in failure to connect to the desired site. The browser will locate and display the desired page. An error message may mean that the URL has not been entered correctly, although website addresses do become out of date, so it may be that the page is no longer available or has moved to another location. Similarly, web pages are sometimes temporarily unavailable, while they are being updated, for instance, or because of some technical difficulty with the server on which the page is stored.

Bookmarking

In order to ensure that a web page can be easily accessed in future, its location can be saved in your own computer's memory. This is usually called **bookmarking** or **favourites**, based on the terms given to this feature by the two most common browsers. In future the site can be accessed directly from this list, without the need to enter the URL.

Practical task

Begin your own list of bookmarks or favourite websites. Find out how to:

- *add a site to your list;*
- *delete a site;*
- *organise your list into folders.*
- *transfer your list to another machine.*

Surfing

Surfing or **browsing** is the term given to exploration of the web in which a user follows links from one web page to another as their interest takes them. As an introductory activity this has value in terms of familiarising the user with the ways in which web pages are interconnected. Not all links are logical or indeed useful and such unstructured activity may quickly become frustrating.

Searching the World Wide Web

Many websites have search facilities built in. These allow the user to search in that particular, often large, site for something specific and access it straightaway. For example, the National Grid for Learning, NGfL, has a search facility *http://www.ngfl. gov.uk/* which enables users to search the entire site. It also provides access to searchable databases of CD ROMs and educational software.

Search tools

Search tools are programs which search the web to help users find a particular website or information on a specific subject. Most web browsers have direct links to a range of search tools. No one search tool searches the whole web, so it may be useful to try similar searches with a couple of different search tools. Search tools are generally divided into two categories depending on the ways in which they work.

SEARCH ENGINES

Search engines are huge databases which users can search with keywords or phrases, e.g. AltaVista *http://www.altavista.com/*. Search engines automatically trawl the web looking for sites and index them by keyword. This can mean that every word in a website is indexed regardless of context or relative importance resulting in huge numbers of hits for any word or phrase searched, many of which will not be useful. Results are usually ranked in order of relevance which can be helpful, although the criteria used to decide relevance may not match with the user's own ideas. Searching with combinations of words or phrases can result in fewer, more appropriate hits. Many search engines support a range of strategies and tools for refining searches. Practice may also improve the user's effectiveness in using a search engine.

 For more information on keyword searching, see page 86, Chapter 4

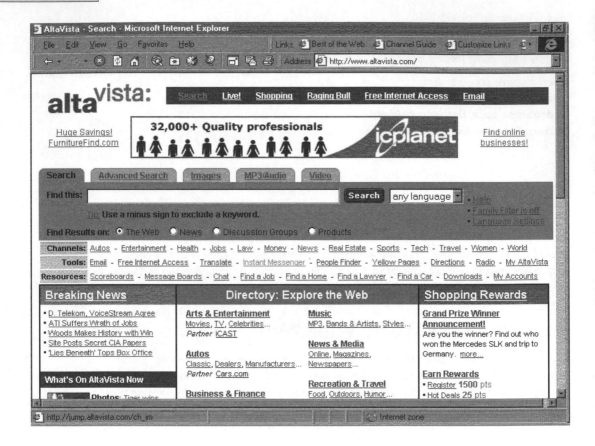

The AltaVista search engine home page

DIRECTORIES

Directories are the second common type of search tool and they allow users to progressively narrow down their search area by choosing categories and sub-categories, e.g. Yahoo! *http://www.yahoo.com/*. There are some similarities to branching tree databases. Some form of human mediation is usually involved in organising these directories and productive searching may as a result be faster. The number of websites included in a directory is likely to be smaller than that covered by a search engine. Most search directories also support keyword or phrase searching.

Meta search tools

These are search tools which themselves search a range of other search tools simultaneously. Ask Jeeves *http://www.aj.com* is an example of a meta search tool which works in a different way from that described above. The user poses a question and the search tool searches for websites likely to provide an answer.

Practical task

Use a range of common search tools to search for:

- *a website you know of;*
- *information related to a specific part of the National Curriculum programmes of study – for instance, the Earth and beyond;*
- *a newsgroup relevant to your subject specialism.*

What do you notice? Do you find one of the tools or types of tools more suited to your needs and interests than another? Why do you think this might be? How can you increase the efficiency of your own searching? What useful knowledge, understanding and techniques have you discovered which you could utilise within the classroom?

Advanced searching

Most search tools now support both keyword and categorised searching. For many users, especially when starting out, search tools can be frustratingly unproductive. Perseverance and the use of some advanced or **Boolean** searching strategies will usually turn up something useful.

Boolean searching involves the use of operators such as AND, OR and NOT. These can be used to refine searches by combining or excluding words or phrases:

- **AND narrows a search, such that only sites that contain both keywords will be displayed, e.g. information AND technology;**
- **OR widens a search, to include sites containing one or other, or both, of the keywords used, eg information OR technology;**
- **NOT narrows a search, by excluding sites containing the keyword which follows it, e.g. information NOT technology.**

Often the Boolean operators must be in upper case, although it is important to check in the search tool being used. Some tools use the plus and minus sign to provide similar functions.

Other useful strategies supported by a number of search tools include:

- **the use of quotation marks around phrases, such as "information technology" – this will ensure that only sites in which the words appear in this order are found;**
- **wild cards – symbols which can be entered at the beginning or end of keywords or phrases, such as tech*, and the search engine will then look for matches which contain words beginning with tech, but with a range of endings, such as technology, technologies, techniques and technical. The symbol used varies between search tools.**

Search tools vary enormously. They also develop and change. It is worthwhile exploring the guidance given by the tools themselves – there is usually a wealth of information pointing towards more efficient and effective use.

Unfortunately, it is likely that standard search tools will find a lot of irrelevant information and even some unpleasant and inappropriate material. There are a range of options that can minimise risks and maximise searching efficiency.

Practical task

Find out more about Boolean searching. Many search tools describe these techniques – look under advanced searching.

Safe search tools

Safe search tools are designed to protect children from inappropriate material. There are a number of these available, such as Yahooligans! *http://www.yahooligans.com/.* Similar in layout to its parent site Yahoo!, this is a search directory through which children can only access pages which have been positively vetted for content. This site is US based.

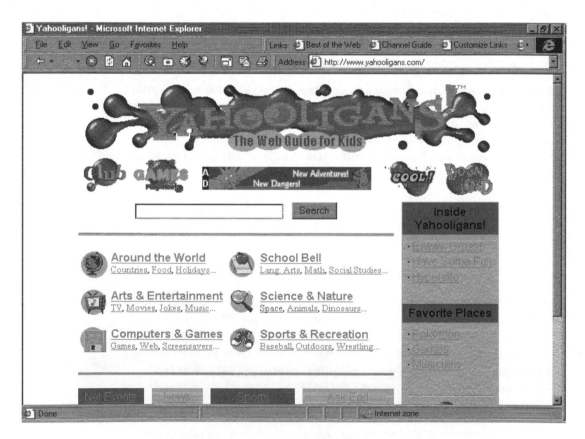

The children's search directory Yahooligans! home page

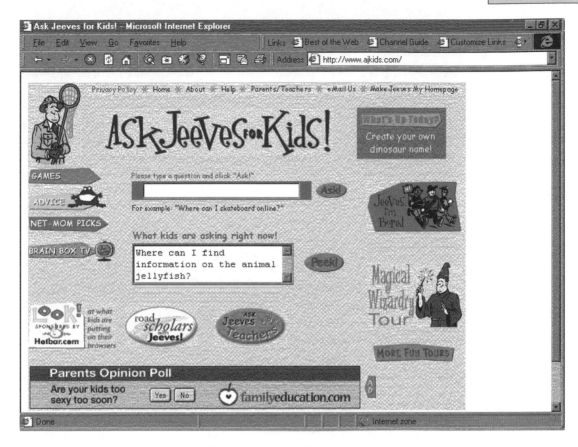

The Ask Jeeves for Kids! home page

Another safe search tool is Ask Jeeves for Kids! *http://www.ajkids.com/*. Ask Jeeves for Kids! works in a slightly different way, inviting children to pose questions and narrowing down their searches through this means. The orientation tends to be more UK-focused and sites are graded for reading level.

Safe searching environments

Some websites are safe environments in which to search, such as the NGfL. This is because all resources and links accessible through the site are carefully monitored and controlled. A range of strategies are used, including the following:

- **Web page authors must apply for inclusion in the NGfL and work within a code of conduct for content providers;**
- **All web pages included must have a designated webkeeper, responsible for quality and currency;**
- **Users can report inappropriate or inaccurate material within the NGfL to GridWatch, a facility which exists to monitor content.**

Filtering software

There is a variety of software available which aims to filter websites with the intention of protecting children against inappropriate material. These are referred to variously as **filters**, **screens** and **firewalls**. Each works in a slightly different way, but generally speaking they screen web pages for proscribed words or images which trigger a blocking device, preventing access. Examples include Net Nanny *http://www.netnanny. com/* and CyberPatrol *http://www.cyberpatrol.com*. Filters can also be used in association with email software.

Some browsers also support screening options based on a system of **page rating**, similar to film certificates. The browser can be set to exclude pages with particular ratings and any pages with no rating at all. The system called PISC (Platform for Internet Content) is voluntary and relatively new.

Filters can be very useful, providing protection and reassurance for users. However, they can be blunt instruments, since there is little or no human mediation. This results in the blocking of access to innocuous sites, while the possibility remains that inappropriate material may not trigger the filter.

ISPs

Many ISPs provide safe searching environments. Two methods are used. The first is a pre-filtered system, utilising filter software as described above, installed on the ISPs' servers. The second is often described as a **walled garden**, which means that all sites accessible have been positively vetted, a system also known as **white paging**. This system may be more limiting as the range of web pages available may be smaller. Teachers can usually contact the ISP to ask for specific web pages to be included within the walled garden. However, there may be a time delay involved while the ISP conducts checks on the pages and links leading from them.

Monitoring software

A number of schools, particularly secondaries, as well as universities and colleges make use of monitoring software rather than filters. These have the advantage of allowing access to the entire World Wide Web, while providing a tool to monitor and record access (especially where a network with individual passwords is used). A frame of reference for work involving the World Wide Web is usually operated, detailing clearly expectations and penalties for improper use.

Focused searching

There are many sites designed for teachers, providing access to resources, teaching ideas and discussion opportunities. Many of these are free, though there are some commercial services for which a subscription is payable. Searching in sites like these is likely to provide results more quickly than using general search tools. Additionally the material provided may also be more closely matched to teachers' needs.

The BBC employs teachers to recommend sites. Their Education Webguide thus provides a searchable database of links to sites which are focused, relevant and accompanied by a short descriptive paragraph as well as the name and address of the site *http://www.bbc.co.uk/webguide/schools/*.

A search tool with a UK focus can be helpful. This will reduce the range of sites searched, but results may be more closely matched to the user's requirements. *http://www.ukplus.co.uk* is an example. Similarly, some search engines and directories will allow the user to search for UK sites only if required.

There is a range of specialist search tools directed at particular needs and interests. A popular one is the UK *Yellow Pages* online at *http://www.yell.com*. Many libraries make their catalogues available online; there are directories of local services, etc. Search Engine Watch provides links to many such specialised directories *http://www.searchenginewatch.com/*.

Publishing on the World Wide Web

Anyone with access to the Internet can publish their own pages on the World Wide Web. ISPs usually provide space on their servers to their subscribers for this purpose. The pages need to be saved onto a server (uploaded) so that they can be accessed from anywhere in the world at any time. Web pages can range from the purely text-based to the fully multimedia. There are a range of programs specifically designed for web page authoring, such as Frontpage Express (Microsoft) and HotDog (Sausage), although increasingly other generic packages such as word processors also support this function – Textease (Softease) and Word (Microsoft) being just two of many. Enthusiasts often write them directly in HTML, the programming language (see below).

```
<HTML>
<HEAD>
<META HTTP-EQUIV="Content-Type" CONTENT="text/html; charset=windows-1252">
<META NAME="Generator" CONTENT="Microsoft Word 97">
<TITLE>index</TITLE>
<META NAME="Template" CONTENT = "K:\OfficeResource\Templates\WEBPAGES\WEBPAGE.WIZ">
</HEAD>
<BODY TEXT="#000000" LINK="#0000ff" VLINK="#800080" BACKGROUND = "m28.jpg">
<B> <I> <FONT FACE="Comic Sans MS" SIZE=7> <P ALIGN="CENTER">School of Education </I>
</FONT> <FONT FACE="Comic Sans MS" SIZE=7 COLOR="#008080">  <IMG SRC="blank.jpg" WIDTH=550 HEIGHT=7> </P> </B> </FONT>
<P> <A HREF="National resources/National resources1.htm"> <IMG SRC="really useful links.jpg" BORDER=0 WIDTH=153 HEIGHT=23> </A> </P>
```

RESEARCH SUMMARY

Abbott (1998) contacted some young authors of home pages on the World Wide Web in 1996. At this time web publishing was first becoming widely accessible. He found that the motivation for the majority was communication with others. Predominantly web-page authors were aiming their work at other young people. Abbott notes that the immediacy, personal control and low cost of publishing on the web is opening up audiences for young people's work which were not previously accessible. He suggests that the impact of the World Wide Web on the way society views publication, especially the relocation of control from editors and publishers to individuals, has widespread implications for the education of children as both the consumers and the producers of media.

Sending and receiving email

Email can be sent and received using browser software, although many people use a separate email package. Email software varies in its sophistication, although most packages support the following common functions:

- **composing and sending new messages;**
- **opening and reading incoming messages;**
- **forwarding messages received on to third parties;**
- **replying to messages – this can be quicker than composing a new message as the recipient's email address, the message title and the incoming message are all automatically included in the reply;**
- **sending attachments – formatted files of any type can be attached to an email – which can be a rapid and efficient way of transferring information from one computer user to another (it is good practice to save an incoming attachment to a disk and scan it first for viruses before transferring it to your computer's hard disk);**
- **organising incoming and/or outgoing messages into folders to ease navigation;**
- **deleting unwanted messages. NB Most email software automatically keeps a copy of each outgoing email; these can quickly eat up memory space so it is important to remember to delete them as well as old incoming messages on a regular basis;**
- **an address book in which to save email addresses, obviating the need to type an address in each time a message is sent.**

Access to email is through user accounts. Users are allocated an email address and a password. Details vary, although email addresses follow a similar formula to URLs:

- **the account name, such as m.smartypants;**
- **@ (at);**
- **the domain name, such as wkac.ac.uk, which identifies the server on which the user's account is located.**

What do teachers need to know about the Internet?

Teachers work with the Internet in two key ways:

- **to teach with and about these powerful communications tools;**
- **to support themselves in their professional roles as teachers.**

In order to do so they need to be competent and confident users of the technologies in these contexts as well as having an understanding of key related issues, such as Internet safety.

Teaching with and about the Internet

Involves teachers:

- *Selecting appropriate opportunities* – **which will be facilitated, enhanced or extended through the use of one or more Internet resource(s). Some teaching and learning opportunities will focus on ICT knowledge, skills, understanding and competence (comparing the results from two or more search tools), while in others the emphasis will be on other curriculum areas (choosing keywords for effective searching).**
- *Selecting appropriate resources* – **there is a very wide range of Internet resources available, from email to downloadable mathematics practice software on the web. It is important that teachers make appropriate selections and assist children in the making and evaluation of their own choices.**
- *Preparing suitable resources* – **to support use of the Internet, such as a list of bookmarks of useful websites for a particular topic or a help sheet for composing and sending an email message.**
- *Making explicit links between related knowledge, skills and understanding* – **the Internet may be used to support any aspect of the curriculum. Teachers therefore have the opportunity to make explicit links between children's learning with ICT and that in other curriculum contexts.**
- *Modelling appropriate use of ICT* – **such as monitoring the temperature in a distant place during the period of a study.**
- *Demonstrating and intervening* – **for instance, demonstrating adding an email address to an address book to reduce the time taken typing it in and the chance of the message not being delivered due to an inaccuracy in the address.**

The list below attempts to identify the knowledge, skills and understanding teachers need in order to teach effectively with and about the Internet.

Using email:

- **detailed knowledge of the school's email policy and protocols;**
- **accessing email accounts;**
- **composing, sending, opening, closing, saving, forwarding, replying to, deleting and printing messages;**

- sending, receiving and saving attachments, including good practice in virus protection;
- using, adding to and deleting from address book;
- compiling distribution lists;
- composing a personalised signature file;
- working off-line.

Practical task

Find out how to access your email account remotely (if possible), from home, school or somewhere other than your usual location.

Using the World Wide Web:

- detailed knowledge of the school's policy and protocols;
- accessing the browser;
- utilising browser functions: forwards, back, home, reload/refresh, stop, print, history, help;
- bookmarking favourite websites;
- navigating via hyperlinks;
- searching safely and productively;
- copying and pasting text, images and URLs from web pages into other applications;
- downloading and saving files, including documents in Portable Document Format (PDF), software, etc.; utilising good practice in virus protection; considering implications of document sizes;
- altering default browser settings, such as filters;
- switching off graphics;
- downloading websites for use off-line using WebWhacker from *http:// www.bluesquirrel.com/* or similar software;
- utilising cache facilities;
- designing, creating, saving, modifying and publishing web pages, including:
  - selecting background, fonts, and colours
  - inserting, modifying and deleting text, graphics, animations, audio and video
  - making and using templates
  - inserting, modifying and deleting tables, bookmarks and hyperlinks.

Practical task

Find out about computer caching. Consider ways in which this feature may be used to advantage in primary schools.

Using the Internet to support the teaching professional

Teachers need to be competent and confident users of the Internet in order to utilise it efficiently and effectively to facilitate a range of professional functions. Such usage includes:

- *Communication with parents* – increasingly the most effective and sometimes immediate way to communicate with some parents will be via email and the World Wide Web. Parents may bookmark the school's website and use this to keep up to date with information and events.
- *Communication with peers* – through special interest listservs and discussion groups, such as the successful **SENCO** forum at *http://www.becta.org.uk/ inclusion/discussion/senfor.html,* through which **SENCO**s, who are usually the only **SEN** specialists in their schools, can exchange ideas and information with others in similar circumstances.
- *Seeking information* – subject knowledge research, teaching ideas and resources, up-to-date information from professional associations, government agencies and **LEA**s.
- *Preparing resources* – downloading up-to-the-moment resources, such as satellite weather maps and current news reports, software for mathematics reinforcement, activity ideas and worksheets, as well as using images and text from the World Wide Web to prepare classroom activities.
- *Publishing* – children's work, information about the school, tried and tested resources for the benefit of others.

The list below details additional knowledge, skills and understanding that teachers need in order to utilise the Internet efficiently and effectively to support themselves as professionals. It should be read in conjunction with the list above:

- subscribing to and unsubscribing from listservs;
- accessing, reading and contributing to discussion fora;
- accessing email remotely;
- checking authored web pages in a variety of browsers;
- uploading web pages to the server/ISP.

Internet safety and acceptable use policies

Internet safety is a significant concern for parents, schools, teachers and perhaps children as well. Concerns centre around the potential for:

- exposure to offensive material, including racist and pornographic material;
- disclosure of personal information, which might place children in danger;
- exposure to viruses.

Such safety issues are just as pertinent to the use of email as the World Wide Web. Fortunately there is a wealth of focused and up-to-date information and advice available, through:

- **BECTa (The British Education and Communications Technology Agency)**
  http://www.becta.org.uk;
- **NGfL** *http://www.ngfl.gov.uk;*
- **ACITT** **(National Association for Coordinators and Teachers of IT)**
  http://www.acitt.org.uk;
- **PIN (Parents Information Network)** *http://www.pin.org.uk/.*

Schools making use of the Internet should have an appropriate policy, often called an Acceptable Use Policy, which clearly outlines the potential benefits and risks and how these are managed within the school. Policies are usually written and reviewed in consultation with parents.

Practical task

Utilising the websites given above, and other sources, produce an A4 handout detailing the key issues to be considered by a school devising an acceptable use policy.

What are the key features of the Internet and World Wide Web?

Communication

The power of the Internet lies in the communication facilities it supports. The range of facilities caters for diverse needs, interests and preferences. Cluster schools doing the same topic might set up a shared area on an LEA Intranet to share resources and ideas. Children can pose questions direct to war veterans or zookeepers or Year 7 children in the local secondary school via email. Video conferencing can be a vehicle for developing questioning (and answering) skills.

Classroom story

Artists in non-residence

A class of Year 4 children and their teacher undertook a research project involving video conferencing with a practising artist. The artist, an abstract expressionist, first discussed and planned a sequence of activities during a video conferencing meeting with the teacher. Over a term groups of children with their teacher met weekly with the artist online. The children showed and discussed their work. The artist was able to share resources, such as images of his own work and that of others on photoCD, to support the discussions. The class asked questions ranging from queries about the artist's influences and inspiration to the price of finished paintings. Together, the teacher, artist and class planned an exhibition to display the children's abstract work. The artist was able to advise the children on issues such as the impact of framing pictures.

The project was an opportunity for professional development for the class teacher as well as an exciting learning experience for the children.

Information

This is the information age. The World Wide Web contains unimaginable amounts of information. Some of it is incorrect, some of it is out of date, some of it is not relevant, but some of it is of a high quality and generously shared by its originator with the worldwide online community. Access to such a wealth of information is revolutionising many aspects of day-to-day life.

Resources

Similarly, there are an unprecedented range of resources available via the Internet, mostly freely available, including:

- channels for discussion and exchanges with peers with similar interests;
- activities developed by others and shared, such as the Argosphere site *http://www.argosphere.net/* and Ambleweb at Ambleside CE Primary School *http://www.ambleside.schoolzone.co.uk/ambleweb/*;
- mathematics worksheet generators at Teaching Ideas *http://www.teachingideas.co.uk/maths/contents.htm*;
- children's work displayed, e.g. Fryern Junior School *http://fryern.hants.sch.uk*;
- free software downloads, e.g. *http://shareware.cnet.com/*;
- portals to useful sites, e.g. Gareth Pitchford's Primary Resources *http://www.primaryresources.co.uk/*.

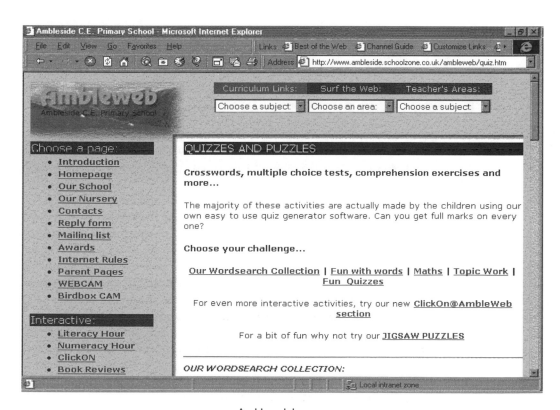

Ambleweb home page

Practical task

Download a lesson idea, worksheet or other resource from a suitable website. Draw up a lesson plan for a stated age group and subject focus detailing how you would make use of the resource to enhance or extend children's learning.

Irrelevance of geographical location

Anyone connected to the Internet can communicate with anyone else similarly connected, irrespective of the distance between them. They can also access any of the world's web pages regardless of the location of the server on which they are stored. Schools in geographically isolated locations can access resources such as online galleries when journeys to traditional galleries would be difficult or impossible. Similarly, virtual field trips allow children to explore a variety of close and distant locations. Email communications between children from schools a mile to a continent apart provide a range of learning opportunities.

Practical task

Access the Cyber Geography Research website http://www.cybergeography.org/ *and explore the Atlas of Cyberspaces. What do you notice about the network?*

What does the Internet have to contribute to teaching and learning?

Finding things out

The opportunities for finding things out via the Internet are almost limitless. Teachers can research subject knowledge, teaching ideas and resources. Accessing such information efficiently and effectively is vital to ensure that they and their classes can benefit from the professional information at their disposal.

Well-organised and managed research activities on the World Wide Web can be visually and intellectually engaging as well as developing children's understanding of electronic texts and the use of a range of media to communicate information effectively. The development and practical application of higher order reading skills, such as keyword searching, skimming and scanning, are key as are strategies for effective use of search tools. Caution must, however, be exercised as not all the information accessed may be current, appropriate or even accurate.

Email and video conferencing provide opportunities for asking direct and purposeful questions, as well as making comparisons and collecting data. Similarly, there are a range of 'ask an expert' websites, through which children can seek information directly from historians or authors.

The World Wide Web also provides children with opportunities to find things out from other children via web pages. This can be valuable in all sorts of ways, such as providing models at levels children can aspire to – children's poems, for instance, as most poems children read are written by adults. Children's science, geography or RE work may be sources of information expressed in language accessible to primary children.

There are a range of tools available via the World Wide Web which enable children, for instance, to calculate their weight on Mars, Saturn and Pluto *http://www.exploratorium. edu/ronh/weight/*. Use of resources such as these can add an extra dimension of understanding or engagement with learning for children. Children may predict whether they will be heavier or lighter on a particular planet and use their understanding to back up their predictions.

Developing ideas and making things happen

Collaboration is facilitated by communication and the Internet provides a variety of channels for this. Children can contribute stories, poems and reviews to a range of websites. They can also respond to others' contributions. Such sites also models authors' story starts and provide plentiful opportunities for reading online.

Children may post part-completed or drafted work on school web pages and invite email responses to help them develop their work. This might be a D&T design, a poem or a piece of music. Responding to others' work can help children articulate and apply their own knowledge, skills and understanding.

Exchanging and sharing information

Many of the points considered above also have relevance for the exchange and sharing of information.

Person-to-person exchanges, such as through electronic pen pals, are facilitated by the Internet. This can add an element of speed to the communication, maintaining interest and relevance for the correspondents.

The global online community works because people are prepared to share information and resources with others, usually without charge. There are a number of sites where schools can access environmental data on weather from around the country and the world. Schools can post their own data, either as a quid pro quo for utilising information from other schools, or merely for the satisfaction of adding to the wealth of available resources. This is particularly easy to achieve where the school has an automatic weather station. Similarly, publishing children's project work on the web enables them to share it with people they know, parents and other relatives, as well as people they don't such as children in an elementary school in the USA. Posting lists of links to useful online resources can save other teachers time and effort.

Sutton-on-Sea's Weather Station response form for 6–8-year-olds

What are the capabilities and limitations of the Internet?

see page 91 in Chapter 4 for more information on evaluation

Evaluation

Websites are not all high quality and perfectly matched to the needs of primary education in the UK. Teachers (and children) must exercise discretion in the selection and use of web-based materials. Developing a system of evaluation may be invaluable.

Practical task

Develop a list of evaluation criteria for websites. Evaluate a range of sites including:

- *a school site;*
- *an NGfL resource;*
- *a commercial site;*
- *a professional association site.*

What were the strengths and weaknesses of each as a resource? What did you discover about your evaluation criteria? How might you revise them? How might you develop them to use with children?

Commercialisation and marketing

Many websites are produced and maintained by commercial organisations, and often include advertising in order to offset costs. Some schools are beginning to do the same. The Internet, and particularly the World Wide Web, provide opportunities to target marketing directly at a range of audiences, children included. Sometimes such marketing can be quite subtle, combining product placement with activities promoted as learning opportunities and/or games.

Speed

Speed of Internet access can be an important consideration. Key factors which affect the time web pages take to download include:

- *speed of connection* – **dial-up connections are slowest, broadband fastest;**
- *computer specification* – **larger memory space facilitates downloading;**
- *traffic* – **after 2pm US users are online;**
- *page design* – **dark colours, graphics, animations and sound take longer.**

It is possible to set a browser so that it will only display the text elements of a website – known as switching off the graphics. This may be a useful option to speed up browsing from a slow connection.

Cost

Use of any aspect of the Internet, be it sending and receiving email messages, taking part in an online quiz or reading web pages for information, has a cost implication. Many ISPs, especially those providing home Internet access, now charge for time online at local telephone rates. Specialist schools ISPs often make lump sum charges which include the cost of time online. Such arrangements make budget planning easier for schools and at the same time act as an incentive to use the Internet in order to maximise value for money. Methods of charging for access are likely to continue to develop and change. Currently, cost is considered to be a significant barrier.

Mirror sites

Popular websites are very heavily used which means that access can be slow. Some such sites have mirrors. A mirror is a duplicate copy of the site located on another server. For example, the Nine Planets Multimedia Tour based in the USA has a mirror located at Exeter University *http://www.ex.ac.uk/Mirrors/nineplanets/*. This mirror is generally a lot less busy that the original site *http://www.seds.org/billa/tnp/*. Some search tools also have mirrors and invite the user to select the geographically closer one. It may be at least as worthwhile to choose one in a time zone where it is currently night.

Information overload

There are certainly times when too much information is almost as unhelpful as no information at all. Making the best selections from a vast number of sources of differing origins can be challenging. Teachers and children will need to develop strategies to manage such difficulties. Searching in environments where web resources are of a guaranteed quality, such as NGfL and BBC Learning *http://www.bbc.co.uk/learning/*, can be helpful as can developing critical site evaluation techniques and refining search skills.

Staying focused

The Internet and especially the World Wide Web can be enthralling – the temptation for random exploration can be hard to resist. Teachers will need to manage children's tasks in order to ensure both their safety and the productivity of the activity. Use of bookmarked sites only, tightly focused tasks and time-limiting can be appropriate strategies.

Reading level and language issues

The vast majority of web pages are aimed at an adult audience and may thus be difficult for primary children to comprehend. There are a number of strategies teachers can deploy in order to provide access to material which is accessible, including:

- **the use of the search tool Ask Jeeves for Kids! which has a reading level option and is designed to select sites which answer the query posed at an appropriate reading level;**
- **utilising web pages specifically written for children;**
- **utilising web pages recommended by other teachers;**
- **utilising children's work on school web pages.**

Teachers may also be concerned about American web pages which display not only differences in vocabulary but also in the spellings of words. Children are exposed to US (and Australian) vocabulary through television, as are adults, and appear to have little difficulty with comprehension. Alternative spellings may provide more of a challenge, although they can also provide a teaching and learning opportunity. Teachers can make explicit the differences and discuss these with children – for instance, searching for information on the theme of 'colour' in a US-based search tool may be unproductive, although a parallel search using the US spelling could also be attempted.

Viruses

It is essential to promote good practice associated with downloading and opening files, whether they be free software from the World Wide Web or attached images received via email. Any file may be harbouring a virus which could do damage to a computer or even a whole network. Prevention is very much better than cure. Schools should have protocols detailing how they deal with downloaded files. Generally files should be saved, preferably on a floppy disk, since if they are infected the infection can be contained, and scanned using antivirus software. Many computer systems are designed to automatically scan any disk or downloaded file. Only when this process has been successfully completed should the document be opened or saved on to the computer or network.

Antivirus software is constantly updated to deal with new viruses and these updates are usually available free of charge (once the software has been purchased) via the supplier's website.

Unfortunately there are time-wasters who circulate email messages warning of viruses contained in email. Such messages often include reference to a source, usually a prominent IT company, and accounts of hard drives wiped clean merely by opening a message with a particular title. More information on such hoaxes is available at *http://www.symantec.com/*. Viruses cannot be spread merely by opening an email, which can only contain text. The risk lies in opening files attached to email messages. It is considered to be a sensible precaution to delete without opening (and certainly without opening any attached documents) any email message received from someone the user does not recognise.

Copyright and the web

Material placed on the World Wide Web remains the intellectual property of the author and is subject to copyright whether or not this is specifically stated. Copyright extends beyond text to images, animation and sound. However, it is generally accepted that material placed on the web is there for other people to use. Sometimes it will not be possible to copy and paste an image from a web page, because the author has arranged the programming to prevent this. Similarly, it may be possible to listen to a sound file, but not to download it. It is good practice to acknowledge the source of any material from the web and to encourage children to do the same. Further information is available from the Copyright Licensing Agency *http://www.cla.co.uk* and the Copyright Web Site at *http://www.benedict.com/*.

For more information on copyright, see page 225 in Chapter 14

Currency and authenticity

There is a lot of concern about the currency and authenticity of materials available on the World Wide Web. The potential to access up-to-the moment satellite weather photographs, breaking world news stories, images from space as they are received from missions or real-time video of bird eggs hatching is exhilarating. However, there are lots of websites which are not regularly maintained and in which the information displayed may be outdated. This can be frustrating and schools must also do their bit to ensure that their own web pages are current. Many web pages include information giving the date on which they were last updated. This can be a useful guide.

Authenticity is often harder to assess. Anyone can upload information to the World Wide Web or circulate it via email, newsgroups or listservs. There is no editing process, as there is with any published book, newspaper or magazine, and thus material, particularly from unfamiliar sources, must be viewed critically. It may be partial, misleading or inaccurate. Comparing information from the Internet with that from other sources for substantiation and corroboration can be a teaching and learning objective in itself. Some high quality websites are subject to an editing process, such as the BBC *http://www.bbc.co.uk* and newspapers, e.g. *http://www.guardian.co.uk*.

Vocabulary and jargon

A vast new vocabulary is emerging related to ICT, a lot of it related to the Internet and some of it found in this chapter. In common with children's language development in maths or science, it is important that they develop a vocabulary which enables them to articulate their ideas, understanding, intentions and problems. Deciding when and how much vocabulary to introduce is an important professional consideration for teachers.

Printing from websites

Web pages can be printed using the icon on the browser, or selecting print via a menu. This will print the whole of the current web page which may be rather more than is expected. There is nothing to limit the length of web pages to the amount visible on screen at any one time, or even to A4. The web page author can make the page any length at all. Printing out long pages can be time-consuming and also expensive. It is useful to get into the habit of copying and pasting text and images to be printed into a word processing package and to encourage this strategy with children. This ensures that only the text and/or images actually required are printed, and the document length can be assessed before a decision on printing is made.

Digital division

There is increasing concern that the Internet is leading to a digital division in society in the UK, with information (and skill) haves and have nots. Concern focuses on the potential for children (and adults) who do not have access to online resources to be seriously disadvantaged as a result. This issue is increasingly relevant for primary schools as home computer ownership continues to expand. Many children live in families for whom computer ownership is never likely to be a reality. Schools are beginning to consider the implications for entitlement and equality of opportunities. Free Internet access is now available via many public libraries and the availability of such community facilities is increasing. Some schools are beginning to make computer facilities available before and after school.

School websites

There are a number of issues that affect a school's motivation to construct a website, including:

- **visible presence – everyone else has one;**
- **curriculum integration – providing quick access to useful web resources, occasionally making available resources to others, e.g. Sutton-on-Sea Primary School** *http://www.sutton.lincs.sch.uk/*;
- **communication – with children and sometimes adults around the world, with parents, local communities and businesses, eg, Llanddulas School** *http:// www.conwy11.u-net.com/index.htm*;
- **government initiatives – such as the current focus on ICT.**

Once they have a site, schools use them for a variety of purposes:

- **Information and resources for a primarily internal audience – the key focus may be use by staff and children, providing information and access to quality websites, resources to support the curriculum and displaying children's work.**

- Advertising and/or information for an external audience – an electronic prospectus for potential new parents, promoting events to the local community, attracting business sponsorship, raising the local as well as national and international profile of the school, sharing resources with a wider audience as well as providing an audience for children's work.

Practical task

What are the issues associated with displaying children's work on the Internet?

Practical task

Involvement in schools' websites is an interesting issue. In some schools it is clear that the site has been designed and maintained by one person. Why might this be? This raises issues about use and ownership by other teachers and pupils. Some sites are clearly child-centred and others are primarily designed and maintained by pupils. Can you find examples of these?

A good school website should be:

- pupil and teacher focused, unless there is a separate Intranet and the site is purely for external consumption;
- easy to navigate, clearly signposted and preferably with some sort of index or map;
- carefully designed for ease of loading while maintaining visual interest;
- up to date and regularly maintained, especially in terms of children's work and links to other useful resources;
- reflective of the overall ethos of the school;
- interactive, facilitating communication within the school, with parents, locally, nationally and internationally.

Issues to consider in planning a school website:

- *Audience.* The site may be predominantly for internal use by children and teachers, it may be a promotion tool for the school. Considerations may include how the site can be made interesting and accessible to the audience.
- *Management.* School websites in which individual teachers and classes have ownership over areas tend to be the most interesting as well as the most well used. The overall management of a site usually rests with one person, called the *webmaster*, although that person usually acts as editor and monitor rather than being responsible for creating, maintaining and removing web pages.
- *Currency.* Keeping a website current can be a time-consuming process. Material can quickly become out of date. Similarly, if the material on the site changes infrequently or not at all users will soon stop revisiting. Many schools decide on an approximate display time for children's work and pictures of sports days and

plays. Older material can be archived so that it is still available.

- *Safety.* Children's safety is paramount. Care must be taken to prevent the identification of children and the publication of personalised information. A number of primary schools where children have their own web pages, or wish to share information about themselves, use first names only and include children's drawings of themselves, rather than photographs.
- *Copyright.*
- *Design.* Good design is essential and must be balanced with other issues, such as download time and ease of navigation. Many sites adopt a common style across all their web pages, while in others the individual pages reflect the personalities and priorities of the authors.
- *Navigation.* The home page of most websites takes the form of an index, providing links to other areas of the site. A home link on each page and hyperlinks to related pages are useful. As a site grows and more and more pages are added, a periodic review of navigation may be needed. Trialling is important.
- *Feedback.* Most schools invite feedback on their website by including an email address. Children enjoy responding to other children's work as well as receiving comments and encouragement on their own. Similarly, if users have found elements of the site particularly good, or difficult to follow, it is helpful to know.

For more information on copyright, see page 225

Practical task

Access a range of school websites. Which sites do you like best and why? Which features would you include if you were designing a school website?

The Internet and core subjects

The ideas and activities introduced below are intended to give a feel for the range of ways in which the Internet can be utilised to support and enhance teaching and learning in mathematics, science and English. They are not intended to be comprehensive, merely to go some way towards illustrating the breadth of possibilities and to provide starting points for the customisation of ideas and the generation of others. Examples introduced under mathematics, for instance, may be just as applicable to one or more of the other areas. Other useful sources include professional journals (*Primary Science Review, Reading, Interactive, Child Education, Junior Education*, etc), websites (National Grid for Learning, BECTa, etc.) and Schemes of Work (Science, ICT, etc.).

Many of the activities mentioned below do not necessarily require a class of children to have direct Internet access. Some relate to resources which can be accessed either by the teacher beforehand or by children sharing a class computer. Efficient use of online resources is a key consideration. Publication on the World Wide Web can provide a real and relevant audience for children's work and there is much evidence to suggest that this can have a positive effect on quality.

English

There are very many websites which support a range of literacy-related activities. For example, Kent National Grid for Learning has developed a range of big books online at Infant Explorer featuring Sebastian the Swan *http://www.naturegrid.org.uk/infant/*. These can be read online and are supported by a range of worked lesson plans and activity ideas and resources. Children are encouraged to email Sebastian with their work, which may be displayed on the pin board.

'Sebastian the Swan' home page

The Children's Story site *http://www.childrenstory.com* enables the user to select a fairy story and hear it being read. Activities such as these can be followed up in a range of ways away from the computer.

There are a range of interactive language-focused activities on the web in which children can engage individually, in groups or as a whole class. Story starts from Sutton-on-Sea Primary School (see page 116), provide a range of story beginnings with drop-down menus for children to make selections. Having customised their start, children can then either copy and paste their beginning into a word processing document or print it out and finish by hand. Such extended writing activities may facilitate work on structuring writing (beginnings, middles and ends), character development, genre and more. Each child could begin with the same story start which might lead to interesting comparisons in terms of choices and outcomes. Similarly a range of interests are catered for.

Online stories are developed with children from different schools, often of different ages, contributing a chapter by email to take the story forward. Other email-related activities might involve analysing an email message as a shared text in literacy as a precursor to work on developing email-writing skills, examining the similarities and differences compared with letter-writing. There are online postcards which children can access and complete – these might require imagination or factual information.

It is possible to download specialist fonts which enable children to write messages in runes or hieroglyphs, similarly to retell stories relevant to the culture, to decode information from the teacher or other children. See, for example, *www.pastforward. co.uk/vikings/runes.html*.

Use of the World Wide Web provides a range of opportunities for the development of higher order reading and reference skills, such as keyword searching, skimming and scanning text. Children may wish to search for poems by particular authors, or by other children, as models and illustrations. There are online dictionaries and thesauruses which may add an extra dimension.

A wide variety of media-focused activities can also be supported using online resources. Comparisons of the ways in which news is reported in different media and/or around the world can be resourced. Consideration may be given to the presentation of information in different media – World Wide Web versus reference book versus CD ROM, focusing on the integration of media (images, video, text, sound, animation), paragraph length and page layout. Such work could inform an enhanced newspaper project, a popular activity in many primary schools, with the added dimension of being more up-to-date than *The Times* or the local evening news.

Science

The World Wide Web enhances teachers' and children's opportunities for monitoring current scientific activity, making science accessible and real. Possibilities include accessing pictures from the Hubble space telescope and tracking the progress of current scientific news stories. Online scientific experts abound and queries may be raised with one of them by email.

Many World Wide Web sites are sources of high quality factual information, in which children can research. Children must, however, consider the validity of material they are accessing, perhaps by making comparisons with books and CD ROMs. BBC resources such as their children's health site are full of high quality, appropriate and engaging material *http://www.bbc.co.uk/health/kids*. Many sites provide teaching and learning resources and opportunities which would not otherwise be accessible.

Projects are organised online in which children conduct similar science investigations in a range of schools and post their results, providing data for comparison and opportunities to explore issues of experimental error and replication.

Areas of science that may be difficult to resource or provide few opportunities for practical activities are well catered for with child-centred web resources, the NASAKIDS site http://kids.msfc.nasa.gov being a good example. This is visually engaging, often modelling through video and animation concepts which are counter-intuitive and otherwise difficult to communicate.

Mathematics

There are a number of World Wide Web sites which provide free software for teachers to download, such as Birmingham City Council's mathematics resources at *http://atschool.eduweb.co.uk/ufal0/resource.htm*. This includes a drill and skill program geared at tables reinforcement. Software can be downloaded and then freely used on school machines without incurring further online costs.

There is a wide range of mathematics activities available online, such as the grid game at the BBC's Megamaths site *http://www.bbc.co.uk/education/megamaths/picknumber2*, which provides timed, randomly assigned mental maths quizzes. There are three levels of difficulty and three choices of time, e.g. 45 seconds. Thus children can return again and again to the activity to improve on their past results. Such activities provide opportunities for reinforcements in an interactive environment, in which immediate feedback is provided.

Similarly, there is a currency converter available at *http://atschool.eduweb.co.uk/ufal0/currency.htm*. Resources such as this can be used to support work on approximating and mental calculation. Online puzzles and mental mathematics practice opportunities abound. Activities available at the BBC's mathsfile *http://www.bbc.co.uk/education/mathsfile/* support number, data handling, algebra and shape, space and measure.

Children and their teachers can access websites to look for mathematics investigations which may then be carried out away from the computer. Such opportunities maximise use of limited computer resources as well as providing access to well-thought-out activities – for instance Bernard's Bag at the primary mathematics enrichment site *http://nrich.maths. org.uk/primary/*.

There are an increasing range of activities to support young children's mathematical activities, such as counting fishes at *http://www.geocities.com/buildnextgen/puzzles.htm*. Such activities may be used to develop hand–eye co-ordination as well as reinforce early mathematics.

Many of the websites mentioned above have teachers' areas with worksheets, activity ideas and lesson plans. The worksheet generator in the mathematics area of Teaching Ideas at *http://www.teachingideas.co.uk/* which also calculates answer sheets may help teachers, for instance, in managing the setting and marking of homework activities.

The Internet:

a summary of key points

____ *The Internet is a global network of computers supporting communication through the World Wide Web, email and conferencing.*

____ *Schools are increasingly active in the online community, searching, retrieving, analysing and synthesising information as well as developing, trialling and publishing their own.*

____ *Critical evaluation of web-based resources is vital to ensure suitability, accuracy and safety.*

____ *Through its many facets the Internet has the potential to support teachers in their day-to-day work in the classroom as well as their continuing professional development.*

Further reading

BECTa (2001) *Acceptable use of the Internet advice sheet*, BECTa.
   http://www.becta.org.uk/technology/infosheets/index
BECTa (2001) *Caching advice sheet*, BECTa.
   http://www. becta.org.uk/technology/infosheets/index
BECTa (2001) *Designing effective school web sites advice sheet*, BECTa.
   http://www.becta.org.uk/technology/infosheets/index
BECTa (2001) *Internet safety advice sheet*, BECTa.
   http://www.becta.org.uk/technology/infosheets/index
BECTa (2001) *School Intranets advice sheet*, BECTa.
   http://www.becta.org.uk/technology/infosheets/index
BECTa (2002) *Broadband advice sheet*, BECTa.
   http://www.becta.org.uk/technology/infosheets/index
BECTa (2002) *Firewalls advice sheet*, BECTa.
   http://www.becta.org.uk/technology/infosheets/index
Bolton Curriculum ICT Centre (1998) *ICT for the Under Fives*, Bolton Curriculum ICT Centre.
Bolton Curriculum ICT Centre (1998) *IT in Primary Literacy*, Bolton Curriculum ICT Centre.
Bolton Curriculum ICT Centre (1999) *ICT in Primary Numeracy*, Bolton Curriculum ICT Centre.
DfEE/QCA (1999) *Curriculum Guidance for the Foundation Stage*, DfEE/QCA.
DfEE/QCA (1999) *The National Curriculum*, DfEE/QCA.
Higgins, S. et al. (1999) *500 ICT Tips for Primary Teachers*, Kogan Page.
Monteith, M. (ed) (1999) *IT for Learning Enhancement*, Intellect Books.
QCA/DfEE (1998, rev. 2000) *Information and Communications Technology: A Scheme of Work for Key Stages 1 and 2*, QCA/DfEE.
Smith, H. (1999) *Opportunities for ICT in the Primary School*, Trentham Books, Chapter 14.
Somekh, D. and Davis, N. (eds) (1997) *Using Information Technology Effectively in Teaching and Learning: Studies in Pre-service and In-service Teacher Education*, Routledge, Chapter 7.

What this section contains

This section is concerned with all issues related to planning, assessing and recording with ICT throughout the whole of the primary age phase. The curriculum for the Foundation Stage will also be addressed in a separate section on ICT in the Early Years setting.

The planning and assessment issues will be addressed in the context of the published requirements for Initial Teacher Training (TTA/DfES, 2002).

Given that good planning depends on a thorough analysis of the situation before you even start working, the opening chapters provide a consideration of the background knowledge you need to acquire in order to deliver real learning opportunities for the children you teach.

See page 9 for a description of the Professional Standards for QTS for the use of ICT in subject teaching

In 'Managing Primary ICT' we will consider the literal, physical management of computers and children. The different levels of resourcing will be characterised so that you can begin to assess the situation in a given school more quickly. We will consider what the various strategies are for dealing with high-, medium- and low-resource situations.

For example, we will consider the very different management strategies to be employed when working with children in a primary school with a network room full of computers and when working with one standalone machine in the corner. We will also look at the implications of recent initiatives in equipment and training in primary schools concerned with the National Grid for Learning and see how some are taking ICT in UK schools forward at a very rapid rate.

As far as possible throughout the parts of chapters which are concerned with resources we have attempted to be completely generic. Some example titles of software may be given, but only where absolutely necessary to explain a concept further. There is so much software available for schools at all levels for all of the computer platforms that it would be impossible to create a list that would be applicable or viable in all settings. Local education authorities and schools themselves should have such lists and justifications for the choices they have made in terms of ease of use, applicability to the age phases they are being used with and so on.

In 'Planning Primary ICT' we will consider the context of the National Curriculum and its impact on the teaching and learning of the subject in its most recent form – Curriculum 2000. We will also look at how to use the QCA Scheme of Work, published in 1998 and revised slightly in 2000 – before the latest version of the ICT National Curriculum. We will look at how to map the Scheme of Work back on to the new curriculum and negotiate the different emphases in the documentation. We will also address the ways in which some LEAs and schools have planned for ICT, using the QCA Scheme of Work as a template, but also adjusting it to suit local needs and priorities. ICT exists in all subjects of the National Curriculum, so this section will also look at how to plan within the core curriculum (English, maths and science) and its associated strategies (National Literacy Strategy, National Numeracy Project) as well as within the foundation subjects in order to maximise the potential of ICT for all learners.

'Planning Primary ICT' will also focus in part on relevant theories of learning with computers and characterise the different approaches to this issue. Analysis depends also on looking at the ways in which what we know about children learning have been applied (or not) within the field of computers in education.

'Planning ICT in the Early Years' will look specifically at ICT in the context of the Early Learning Goals as defined for children who are in the Foundation Stage (cf. *Curriculum Guidance for the Foundation Stage*, QCA, 2000). We will look at how this relates to the additional standards for Early Years specialists.

'Assessing and Recording Primary ICT' will look at how to go about evaluating children's development with ICT in order to inform planning. It will consider a range of strategies designed to provide a quick overview of a class as well as a more detailed and individually targeted assessment of the needs of a given learner.

'Monitoring and Researching ICT' will be of particular interest to those training in the primary phase as ICT specialists. This section will look at the role of the national reporters on standards (OFSTED) as well as the monitoring of the curriculum which should go on at school level in the work of the ICT co-ordinator. It will include an activity looking at recent classroom-based case studies.

Professional Standards for QTS

There will be references throughout this section to the guidance from the TTA and the DfES. This is set out in three documents. Qualifying to Teach (TTA/DfES, 2002) sets out the Professional Standards for Qualified Teacher Status and the Requirements for Initial Teacher Training. These are the Standards that you must meet during your training written out alongside the requirements for your course providers, setting out standard levels of provision. A Handbook gives examples for both trainees and training providers on how to meet the standards. It is divided into Guidance on the Requirements for Initial Teacher Training (TTA/DfES, 2002a) which is aimed at training providers and Guidance on the Standards for Qualified Teacher Status (TTA/DfES, 2002b). These documents are all available in full from the TTA website at www.canteach.gov.uk

As you will realise from reading the booklet of Standards for QTS, ICT is in a different position to any of the other subjects. It requires you to develop in three separate but related areas.

1. A set of skills with new technology for your professional use.
2. Knowledge and Understanding of ICT as a discrete subject in the National Curriculum.
3. Knowledge and Understanding of ICT in the teaching of all other subjects.

You can find the relevant references in Qualifying to Teach (TTA/DfES, 2002) as follows:

For the general, professional use of ICT, para 2.5 says that those awarded QTS must demonstrate that they know how to use ICT effectively to support their wider professional role.

For the knowledge and understanding of ICT as a subject in its own right, para. 2.1 b states that those awarded QTS must demonstrate that they have sufficient understanding of a range of work in ICT.

For the knowledge and understanding of ICT in the teaching of all other subjects, para. 3.3.10 states that those awarded QTS must demonstrate that they can use ICT effectively in their teaching.

In Section B we will refer to all the relevant guidance and handbooks throughout and give you the references you may need for auditing purposes.

This chapter is intended to focus thoughts on the organisational issues around teaching with computers in primary schools. We will consider the practical, physical aspects of locating equipment and look at how this impacts on planning. We will look at strategies for organising in the different resource settings in schools. We will also consider the pressure on the timetable and how best to meet the needs of the children and deliver their pupil entitlement. We will consider some of the background to the introduction of computers into schools and how the various central government strategies in the years from 1997 onwards have impacted upon equipment provision and teacher education.

The national background

New entrants to the teaching profession are fortunate to be joining it at a time of such accelerated change in ICT in schools. From 1997, with the newly elected government launching a National Grid for Learning (NGfL), spending on computer equipment increased exponentially to the point where, at the time of writing (Summer 2002), £1.6 billion has been committed to ICT in education.

However, change on such a huge scale is not without its logistical difficulties and much still depends on how the growth in funding for ICT in schools is managed at the local level, either by the local education authority (LEA) or by the management within the school.

The evidence, from inspections by OFTSED and others, has suggested year on year that the take up and quality of use of computers in our classrooms is actually low. Even in areas where there is rich provision of equipment, and/or Internet connections, it is possible to find little evidence that the computer is fully or usefully integrated into the curriculum.

 For more information on monitoring ICT see pages 208–211, Chapter II

Part of the issue lies in the variation in the quality of the development plans at local and school level as well as in the wide variation in advisory support to schools. In turn, some of the variation can be put down to the 'bid culture' in which the innovation has taken place. Local education authorities (LEAs) make bids for funding to central government on the basis of their development plan. Schools bid to LEAs for a share and so on.

The huge programme of investment, backed up by training, arises out of the government's commitment which was spelled out in *Connecting the Learning Society* (DfEE, 1997). This in turn arose from the work of Sir Dennis Stevenson who had been commissioned by the Labour Party to write a report before the election of 1997 into the state of IT provision in UK schools.

Stevenson found that the actual age of the computer equipment in classrooms throughout the UK was such that it made the use of computers in the classroom difficult or impossible. His committee also found that what use there was of computers in schools was of hugely variable quality. He warned about the consequences of this situation being allowed to continue into the new century, writing that:

> if the next government does not take steps to intensify the use of information and communications technology (ICT) in our schools, a generation of children – and a generation of adults as teachers – will have been put at enormous disadvantage with consequences for the UK that will be difficult to reverse.
>
> (Stevenson *et al.*, 1997)

As a consequence the government, when it came to power, in 1997 committed huge amounts of spending to the development of what it called 'The National Grid for Learning'. As a trainee in a placement school you will be joining at a time when such changes are taking place or are about to take place.

The National Grid for Learning was envisaged as:

> A way of finding and using on-line learning and teaching materials [and] A mosaic of inter-connecting networks and education services based on the Internet which will support teaching, learning, training and administration in schools, colleges, universities, libraries, the workplace and homes.
>
> (DfEE, 1997)

With huge numbers of computers in schools discovered to be older than five years, there would clearly be no way of building such a grid. As a consequence the first wave of spending was on new computer hardware. LEAs prepared bids to central government to what was called the Standards Fund. They had to prepare a five-year development plan in order to access the money for their schools on a match-funded basis. Money was then devolved to schools according to local plans and priorities. No two neighbouring LEAs have done this in exactly the same way, so you will notice variations when you move between your placement schools. However, in schools which have made a big spend on ICT in the last couple of years it is possible to note the rise in popularity of the network room full of new computers as the answer to all of the problems around the organisation of ICT in the school. We will discuss this further below.

The second major element of spending was an acknowledgement of the need to train teachers in schools. The New Opportunities Fund (NOF) was set up with Heritage (Lottery) money. The government established a set of standards to be reached by prospective training providers. A list of approved training providers was then circulated with details of how to apply for the training. Schools would have to complete an application process, including a detailed development plan, in order to access the funding. The training provided was intended to raise the standard of ICT competency in subject teaching for serving teachers in the same way as the ICT Teacher Training Requirements were expected to raise the standard of pre-service training for trainees in ICT in subject teaching. The two programmes are intended to raise such standards to the equivalent of Level 8 of the National Curriculum in ICT.

The third major element was a plan for subsidised laptops for teachers. Significant pilot projects, such as the BECTa multimedia Portables for Teachers pilots (see *www.becta.*

org.uk for further information) had found that giving teachers laptops greatly increased their use of ICT in the curriculum for teaching and administration. In order to benefit from the scheme teachers had to be part of a school which was registered with an NOF training provider and about to start (or currently undergoing) NOF training on ICT in subject teaching. It would be useful for you to discover levels of ownership of laptop computers under the laptop purchase scheme in your placement school. High levels of ownership might indicate that you are likely to receive significant levels of support. Remember to ask tactfully about this scheme since, like all attempts to give money away, it was not without its problems.

The local background

When you visit schools for your placements you will find that they are at many different points in the process described above:

- **they may have already completed their NOF training;**
- **they may be in the process of completing it during your training year;**
- **they may be about to bid for the training for the following academic year.**

It is important to know about NOF training because it will impact on the background atmosphere of ICT in subject teaching in the school. Practising what you know along-side serving teachers who are engaged in their NOF training may be of benefit to all involved in the process. Indeed, many schools may welcome your input if they feel you have skills gleaned in college training to contribute.

If you find that ICT does not have a high profile just at the moment in the school it could be because the senior managers are planning it for the future. Remember that NOF training, indeed the whole National Grid for Learning, has arrived in schools at a time of great innovation in the core curriculum in the past two years. There was the National Literacy Strategy (main introductory INSET in the year 1998–9), followed immediately by the National Numeracy Project (main introductory INSET in the year 1999–2000). Some schools are suffering from what one former headteacher has described as 'innovation overload'.

In more general terms there has been a perceived lack of confidence on the part of some teachers. Occasionally, this is characterised as 'reluctance'. It is certainly true that some teachers find it enormously threatening to be delivering a subject which employs skills which they do not feel they themselves have.

There may also be no support structure for teachers in their school situation. At school level, there may be no ICT co-ordinator. Good ICT co-ordinators who attend training, pass it on to colleagues and give generously of their time and knowledge are in short supply. At LEA level, it may be that there is no advisory team encouraging good practice and recommending hardware and software. In both these cases there has been a failure of management to see the necessity of putting money into human resources. Too much time and money can sometimes be spent on hardware and software and not enough on the human resources needed to develop and promote excellence in ICT in the classroom.

One other issue to note is the perceived 'skills gap' between teachers and children at home. Year on year, home ownership of computers is increasing. It would be wrong to assume that it was all going into the study bedrooms of middle class students. It is possible to find levels of computer ownership in deprived areas of Inner London, for example, where six-year-old children are experienced users of the latest Office software. Many of these children are, when they get to school, used as surrogate ICT co-ordinators, showing both teachers and children alike how to sort out printing problems and how to close down the computer properly so that the computer comes back to life the next day.

It would be wrong, however, for teachers to allow the feeling to grow that children know more than they do. They may sometimes know more about the mechanics of the software and hardware at a basic level (and NOF training more than adequately allows teachers to catch up with this). What children do not know, and the reason why they need the teacher to be using it with them, is how to apply it in their developing subject knowledge.

Resource levels in schools: a rough guide

This section attempts to categorise schools according to the resource settings at different levels. Three types of resource setting are described on a sort of continuum from high resource through medium resource to low resource. It is useful to characterise resource settings in this way because you will be able to make a judgement about particular organisational strategies if you can learn to observe and sum up the situation in a placement school quickly.

The school in which you are placed will be somewhere along the line of development and will not necessarily have all elements of the different resource settings represented. Furthermore, schools are not static places developing and changing year on year. A school previously described as being low resource may move on quite rapidly in a year, for example, in the case of a school just receiving its allocation of government funding.

A further issue – which is partly included below – is the human resource setting in the school. A school with very low numbers of computers may still be doing well in ICT owing to excellence in organisation and involvement of all staff. Similarly a school which looks good with a network room full of computers may in fact be keeping the door locked and doing nothing with them. The situation is complex.

Central organisation of computers: some issues

Some schools are organising their computers centrally, even where they are not actually part of a computer network. There are issues to consider where schools have set up computer suites.

Firstly, where all the computers in a school have been gathered together in a room this might look like a computer lab, a high resource setting. However, unless they are networked together, the school has not necessarily made the best of the provision.

High resource setting:
Network room, printing – sometimes in colour– is available at every station.
Internet connection is cheap and quick, via an ADSL broadband connection or better and moderated by an LEA.
There is a technician who regularly comes to repair computers, change cartridges, load new software, etc.
Appropriate software is available for every age phase.
There are also stations connected to the network available in the classroom to carry on with work begun in the network room.
The school is implementing a cohesive strategy, including an ongoing development plan with high levels of LEA support.
There is a policy for acceptable Internet use.
There is a fully implemented scheme of work.

Suitability for placement as a trainee:
This is an excellent setting for learning how to integrate ICT fully into the curriculum and develop ICT capability at the same time. It won't prepare you for the transition to a school in the bottom category!

Medium resource setting:
A working computer and printer in every classroom.
An Internet connection somewhere in school *or* a network room with computers removed from class-rooms and placed there to capitalise on resources.
Some programmable toys are available.
Repairs are dealt with fairly promptly.
A scheme of work is being implemented.
The school has the first stages of a development plan in operation.
There is a sense that ICT is valued and that within the next two or three years the school will move forward and become a high resource setting.
A policy on safe and acceptable Internet use is being developed.

Suitability for placement as a trainee:
Although not at the very cutting edge, this is a good situation in which to develop skills of organising for ICT.

Low resource setting:
An older, frequently broken computer in the classroom or one between two.
A shared printer.
Low staff morale, low spending on ICT, no ICT co-ordinator, no technician.
Frequent sightings of batik and plant pots placed over computers.
No scheme of work in place.
No ink cartridges or ribbons in the printers.
Poor software titles with children from Year 1 to Year 6 doing the same thing on the computer (copy typing, doodling in a Paint package or playing a number game).

This situation is often only brought to an end by an imminent OFSTED inspection when, suddenly, all the machines are repaired and the head asks that they are, at least, switched on. With the right support, a development plan might begin to emerge which will see a year-on-year effort to take the school forward into the medium resource setting. At the present time, the school is not providing the entitlement to ICT for its children.

Suitability for placement as a trainee:
This is a very difficult placement in which to gain the required standard in ICT in subject teaching and you will be heavily dependent upon your college for support.

Resource levels in schools

Each computer requires separate maintenance and installation of software and separate connection to printers and other resources. This is a high management and servicing overload. Furthermore, the machines have been divorced from the classroom with no discernible advantage to anyone. If, on the other hand, the computers are networked via a hub and server, then administration is carried out centrally. Users are set up by the ICT co-ordinator and groups for specific projects can also usually be established. Software installations are made easier by copying setups to all the workstations. Printing is often centralised and children's work is stored in their own user area.

Secondly, where a network room has been set up and there is no physical, cabled connection as yet to the classroom, there still needs to be some ICT work going on back in the classroom. Although the provision has undoubtedly improved in such a school, the one hour a week in the network room is not sufficient to develop ICT in subject teaching. The ICT is divorced from what goes on in the rest of the curriculum. The various curriculum strategies in numeracy and literacy and the learning in science and the Foundation subjects are all enhanced by the judicious use of ICT (see the chapters which follow). In other words, children need to work in both situations with ICT and, indeed, to bring work to and from the network room in electronic form so that they can carry on through the week in their groups, in whatever rota system there is on the classroom computer.

Finally, the most flexible (and, admittedly, costly) organisational strategy for ICT in the school is the computer suite fully networked and fully connected to terminals back in the classrooms. Work can be commenced in the network room and accessed over the network through the week. Indeed, there are networks in some schools which are delivered over a wireless connection to children using portable computers in classrooms. In this situation ICT really can become part of the world of the classroom.

Observing the local situation

The following three interrelated observation tasks look at the three areas which impact strongly on ICT in primary schools, namely, the hardware, the software and the people therein.

Observation task 1:
the computers and other hardware

This would make a good observational task, early on in your time in the primary school before you have to take responsibility for too much of the timetable. Have a look at all the classes, all the places in the school where computers may be in operation. What do you see? Make a list and answer the following questions:

- *Do you find that there are computers in all the classrooms?*
- *Are they all in a network room?*

- *Are they in a room all together but not connected to each other?*
- *Are they all the same type? That is, are they PC? Or AppleMac? Or Acorn? Or older RM Nimbus 186s?*
- *Are they all roughly the same age?*
- *Which classes seem to have the older equipment?*

- *Are there any working printers? For example, large, robust dot matrix printers with continuous feed paper – very noisy in a classroom but economical (when it isn't jammed)?*
- *As above but smaller with a cut sheet feeder?*
- *Higher quality inkjets – quieter, cheap to buy but very expensive to maintain?*
- *Laser printers, colour or black and white?*

- *Are there any portable computers for you and the children to use?*
  Acorn Pocketbooks, I or II or III (which are the same as Psion Organisers series 3)
  Apple e-Mates
  laptops from Acorn or Apple or RM
  Multimedia laptops from a pilot project
  Dreamwriters
  AlphaSmarts
  others?

- *Is there equipment for supporting access to ICT for children with Special Educational Needs?*
- *For example, are there Concept keyboards, touch windows, large keyboards, smaller or larger mice?*
- *Is there anything else used for specific children?*

- *Is there Internet access for you and the children? If so, what kind is it?*
  via a modem (external or internal) of varying speed and quality
  or via an ISDN line
  or via cable
  or via a local authority or higher education Internet connection?
- *How fast does it appear to be?*
- *Where is it available? For example:*
  on one computer in the library
  on three computers linked together
  in the network room
  in the network room and in the whole school in every class
  any other variation?

- *Is there a large training monitor or an interactive whiteboard so that all children can see the screen when you are talking to the whole class about the ICT activity?*
- *Has a large TV been connected via an adaptor for this purpose?*

- **Are there programmable toys for you to work on those aspects of controlling and modelling in the various subjects of Curriculum 2000? For example:**
    a Roamer, Pixie, Pip
    a Valiant turtle (infrared linked to an Acorn usually)
    a Jessops turtle (linked by cable)?

- **Are there any digital cameras?**
- **Do you have to connect them to a computer to download the pictures?**
- **Do they shoot straight to a disk?**

- **Do you have access to a video camera?**
- **Is there any way you can download the video clips?**

- **Have you and the children got access to a scanner somewhere:**
    hand scanners
    flatbed scanners?

- **Are there any electronic keyboards?**
- **Can you record into a computer using MIDI equipment?**

- **Is there a microphone for recording speech in multimedia presentations or music-making?**

- **Do you have access to the range of non-computer ICT equipment that you need to support your subject teaching:**
    tape recorders
    video recorders
    CD players?

Observation task 2: the software

Find the software associated with your age phase in the first instance. Note down particular curriculum content or applicability. Then widen your search to see if there is a similar range available for other classes in the school.

See how the software titles have been arranged. These are the sorts of things you may see:

- *Software which came bundled together with the computer. It was pre-loaded and intended to form a basic toolkit of software which could be used as a starting point for the school. The toolkit is a common concept across platforms and is usually organised to the following labels or similar:*

    word or text processing
    (e.g Talking WriteAway or Textease – PC, Talkwrite or Pendown – Acorn)

desktop publishing
(e.g. Microsoft Publisher or Creative Writer – PC, Ovation Pro – Acorn)

controlling and modelling software
(e.g. Logo or WinLogo – all platforms)

monitoring or datalogging software
(e.g. Junior Insight – all platforms)

image processing or graphics
(e.g. Dazzle or First Artist – PC or Acorn)

data-handling
(e.g. First Workshop or Information Workshop – PC, Junior Pinpoint – Acorn or PC)

Early Years
(e.g. MyWorld – PC or Acorn)

multimedia authoring
(e.g. Hyperstudio – PC, Acorn or Apple)

web browser
(Netscape or Internet Explorer or similar)

web authoring
(Netscape Composer, Front Page Express or similar)

- **There may be additional CD ROMS in use, bought for specific teaching purposes, such as Animated Alphabet *from Sherston (for early literacy) or* The Way Things Work *from Dorling Kindersley (for science, design and technology).***

Observation task 3: human resources

Observe how the class teachers organise the ICT for their children. Remember that unless they have supportive ICT co-ordinators or senior managers, a programme of staff development and working equipment, they may well be struggling with ICT. They will welcome your support but you must never make them feel threatened by your access to more recent knowledge and ideas, previous career in systems analysis or dot.com companies, etc. Remember that the teachers are there to help you learn. Whatever you can give back to the school as a trainee who is learning about ICT in subject teaching has to be offered tactfully and with due regard for the teachers' professionalism.

Observe the children themselves as they work with ICT in the school. They are the best source of information about what is going on with computers in the classroom. They know about the equipment. If it is old, they know which keys stick. They tend to know how to get round the deficiencies of the equipment, such as the printer which jams regularly.

Many children now have access to computers at home. What they say about the computers in school can be quite interesting in this regard. It is possible to hear young children discussing the relative merits of the latest Office software over other writing packages, with others talking knowledgeably about computer viruses and what can be done about them.

The games-playing children, those who have computer games consoles at home of one kind or another, often have a robust attitude towards computers of all sorts. They are aware of 'cheating' to get to different levels. Sometimes they will indulge in various key presses which may cause havoc with onscreen displays; sometimes they may discover for the class newer, more efficient ways of doing things.

Whatever the situation, it is always worth listening to what children say about computers and considering and valuing their contributions to the whole class body of knowledge about ICT.

Observe the classroom and learning support assistants wherever possible. Where available, they are a valuable source of knowledge and support about computers in the classroom. Some authorities are already in the business of providing training for classroom assistants in classroom ICT. Listen to what they say and involve them in your planning. Mutual respect and good communication are the keys to working well with classroom assistants.

Find out about the parents and governors and ICT. Parents, like children, have a wide range of ability and experience and an even wider range of concerns with ICT. They may be thinking about a purchase for their child and will often ask about a particular piece of hardware or software. They will assume, rightly or wrongly, that you are an individual, fully trained to deal with such enquiries.

Some parental concerns will be around the use of the Internet in your school, how it is organised and so on. They may be hinting at whether or not the school has an acceptable use policy and adequate protection for their children from unsuitable material on the World Wide Web.

Governors may raise many of the same issues with you and the school will be held responsible for the materials which the children may, in all innocence, be accessing if the school is not providing access through an education provider or through a filter which it is maintaining itself.

Organisational strategies for working in different resource settings with children

ICT is an entitlement no matter which situation you are working in. In all settings there are organisational issues which need addressing. This section looks at bringing ICT into the world of the classroom in the low resource setting and the high resource setting.

Organising ICT in low resource settings

On a regular basis and always with new computer programs in the classroom, arrange a whole class session. In a low resource setting, i.e. a single computer to a class of thirty children, first bring the computer to the carpet area where it can be seen by everybody. This immediately brings the computer out of its corner and into the world of the classroom. There may, of course, be physical reasons why you cannot do this. If there are, do what you can to overcome them or borrow areas big enough to do it somewhere else in the school. Just getting started with a piece of software should involve the whole class. This does not need to be of the same order of time as for the initiatives in literacy and numeracy, although at the beginning with a new package, when screens look very unfamiliar to the class, it would be worth spending longer on them.

The aim is to allow the computer to come into the world of the classroom more fully. A question and answer style lends itself to this situation. Allow the children to contribute, even to provide tips for other users. Discuss with them the difficulties that they have overcome in familiarising themselves with the onscreen layout of the particular piece of software. Whole class sessions can be enhanced by the following examples and principles:

- **Ask the children to discover during the session, and then report back on, different ways of doing the same thing. In a writing program, for example, how to make text appear in a different font size or colour.**
- **Stress regular, practical instructions by giving a mantra-like tone to them. One such regularly repeated instruction should be 'Save Before You Print', droned to children day in day out in order to persuade them that they should indeed save before they print in order to avoid the inevitable heartache which arises when a document gets lost in a malfunctioning printer.**
- **As is the case with all good primary practice, question children who don't always jump up and down with the answer (don't favour the loud over the quiet).**
- **Invite children to contribute to the discussion strictly girl – boy – girl – boy, etc.**
- **Do not allow one sex or group of children to dominate.**
- **Stress the team-building aspects of sharing strategies so that they/we can all use the computer efficiently and safely.**
- **Involve children in a discussion about safety – monitor position, length of time, seating and so on.**
- **Let everyone become an expert – don't always ask the same child who is managing their own Internet business from their bedroom at home.**
- **Value what they say even when it is patently wrong. Help them to discover a better way constructively (That's a good suggestion but …).**

Regular whole-class input increases the shared level of knowledge in the classroom about the use of the computer. It increases the overall standard of ICT work and the number of areas for which you can use ICT with some feeling of security.

It will also repay you in terms of stress reduction to have a regular period of whole class instruction in the basics of a particular piece of software. You will reduce the number of times that you have to say the same thing over and over again to groups of two to three children.

Becoming independent and increasingly competent in basic ICT skills will engender in the children a sense of responsibility for their work. From an early age, as children progress through the school, they are expected to take on more responsibility for knowing where their equipment is, where their possessions are, where they're going next and so on. It should be the same for ICT. Children can be shown the importance of looking after electronic forms of their work, just as they learn the importance of looking after their draft books. They will need to be shown how to save and retrieve their work and the importance of backing up work.

All of these activities allow you and the children to start to think of the computer as more a part of the world of the classroom. More than that, they foster a belief amongst all users in the classroom that they can become competent and confident manipulators of ICT.

The alternative model of instruction, a version of the cascade model, whereby one or two children learn it and teach others over a period of time discreetly while other children get on with the real work, allows the more negative messages about ICT to be disseminated. Amongst these more negative messages are:

- **There are ICT experts who know everything and must always be consulted before you do anything.**
- **ICT is something that happens in a corner of the room away from the mainstream and is never discussed and nothing to do with the rest of the school day.**

Show children that you are also a learner. ICT will be less threatening to you as a teacher if you enter into the situation as a learner alongside them. It is wrong to give children the impression that you or anyone else knows all they need to know about computers. Frustrating as it may be, the truth of the matter is that we are all always learning about ICT. Once one thing is learned you can be sure another parameter will enter the equation. It is OK to make mistakes. If the basic care of the equipment is known and respected, there is not much harm that can be done.

At the same time it is important in the low resource setting to establish and maintain a rota. Rotas ensure that there is equality of access and of opportunity in the classroom. However, they should not be fixed once and for all at the start of an academic year. The acquisition of ICT skills is a dynamic process, always changing. After whole class input, in the beginning of working with a new piece of software or hardware, children need time to practise. Longer rota periods can be gradually shortened as children become more skilled.

Rotas should always be public. They should be large, on the wall, clearly visible so that children can see that there is equality of provision. Older children can be involved in the drawing up and monitoring of time on the system. With software which has specific content, such as a game or simulation or where the software is of the drill and practice sort – such as integrated learning systems – there are fixed, tighter, more specific timetables of use involved. These are monitored by the software itself.

Organising ICT in high resource settings (networked computer suites)

Many of the same principles from the previous section apply in networked computer suites.

In a high resource setting, it is quite likely that you will be able to show all the children exactly what the session is about by means of a large display. This will be in the form of a large monitor, projection onto a screen or an interactive electronic whiteboard. It could be by being able to take control of the screens at the individual stations and replacing them with the teaching screen via some network software. In schools where there is no such display facility you will have to gather the children together in a space in front of one of the monitors. Teaching in network rooms without a large display is very, very difficult.

There are additional levels of complexity in network rooms and you must be on the alert for children who are still thinking in terms of standalone use. In the first place, make use of the large display or screen grabbing facility to demonstrate the procedure for logging on. Remind the children that they do not have to sit at the same machine each week. Remind them about the importance of their password. Here are some different models of practice:

* **whole class log on with the same username and password into a general area on the network for that class;**
* **the children have a unique username and password;**
* **the children have group log-on names and passwords.**

Before teaching the children on a network, make sure that you understand the process of logging on yourself. Ask the ICT co-ordinator (or technician) before starting (remember to ask for your own username and password as a guest on placement at the school!). Children are often given their own area on the network in which to save their work. It is important that you follow the same protocols as they are used to.

As a rule, unless the children are very young, they should be taught how to log on and log off their network. This is part of learning about network literacy, a concept that is new to primary schools where previously children and teachers worked with one standalone computer in the corner of the classroom. One strategy is to have all the passwords and usernames on index cards, used at the beginning of the session and collected at the end.

Whole class demonstrations can and should still take place, but they need to be a sensible length, enabling the children to make the best use of what may be their only time in the week when they are on the machines. After all, lesson management ought to be easier with no other activities going on other than computing. The teacher can provide more direct input for the children. Where these grouped computers are networked, saving and logging of progress is even easier.

For more information on planning, see pages 147-200, Chapter 7

The planning chapter and sections will look in detail at content across the curriculum. It is important to remember that children can contribute to the whole class under-standing and skills development in ICT and that there should be an opportunity for them to do so at the end of the session. The plenary can really come alive in a networked environment if the children are encouraged to use software for presenta-tion and present their projects for all to see. Schools in high resource settings which are capable of publishing on the Internet or their own Intranet will be able to further enrich the motivational opportunities for children writing or creating multimedia for a wider audience.

Organising ICT for Special Educational Needs

Children who have Special Educational Needs have the right to access to the whole curriculum including ICT. The nature of the need dictates your response to it as a teacher. Often ICT has been identified as being of particular benefit to a given learner in a given situation. Sometimes, if the child is on the SEN register, the child will have ICT hardware and software use identified as part of her or his Individual Education Plan (IEP) and you will need to incorporate this in your planning and organisation. Some examples might include:

- **software which addresses the needs of a dyslexic child;**
- **hardware which allows access to the computer for a child with motor impairment;**
- **browser windows which open up in larger fonts for visually impaired children;**
- **portables or laptops with specialist software loaded for very particular needs (this might include one specialist device or laptop assigned to one child in particular);**
- **specialist hardware for those who are using wheelchairs, such as specialist keyboard mounts or switching devices.**

Some companies are dedicated to finding solutions for access for children with SEN and they will welcome enquires about their software and suggestions for future develop-ment. They are usually smaller companies who depend on a close relationship with the schools and children with whom they work. The annual British Educational Technology and Training exhibition (known as the BETT show) includes a Special Needs Village for you to examine at first hand such solutions.

For children with SEN in your class it is important to discover if they require any additional access to the computer in the form of hardware that makes it easier to point and click at menu items or enter text. Some examples include:

- *A Concept keyboard* – a device which allows touch sensitive areas to be created on a flat A4 or A3 board which can be set up to input particular items of text or commands. Teachers can tailor the Concept keyboard to the particular needs of an individual child using authoring software provided. The software also includes printing facilities.
- *A touch window* – a device which attaches to the front of a monitor allowing the user to touch areas of the screen as a replacement mouse click to gain access to the menus in given software.
- *Big keys* – a larger format keyboard for children with fine motor control difficulties.
- *Switches* – on/off rack-mounted switches for wheelchair users and others which equate to left and right mouse clicks.
- *Trackballs* – large inverted mouse systems where the user is able to move a larger ball over a bigger area to point and click.
- *Small mice* – smaller point and click devices for smaller hands with motor control difficulties.

In terms of software for Special Educational Needs, there is a very wide range indeed. Most of it can be used to access the curriculum including the units of work in the ICT scheme of work by means of levelled menus and different screen setups.

There is also a case for appropriate tutorial software for some children with dyslexia or language delay because it will address very specifically the multi-sensory approach needed to allow such children to acquire strategies to catch up with language development.

As before, when organising for ICT with children who have Special Educational Needs:

- Find out about children in your class with **SEN**.
- Does their **IEP** require that they use **ICT**?
- Is there, in fact, dedicated equipment for use by one child?
- Would this be hardware, software or both?
- Does the child have a Special Needs assistant who will work with them on their **ICT**?
- How does their need for specialist **ICT** input impact on your organisation of the class?
- Is there a programme of review for determining success levels of the **ICT** equipment with their Special Educational Need?
- Is there someone you can discuss the situation with?
- What are the feelings of the parent on the use of **ICT** by their child during the week? Do they have materials or equipment at home which they are using to support her or him? Does it complement what you are doing or do you need to make adjustments to it?

One example of a piece of research into Special Needs is the study by Lie, O'Hare and Denwood (2000) in Scottish schools. This study finds that although word processing is believed to have a positive effect on the compositional process for children with specific writing difficulties, there are further significant background factors around motivation, cognition, medical factors and the whole learning environment.

The argument throughout this book and this chapter in particular is about seeing the possibilities for ICT use within the context of the whole class, or, in this case, the individual learner with Special Educational Needs. ICT is a tool for the enhancement of the learner's education within the context of the whole child and not simply an intrinsically 'good thing'. Its successful use depends on a thorough understanding of the background factors and appropriate planning and organisation.

Organising ICT for children with English as an Additional Language

ICT offers many benefits to young learners in the primary classroom who are learning and using English as an Additional Language. The computer brings many audio and video resources across the curriculum within reach. Children who are learning English at the earliest stages can access parts of the curriculum by means of such media.

As the child begins to acquire more English the computer, if properly managed, allows the child to experiment with forms of written and spoken English in an unthreatening and motivating environment. Some additional tutorial software may be appropriate but talking word processors can be just as effective with immediate feedback provided on composition. The biggest benefit is in areas where the child can experiment with open-ended software alongside peers.

Community languages with their own alphabets and letter systems are available through specialist software or as font add-ons in Office software. These can be used to produce signs and instructions in the appropriate language. In turn, this goes some way to demonstrating that the language of that child is valued in the context of the school and is an excellent way, again, of bringing ICT into the world of the classroom.

For younger children in this context, sensitive adult intervention and peer support are crucial. There should be plenty of opportunity to try to move conceptual development along by talk in the home language alongside support for learning English.

The choice of software should include elements which allow for the child to choose menu items by pointing and clicking, to have sections of text spoken, to allow access to pictures, music and video. Multimedia authoring packages can be useful in this context. There is enormous potential for producing home-grown resources in dual language format. This would be an exciting project for Year 6 for the Multimedia Authoring Unit. Resources could be created for any age in the school by the older children asking parents, siblings, other adults to help to record in the home language.

Organising ICT for children with English as an Additional Language carries the same responsibilities and requirements as for organising any area of the curriculum for them, namely:

- **Never assume the level of language learning – find out.**
- **Differentiate for levels of English appropriately; do not assume that all EAL learners are the same or have the same learning style.**
- **Make sure that EAL children understand all of the processes involved in switching on and off, logging on and off and saving work.**
- **Check and re-check understanding with sensitive questioning.**

Managing primary ICT:

a summary of key points

This chapter has considered the background to the situation in UK schools from the local and national perspectives. It has suggested that an understanding of these factors will provide a perspective on the differing resource settings which you will find in primary schools. In turn, the impact on classroom ICT of working in schools with differing levels of resource provision has been examined alongside several strategies for working in all settings.

We have also seen that there are different sorts of management strategies to consider for primary schools which have network provision of ICT. The ongoing deployment of these networks brings with it new challenges for teachers in their everyday work, not least the challenge of preventing ICT from being divorced from the rest of the curriculum. The emphasis throughout this chapter has been on practical solutions and on bringing ICT much more into the world of the primary school and the primary classroom.

Later in the chapter, three sets of observational activities were set out which would be useful to carry out to understand further the impact of different forms of organisation on teaching with ICT. These are the sorts of observations to carry out early on in your time in a school when you are in a position to observe, before you have a higher teaching load.

Finally, the chapter has also considered organising ICT for Special Educational Needs and for those children with English as an Additional Language. In either case, successful use of ICT depends on an understanding of the learners' abilities and needs.

Further reading

Ager, Richard (1998) *Information and Communications Technology in Primary Schools* David Fulton.

Beynon, J. and MacKay, H. (eds) (1993) *Computers into Classrooms: More Questions than Answers,* Falmer Press.

Cook, D. and Finlayson, H. (1999) *Interactive Children, Communicative Teaching: ICT and Classroom Teaching*, Open University Press.

DfEE (1998a) *Teaching: High Status, High Standards – Circular Number 4/98: Requirements for Courses of Initial Teacher Training*, DfEE.

Freedman, T. (1999) *Managing ICT*, Hodder & Stoughton.

Harrison, M. (1998) *Co-ordinating Information and Communications Technology across the Primary School.* Falmer Press.

Kyriacou, C. (1997) *Effective Teaching in Schools*, Stanley Thornes.

Leask, M. and Meadows, J. (eds) (2000) *Teaching and Learning with ICT in the Primary School,* Routledge.

McFarlane, A. (ed) (1997) *Information Technology and Authentic Learning: Realising the Potential of Computers in the Primary School*, Routledge.

Passey, D. *et al*. (1997) *Improve your Use of IT in Teaching,* Folens.

Somekh, B. and Davis, N. (eds) (1997) *Using Information Technology Effectively in Teaching and Learning: Studies in Pre-service and In-service Teacher Education*. Routledge.

Tagg, B. (1995) *Developing a Whole School IT Policy,* Pitman.

Trend, R. Davis, N. and Loveless, A. (1998) *Information and Communications Technology,* Letts Educational.

ICT planning in the Professional Standards for QTS

The curriculum for teacher trainees for ICT in subject teaching is set out in paragraph 3.3.10 of *Qualifying to Teach* (DfES/TTA, 2002), which says that those awarded QTS must demonstrate that they can use ICT effectively in their teaching. There is further guidance in the Handbook that accompanies the Standards (DfES/TTA, 2002b).

During the ITT course, trainees are expected to develop skills of planning for the use of ICT in their subject teaching which, amongst other items, stresses learning about the appropriateness of using ICT. This sense of appropriateness is reflected in the Handbook that accompanies the Standards. On page 51 it says 'Trainees will need to be able to use ICT with discrimination, knowing where and how it can be used to the greatest effect on pupils' learning' (DfES/TTA, 2002b).

In other words, the Standards demand that trainees focus on subject-related opportunities to work with ICT that make a significant contribution to the learning of the pupils. At the same time as acquiring these skills of planning within subject teaching, however, trainees *will* need to be mindful of the developing IT capability of their children. The capability and the application in subject teaching are very closely bound up together. Planning which addresses one without at least considering the other will not work. Good planning depends on a thorough analysis and negotiation of factors around the children, including their capabilities and needs.

While learning how to plan for ICT in subject teaching, trainees will be cognisant of the need to know about their children's IT capability in order to pursue opportunities to exploit and extend it. It will be part of a set of factors which makes up good lesson planning in the same way that planning a useful daily mathematics lesson in Shape and Space, for example, takes into account the children's wider mathematical capabilities and opportunities to enhance and develop them. They do not exist in a separate world; they are inextricably linked.

For more information on ICT spending in schools see page 130, Chapter 6

We will see in another section (in the context of understanding what is happening with ICT in schools) that this focus on subject teaching, as opposed to IT capability, is what underpins the INSET programme running until 2002 (otherwise known as the New Opportunities Fund – NOF – training). Teachers currently serving in schools are being trained in the same curricular context as trainees on initial teacher training courses.

The Handbook of guidance on the Standards gives examples of evidence of meeting the standards for the use of ICT in subject teaching which takes account of many of the functions of ICT. In terms of planning with ICT you will need to develop the necessary skills to make use of at least some of the following in your teaching:

'…Internet-aware computers and the relevant peripherals e.g. CD ROM, subject and professional software, projectors, interactive whiteboards, digital cameras, scanners, video, control and sensing technology and calculators' (DfES/TTA, 2002b, p. 51).

There is recognition in the handbook that not all schools will be able to provide you with all these opportunities and we have discussed resource settings in the preceding chapter (Managing Primary ICT). The Handbook states that:

'Trainees' opportunities to demonstrate that they have met this Standard will be dependent on school software, hardware and access to the Internet, and these may be limited for some trainees. Some evidence will come from their work in the classroom but other evidence may come from out-of-school contexts.' (DfES/TTA, 2002b, p. 51).

However, where such resources exist you need to develop skills of planning for their use in subject teaching. This means being very clear about the learning objective. In fact, the *Requirements* state clearly that:

For those aspects of lessons where ICT is to be used, trainees must be taught to identify in their planning:

a. the way(s) in which ICT will be used to meet teaching and learning objectives in the subject;

b. key questions to ask and opportunities for teacher intervention in order to stimulate and direct pupils' learning.

For more information on subject teaching, see page 167, Chapter 8

We will see, below, how we might identify these learning objectives and opportunities in subject teaching in all subjects. For the purposes of the award of QTS this means each trainee knowing about objectives and opportunities in English, mathematics and science and in their chosen specialist subject. The sections which follow will analyse the situation further in a range of contexts and will then go into each individual subject area (including the strategies for the teaching of literacy and numeracy) in search of such opportunities.

Effective planning – analysing the situation

Effective teaching depends heavily on effective planning. ICT in subject teaching and ICT as a subject in its own right are no exception to this rule. In turn, effective planning depends on a thorough analysis of the situation at the outset. Many writers have identified this link and some have produced books for teachers in training which summarise and synthesise the best of the available research. Chris Kyriacou provides an overview of studies which have looked at lesson effectiveness in his book, *Effective Teaching in Schools* (Kyriacou, 1997). One of the studies reported, that of Cooper and McIntyre (1996), looked at the teaching and learning in a series of lessons in terms of what both the teachers and the children felt. Analysis produced the following list of key items which contributed to lesson effectiveness:

- **clear learning goals for children's learning;**
- **helping children to contextualise the content in terms of their own experience and knowledge;**
- **providing a supportive social context for learning;**
- **enabling children to engage in the learning process in a number of different ways;**
- **willingness of the teacher to modify learning tasks in the light of children's circumstances.**

(Kyriacou, 1997)

All of these factors are of immediate direct relevance to teachers planning for any subject in the curriculum. When it comes to the use of ICT in subject teaching or ICT in its own right, there is an added layer of complexity because of the impact of the resource setting of the school. Some questions need to be raised to take account of this and added to the generic areas above. At the outset, as a minimum, teachers preparing to use ICT in their teaching need to be asking at least these few questions:

 For more information on resource settngs see page 133, Chapter 6

- **What do we know about the children's existing knowledge, skills and understanding in the subject?**
- **What has been their previous experience with ICT?**
- **What does the National Curriculum – Curriculum 2000 – set out for the children in this class? In the subject? In ICT itself?**
- **What am I therefore expecting the children to achieve?**
- **How will I differentiate the activity to reflect the different needs and abilities in the class?**
- **What relevant pieces of theoretical writing and/or case studies are there to support my planning?**
- **What will be the demands on me in terms of my own knowledge, skills and understanding of ICT?**
- **What is the resource setting for the school and how does this impact on what I can plan for the class?**
- **What are the additional time costs and constraints on me when planning to use ICT?**
- **What kind of grouping or organisation am I planning for?**
- **How will I go about the physical management of the activity?**
- **Are there any further cross-curricular links?**
- **How will I go about including the whole class in the activity?**

For more information on assessment and recording, see page 200, Chapter 10

Finally (and we will consider this in far more detail in the relevant chapter below):

- **What are the assessment and record-keeping opportunities in the activity?**

Planning is, of course, cyclical in nature. No sooner have you reached the last question than you realise it must be used to answer the first question in the next batch of planning. Good planning should create assessment opportunities because good assessment informs good planning.

Towards a lesson planning proforma for ICT

It makes sense to try to collect these questions into headings which you can use to ensure that you cover all of the necessary elements, each time you plan. As part of your training year, you will develop or, more likely, be given a great deal of assistance in developing, lesson planning proformas of various kinds. Some will provide very detailed outlines of what is going on in a session whereas others will be shorter. As you gain experience through the year, what seems like a very detailed and time-consuming activity initially will become part of your professional life and almost second nature.

Without attempting to prescribe a model which works in all settings, on all courses, in all classrooms, here is a possible set of headings for a detailed, longer format, plan. Most of the headings are in common use for curriculum planning in all subjects and are relatively easily adapted to ICT in subject teaching and ICT as a subject in its own right:

LESSON OVERVIEW
Describe the lesson in brief before going on to outline the detail of how it will operate and the rationale under the remaining headings.

SCHOOL/CLASS CONTEXT
Describe under this heading the context of the children, their school, their class within the school.

LEARNING NEEDS OF THE CHILDREN
Use this part of the plan to map out the learning needs of the class in both general and specific terms.

GROUPING/TIMING
Is this lesson plan for the whole class, a group, a pair or an individual? Is it an activity which you would like a group to work on all week, or different groups of children to work on through the week? How long will the activity last?

RESOURCES
Outline here how the resources for ICT are set out in the school. What, in particular is available to you to use during the session you are planning? Make a list of everything you need to hand to make the lesson work.

THEORETICAL CONTEXT

Are there any readings which underpin the thinking behind the plan for this lesson, either for you or for the children? An example for you might be one where you have identified, through your use of ICT, a different way of approaching a particular lesson. You find that, for example, 'IT can support the process of professional development as well as providing a stimulus to rethinking the teaching process' (Somekh and Davis, 1997).

NATIONAL CURRICULUM/FOUNDATION STAGE CURRICULUM CONTEXT

What aspects of the programmes of study from Curriculum 2000 are you teaching? Consider the ICT and any links to other subjects. List the main cross-curricular focus. If you are working in an Early Years setting, what elements of the curriculum for the Foundation Stage are you hoping to work with during the activity?

SCHEME OF WORK CONTEXT

From the school scheme of work, or the QCA Scheme of Work, outline the unit, or aspect of the unit, that you are covering with the children. Show how it progresses from the previous one studied.

YOUR OWN LEARNING NEEDS

Take some time to note down any concepts you need to revise and review before teaching the children. Are there any aspects of any hardware, software or websites you are using which you need to consider before starting the activity?

ORGANISATIONAL MEMORY JOGGERS

Do you know all you need to know about passwords, location of keys to the computer suite, computer cupboard, etc.? Have you checked on availability of all of the items you need to run the lesson?

OTHER ADULTS

Do you know how many, if any, other adults are available to support the teaching of the lesson? Have you copied the plan for them and indicated what you would like them to do?

LEARNING OBJECTIVES

List the main objectives of the activities using the scheme of work as a map for learning.

DIFFERENTIATION

What do you expect different members of the class to achieve in terms of their different ability levels? How will you help children who are experiencing difficulties with ICT? How will you develop further the skills, knowledge and understanding of the most able in the class? What do you expect the majority to have achieved by the end of the lesson? There is some good guidance given in the QCA Scheme of Work which can be used as a starting point for differentiation.

For more information on the QCA Scheme of Work see page 157, Chapter 7

LEARNING NEEDS – EAL

How will you support children in your class who have English as an Additional Language?

LEARNING NEEDS – SEN
How will you support any children in the class with Special Educational Needs? Are there particular physical needs, for example, which could be met by means of alternative access devices?

For more information on Assessment see page 200, Chapter 11

ASSESSMENT OPPORTUNITIES
What are the assessment opportunities in this particular lesson? Will you focus on the whole class, or an individual? How will you use other adults who may be around to assist in the process?

KEY QUESTIONS
What are the key questions which you will ask the children during the lesson which draw out the teaching and learning objectives? How will you maintain the dialogue with children who are experiencing difficulties? Record a few possible prompts which you could use.

LESSON FORMAT
Depending on your resource setting, whether you are in the classroom with one computer, or in a computer suite or a corridor, how long will the different phases of your lesson last? Give timings for:

- **an introduction outlining the learning objectives;**
- **development of the lesson through focused activities and integrated tasks;**
- **a plenary, wherein all the strands are drawn together and children have an opportunity to share successes and problems.**

EVALUATING THE LESSON part 1 – OPERATIONAL ISSUES
Good planning includes a space in which to reflect on how the lesson actually proceeded. It only needs to be a few lines, written at the time or soon after, which can give you a perspective on things you needed to change to make the lesson work (and which could, in turn, inform your planning later). Did you need, for example, to alter the timings of the introduction to ensure understanding of what was required for all the children?

EVALUATING THE LESSON part 2 – LEARNING OUTCOMES
How far did the lesson achieve the intended learning objectives? Make a judgement based on your identified assessment opportunities. If it is part of a sequence of lessons, how much is there still left to do? Comment on how the lesson went for the children experiencing difficulty or for those children of high ability. How well were you able to meet the needs of those with English as an Additional Language? Did children with Special Educational Needs have full access to the activity and were they able to succeed?

EVALUATING THE LESSON part 3 – NEXT TIME
Make some brief notes about what needs to happen next on the basis of your comments above. Identify some issues which need to be addressed for the next lesson in the sequence to be successful. What will you do differently next time? What went well?

ICT as a subject: working with Curriculum 2000

This section is concerned primarily with the curriculum as it is outlined for children entering Year I of the primary school up to Year 6. The curriculum for the Foundation Stage, from the age of three until the age of five/six, is covered in a separate chapter below.

For more information on the Foundation Stage, see page 194, Chapter 9

The most recent version of the National Curriculum for schools in England was published early in 2000 and was expected to be implemented in schools from September of that year. In the text, in order to make distinctions from other versions, the National Curriculum will be referred to as Curriculum 2000. It makes several changes to previously existing frameworks for those working with computers in schools.

Curriculum 2000 responded to the changes in the nature of educational IT, including the arrival of the Internet and communications technology in schools signalled by the National Grid for Learning. It changed the emphasis in its programmes of study and grouped them under the following headings:

For more information on the NGfL, see page 130, Chapter 6

- **finding things out;**
- **developing ideas and making things happen;**
- **exchanging and sharing information;**
- **reviewing, modifying and evaluating work as it progresses;**
- **(the breadth of study for the above).**

The following tables summarise the changes that arose as a result of the introduction of Curriculum 2000. They are provided as a historical context and in case you encounter references to planning in school which are connected to the previous curriculum for IT.

Previous National Curriculum 1995–2000	SUBJECT TITLE: Information Technology (IT) Content headings:
IT LOCATED IN ALL CURRICULUM SUBJECT TEACHING, EXCEPT PE	1. General opportunities and awareness of IT
	2. Communicating and handling information
	3. Controlling/modelling (KS1) Controlling, modelling and monitoring (KS2)

Curriculum 2000	SUBJECT TITLE: Information and Communications Technology (ICT) Content headings:
ICT LOCATED IN ALL CURRICULUM SUBJECT TEACHING	1. Finding things out
	2. Developing ideas and making things happen
	3. Exchanging and sharing information
	4. Reviewing, modifying and evaluating work as it progresses
	5. Breadth of study

You will have noticed by now that a major change was that of the subject name from Information Technology (IT) to Information and Communication Technology (ICT). There was much debate around the loss of the old name for the subject, particularly from our colleagues in secondary education and in secondary teacher education. Much of the exchanges centred on the fact that IT was an already established discipline with a history and a set of syllabuses in many different educational contexts. Furthermore, IT is widely understood as a term outside the world of education. Whole professional career structures exist to support IT.

Furthermore, IT was previously defined quite specifically as the skills, knowledge and understanding necessary to apply technology to teaching and learning. ICT, on the other hand, comprised the facilities and features that 'variously support learning and a range of activities in education' (QCA, 1998). In other words, one was the technology around the learning activity (ICT) and the other (IT) was the knowledge required to employ ICT 'appropriately, securely and fruitfully in learning, employment and everyday life' (QCA, 1998).

ICT as a subject title arrived with Curriculum 2000 and, according to the revised guidance, reflected the 'growing importance of communication to information technology'. The distinction between IT and ICT effectively disappeared for schools in England in the curriculum documentation in primary schools ('annex B of the original Information Technology scheme of work teacher's guide no longer applies'). As a result, in schools it is possible to find ICT schemes of work where previously there were IT schemes as well as ICT co-ordinators where previously there were IT co-ordinators. LEAs have ICT advisors where previously there were IT advisors and so on. This explanation is offered in case, once you get into schools, you still see references to IT and wonder what it all means.

What do the headings of Curriculum 2000 mean in practice? The headings of Curriculum 2000 describe what should be studied by all children in schools in England. Working with them means finding curricular opportunities within ICT as a subject and within ICT in subject teaching to develop their skills under the headings of:

- **finding things out;**
- **developing ideas and making things happen;**
- **exchanging and sharing information;**
- **reviewing, modifying and evaluating work as it progresses.**

Additionally, a statement about breadth of study at Key Stage 1 and Key Stage 2 is included to provide a context for teaching and learning about the characteristics and purposes of information and its representation.

Beginning with 'Finding things out' sees Curriculum 2000 requiring that children are taught how to gather information, how to enter and store information, and how to retrieve information (Key stage 1). At Key Stage 2 'Finding things out' develops a more critical sense whereby children are able to discuss the sort of information they need, learn how to prepare it from different sources for development using ICT, and how to interpret it and verify it. Elements of what used to be 'Communicating and Handling Information' have become 'Finding things out'.

'Developing ideas and making things happen' is concerned at Key Stage 1 with developing ideas using ICT by means of text, tables, images and sounds as well as adding to that information for a particular purpose. Also at Key Stage 1 is the requirement to plan and give instructions and to explore what happens in simulations onscreen. For Key Stage 2 children working in this area of ICT knowledge, there is a requirement to deepen their understanding of these concepts, in other words, to refine organisational skills, skills of programming and testing, using simulations, etc. Elements of both 'Communicating and Handling Information' and 'Controlling and Modelling' have become subsumed under the heading of 'Developing ideas and making things happen.'

'Exchanging and sharing information' is the element of ICT knowledge which has been added to take account of the use of the Internet in schools. At Key Stage 1 there is a requirement that children begin to share ideas by presenting work using ICT in a variety of ways and presenting it effectively for public display. At Key Stage 2, the use of email and publishing on the Internet has been suggested to meet the requirements to develop children's sense of what ICT can do to help us to communicate to different audiences. Elements of what used to be 'Communicating and Handling Information' have become 'Exchanging and sharing information'.

Finally, in the targets for developing skills, knowledge and understanding, comes 'Reviewing, modifying and evaluating work as it progresses'. At Key Stage 1 children are asked to develop a sense of reflection about the work produced with ICT which allows them to think about what they might change on a future occasion. At Key Stage 2 this becomes reflecting in detail about the particular effectiveness of ICT compared to other methods for carrying out similar tasks. Elements of what used to be 'Communicating and Handling Information' have become part of 'Reviewing, modifying and evaluating work as it progresses'.

The 'breadth of study' of ICT in Curriculum 2000 requires that children become familiar with a very wide range of ICT tools and applications from floor turtles to word processors and from database packages to the Internet and email. All the time, there is the requirement that they understand real and work-related examples and discuss the uses (and occasional misuses at Key Stage 2) of ICT in school and in the outside world.

These are the requirements for ICT in schools in England. They also represent an entitlement and a right for every child to expect to meet the necessary teaching and teaching resources in their school career throughout Key Stages 1 and 2 (and, we will see in a later chapter, there are benefits to using ICT in the pre-school setting too).

Looking briefly at resource provision for planning with Curriculum 2000, as a minimum, the table below indicates the kind of resources in terms of hardware and software which you would expect to see provided in order for children to have their entitlement to ICT met:

For more information on resource settings see page 133, Chapter 6

Area of knowledge, skills and understanding	Resource entitlement for KS1 and KS2
Finding things out	A range of CD ROMS, Internet access, videos, TV, databases and data-handling packages.
Developing ideas and making things happen	As above with word processors, desktop publishing, multimedia software, digital cameras and/or scanners, floor turtles, onscreen logo, monitoring and datalogging equipment.
Exchanging and sharing information	As above and including email, online forums, music composition software.
Reviewing, modifying and evaluating work as it progresses	All above with opportunities to print and compare.

Resource entitlement in Curriculum 2000

Working with Curriculum 2000 means the same as the earlier versions of the curriculum in effect: creating opportunities to use ICT to develop subject knowledge in all areas of the curriculum, at the same time as developing ICT itself. The following two sections address planning for ICT itself and for ICT in subject teaching.

Planning for ICT with the QCA Scheme of Work

What is the QCA Scheme of Work?

The Scheme of Work for ICT has, since 1998, provided a detailed framework for teaching which combines provision for developing subject knowledge within ICT at the same time as using it as a tool in other subjects. It is possible to find cross-curricular links in virtually every study unit to virtually every other subject.

It is therefore no longer adequate for a teacher to think in terms of putting 'USING CD ROMS' on a term planner under the heading 'ICT for Spring Term' and hope that this will cover children's developing ICT subject knowledge. There can't be many other National Curriculum subjects where this might even be considered a possibility. Imagine a teacher's plan for mathematics which said 'USING DIENES CUBES' and nothing else. It indicates nothing about the context or the subject knowledge that is being developed in the ICT lesson. Placing 'USING CD ROMS' in a planner for another subject as a resource to use, by a detailed plan for the learning outcomes in that subject, is, of course, a different matter.

What this section is concerned with is the use of the QCA Scheme of Work in planning for children's developing subject knowledge in ICT itself.

The Scheme of Work codified for teachers the stages of development of subject knowledge through which children must be allowed to progress. There is substantial guidance for schools in the document even in terms of the vocabulary to be used with children. Schools must have at least this Scheme of Work in place (or equivalent, see below) as a fundamental aid to planning, a map of the learning outcomes for ICT in their school and as a statement of intent and entitlement. However, it is worth pointing out that the scheme is guidance only and is not a legal requirement. As the Teacher's Guide notes at the outset, 'The original Scheme of Work and the additional units can be used as a basis for work in ICT if a school wishes. However, there is no compulsion to use them and schools may use as little or as much of the material as they find helpful' (QCA, 2000a).

Not all schools are using the QCA Scheme of Work. Some have schemes which are based on the QCA model or are based on a similar, local authority one. Good schools will not be leaving it up to chance. OFSTED has identified a lack of scheme of work (or development plan) as significant in keeping standards in ICT low. A school which is delivering ICT well, on the other hand, will have a clear idea of the model of progression through the curriculum which a scheme can provide.

For more information on Monitoring, see page 208, Chapter 11

Try to establish early on in your placement school which scheme is in place and use it in your ICT planning. If there is no obvious plan for ICT year on year other than the ubiquitous 'Use CD ROMS' in the term planner you need to be proactive and use the QCA Scheme of Work at the right level for your placement. If you are working in an Early Years setting, see the relevant section below for some starting points to planning using the Curriculum Guidance for the Foundation Stage.

For more information on planning ICT in the Early Years, see page 194, Chapter 9

Using the QCA Scheme of Work for ICT

The document is relatively easy to use once you get used to the different sections. It is set out in a folder with a Teacher's Guide, an index card linking the various units to the Programmes of Study contained in Curriculum 2000, and a pocket full of the various scheme units in A3 format. It may be that your school is using the original version and has missed out on the update provided to link it to Curriculum 2000 and to set out five new units of work (two at Year 1, and one each at Years 2, 5 and 6). If this is the case, you should be able to get the update through the school by asking them to contact the DfEE document centre or by downloading the units yourself from the Internet.

As another piece of advice, printing or photocopying the units onto A4 and re-filing them in another personal folder is a useful activity. The A3 sheets can go missing from the only copy in a school at a time when you most need them.

The units of work are related directly to the wording of the programme of study for Curriculum 2000 by means of the index card. A key is provided which refers the units back to statements in Curriculum 2000 which define knowledge, skills and understanding under the four headings, namely:

1. Finding things out.
2. Developing ideas and making things happen.

3. Exchanging and sharing information.
4. Reviewing, modifying and evaluating work as it progresses.

Thus, if a particular unit refers to Curriculum 2000 statement (2a) it refers to statement (a) of Developing Ideas and Understanding (namely, children should be taught *to use text, tables, images and sound to develop their ideas*).

Written out in full as an example, for Year 1, the five units described relate back to the curriculum as shown opposite.

Like any other document used for planning, there is a learning curve. However, the more you use the document, the more familiar the language becomes and the more straightforward it is to adapt to the particular resource setting in which you find yourself. Furthermore, the notes of guidance explain very clearly how to navigate the A3 unit planners. The A3 sheets are organised into sections as follows:

- **On the first page is the unit title (see examples 1A to 1E in the table opposite). The letters are not there to indicate any particular order in which the units should be taught. Underneath the title is a section labelled ABOUT THE UNIT which gives an overview of the unit. This is followed by descriptions of the unit in relation to other parts of the scheme (WHERE THE UNIT FITS IN), the vocabulary you need to introduce to the children (TECHNICAL VOCABULARY – similar in concept to the National Literacy Strategy vocabulary lists), and the resources you will need (RESOURCES, both computer based and other forms of technology).**

- **The element of differentiation is supplied in the section labelled EXPECTATIONS. This is a series of outcomes for 'most children', 'some children (who) will not have made so much progress' and 'some (who) will have progressed further'. These broad statements require much greater fine tuning at the classroom level.**

- **The unit descriptions continue across the A3 sheet on the following sides under four headings, namely:**

  Learning Objectives
  Possible Teaching Activities
  Learning Outcomes
  Points to Note.

For more information on Assessment, see page 200, Chapter 10

'Learning Objectives' outlines the steps towards full understanding of the unit. 'Possible Teaching Activities' are described under three potential headings (see below). 'Learning Outcomes' describe the indications of a child's progress and are intended to inform assessment. 'Points to Note' outlines the misconceptions which a child may have and includes suggestions to overcome these issues.

Year/ unit	Title of unit	Related elements of Curriculum 2000 programme of study
1A	An introduction to modelling	From (2c and 2d) Developing ideas and making things happen, pupils should be taught: (c) how to plan and give instructions to make things happen [for example, programming a floor turtle, placing instructions in the right order] (d) to try things out and explore what happens in real and imaginary situations [for example, trying out different colours on an image, using an adventure game or simulation]. From (4b and 4c) Reviewing, modifying and evaluating work as it progresses, pupils should be taught to: (b) describe the effects of their actions (c) talk about what they might change in future work.
1B	Using a word bank	From (1a and 1b) Finding things out, pupils should be taught to: (a) gather information from a variety of sources [for example, people, books, databases, CD-ROMs, videos and TV] (b) enter and store information in a variety of forms [for example, storing information in a prepared database, saving work]. From (2a and 2b), Developing ideas and making things happen, pupils should be taught: (a) to use text, tables, images and sound to develop their ideas (b) how to select from and add to information they have retrieved for particular purposes.
1C	The information around us	From (1a and 1b) Finding things out, pupils should be taught to: (a) gather information from a variety of sources [for example, people, books, databases, CD-ROMs, videos and TV] (b) enter and store information in a variety of forms [for example, storing information in a prepared database, saving work].
1D	Labelling and classifying	From (1a) Finding things out, pupils should be taught to: (a) gather information from a variety of sources [for example, people, books, databases, CD-ROMs, videos and TV] From (2b), Developing ideas and making things happen, pupils should be taught: (b) how to select from and add to information they have retrieved for particular purposes.
1E	Representing information graphically: pictograms	From (2a) Developing ideas and making things happen, pupils should be taught: (a) to use text, tables, images and sound to develop their ideas. From (3a and 3b) Exchanging and sharing information, pupils should be taught: (a) how to share their ideas by presenting information in a variety of forms [for example, text, images, tables, sounds] (b) to present their completed work effectively [for example, for public display].
1F	Understanding instructions and making things happen	From (2b and 2c) Developing ideas and making things happen, pupils should be taught: (b) how to select from and add to information they have retrieved for particular purposes (c) how to plan and give instructions to make things happen [for example, programming a floor turtle, placing instructions in the right order].

Relationship between QCA Scheme and Curriculum 2000

- As stated above, 'Possible Teaching Activities' are further grouped under three different types of teaching activities:

  Setting the scene – introducing the unit to the children and taking only a few minutes.

  Short focused tasks – instructing on a specific IT task and introducing key ideas such as cutting, copying and pasting.

  Integrated tasks – more complex projects which build on the shorter tasks and require several sessions to complete.

For more information on resource settings, see page 133, Chapter 6

The units of work are adaptable to the range of resource settings discussed earlier and identified as low, medium and high resource settings.

Planning example from the QCA Scheme of Work

An example follows of a longer format lesson plan which is taken from a unit of work from the QCA Scheme. It assumes a high resource setting, a school with a networked suite of computers. The context is the unit for year 2A: Writing Stories: communicating information using text:

LONGER LESSON PLAN FOR ICT AT YEAR 2
FROM ICT UNIT 2A: Writing stories: communicating information using text:
CROSS-CURRICULAR LINK: English (NLS Objectives for Y2, term 1)

LESSON OVERVIEW
The children will work on a pre-prepared file which contains no full stops and capital letters and connects ideas using the word 'and' repeatedly and inappropriately. They will identify where the sentence breaks should be, delete each inappropriate 'and' in question and replace it with a full stop and capital letter. There will be opportunities to extend the work into wider kinds of connectives if this is appropriate.

SCHOOL/CLASS CONTEXT
The school is a large, inner-city primary school with a wide range of ability. Some 20 different languages are spoken, of which the majority speak Sylheti-Bengali. There are 29 children in the class, an average size for the school. The children are all in Year 2.

LEARNING NEEDS OF THE CHILDREN

FOR ICT: Most children are confident at logging on and using the computers in the network suite. The children need experience of dropping into text and changing it using the mouse and the keyboard.

FOR ENGLISH: The aim of the lesson is to back up literacy lessons on improving drafts of writing by looking at changing writing containing too many long sentences (deleting 'and' and replacing with full stop and capital letter of the next word). See Objectives for Year 2, Term 1 in Sentence Level work in DFEE, 1998b).

GROUPING/TIMING

The lesson will last one hour, not including a ten-minute outline of how to use the software. We will go into the room at about 1.30 and leave at about 2.45 in time for the afternoon break. The class will be split into two groups. Half will log on for 30 minutes then the other half will swap. The middle group, not using the computers, will have work to do which relates to the lesson, correcting drafts from their own written work.

RESOURCES

The computer suite comprises 15 stations arranged around the outside of the room with a central table-based working area for work away from the computer.

THEORETICAL CONTEXT

From Angela McFarlane's 'Thinking About Writing' (Chapter 8 in McFarlane, 1997). 'The use of word processors helps to present text as something to be experimented with, redrafted and developed as ideas develop, or as the purpose or audience change. It liberates the writer from the heavy burden of manual editing and presentation.'

NC/FOUNDATION STAGE CONTEXT

Developing ideas and making things happen (Programme of Study 2a), pupils should be taught to use text, tables, images and sound to develop their ideas.

Exchanging and sharing information (Programme of Study 3a), pupils should be taught to share their ideas by presenting information in a variety of forms [for example, text, images, tables, sounds].

Reviewing, modifying and evaluating work as it progresses (Programme of Study 4a), pupils should be taught to review what they have done to help them develop their ideas.

SCHEME OF WORK CONTEXT

Lesson ideas from QCA Scheme of Work for ICT, Unit 2A: Writing stories: communicating information using text.

YOUR OWN LEARNING NEEDS

Preparing text in a word processor for the children to work on.

Making sure that I know how to save the work in the children's user areas as a template to work on.

Understanding the context of the work on grammar and punctuation in the National Literacy Strategy teaching objectives for Y2.

ORGANISATIONAL MEMORY JOGGERS

Can I get into the network room during the lunch hour to make sure that the pre-prepared file is in the right area on the network? Do I have the appropriate access rights to the network in order to do this?

Do all children know how to log on?

Are there spare USER IDs in case of emergency?

For more information on logging-on, see page 141, Chapter 6

OTHER ADULTS

Assuming a learning support teacher for a child who is experiencing difficulties with writing, remember to copy the lesson plan and talk to them before the lesson takes place if at all possible.

LEARNING OBJECTIVES

FOR ICT: The key idea that ICT can be used to improve text and make a message clearer by means of onscreen editing. Learning deleting and inserting text to improve readability.

(Part of QCA Scheme of Work Unit 2A.)

FOR ENGLISH: The key concept of full stops and capital letters to create sentences and improve sense and understanding of writing. As an extension: the key idea that writing can be connected by a wider range of connectives than just the word 'and'.

(Part of National Literacy Strategy Sentence Level work Year 2/Term 1.)

DIFFERENTIATION

For Blue Group (lower ability), a slightly simpler form of the file with highlighted 'and's.

For the Red Group (higher ability), a longer version of the file and extension into creating their own files for each other to correct (if time allows). Other connectives to be suggested for the longer sentences.

For other groups in the class – the basic file and questions.

See also: key questions, below.

LEARNING NEEDS – EAL

Remember that children who have English as an Additional Language are all at different stages of acquiring English. Partner the children appropriately according to language needed to access the activity. Consider allowing some pairs to work at the same computer if they are experiencing difficulties. Remember to check and re-check understanding of the task.

LEARNING NEEDS – SEN

For the child with difficulties with motor control, remember to ensure that the Touch Screen driver is loaded and that the support teacher has space to sit with her.

For more information on assessment and recording, see pages 203–5, Chapter 10

ASSESSMENT OPPORTUNITIES

Complete observation proformas on targeted children or on the whole class profile.

KEY QUESTIONS

Remember to focus on the language being developed for ICT in the QCA unit, i.e. shift, spacebar, return/enter, insert, backspace, delete. For English, refer questioning to texts and units currently under study during the Literacy Hour.

Some questions for ICT development, differentiated according to ability, might include:

Which keys do you use to delete or rub out words? (Lower)

How do you change letters from lower case to upper case? (Lower/Middle)

How do you move around in the text and/or how do you place the cursor where you want it to go? (Middle)

Do you know a quick way to locate the word 'and' in the text? (Higher)

LESSON FORMAT

5–10 minutes: Opening with demonstration at the whiteboard. Invite some participation from the children. Ask questions. Check and re-check understanding of the task. Share the learning objective with the children.

20 minutes: Group 1 at the computers, Group 2 at the tables. Allow pairing of children where appropriate and supportive.

5 minutes: Changeover and recap on purpose of the activity.

20 minutes: Group 2 at the computers, Group 1 at the tables. Allow pairing of children where appropriate and supportive.

5–10 minutes: Plenary with contributions/questions from children. Allow them to demonstrate their work at the whiteboard.

Remember to allow for questions from across the ability range.

EVALUATING THE LESSON part 1 – OPERATIONAL ISSUES

As stated above, note here any changes during the lesson which might affect the way you work on this unit on the future. Issues which might have arisen include:

All children needed more time. Allow the whole class to log on together for longer and share the equipment, *or*

The 20 minutes was fine for the activity as it occurred, some children needed to be partnered within the groups to make it work, *or*

The pencil and paper activity was too short. The children needed more work away from the computers, *or*

The plenary was too rushed and there was insufficient time to draw the understanding together and revisit the learning objectives with the children.

EVALUATING THE LESSON part 2 – LEARNING OUTCOMES

Note in this section any particular achievements which children demonstrated. Were you able to carry out the assessments planned for during the session?

EVALUATING THE LESSON part 3 – NEXT TIME

What aspects of this work need to be repeated? How could you deepen understanding of the ICT concepts behind the work? What will you do next time in the light of the organisational changes you had to make?

Practical task

Identify a unit of work in the QCA Scheme which refers to the age group you are teaching. Find an activity from within the unit which fits in with the current units of work being undertaken in any of the other subject curriculum areas. Follow the pattern for the example lesson plan from above, identifying the cross-curricular links in detail.

LESSON OVERVIEW
SCHOOL/CLASS CONTEXT
LEARNING NEEDS OF THE CHILDREN
GROUPING/TIMING
RESOURCES
THEORETICAL CONTEXT
NC/FOUNDATION STAGE CONTEXT
SCHEME OF WORK CONTEXT
YOUR OWN LEARNING NEEDS
ORGANISATIONAL MEMORY JOGGERS
OTHER ADULTS
LEARNING OBJECTIVES
DIFFERENTIATION
LEARNING NEEDS EAL
LEARNING NEEDS SEN
ASSESSMENT OPPORTUNITIES
KEY QUESTIONS
LESSON FORMAT
EVALUATING THE LESSON part 1 OPERATIONAL ISSUES
EVALUATING THE LESSON part 2 LEARNING OUTCOMES
EVALUATING THE LESSON part 3 NEXT TIME

AUDITING
After the lesson, discuss the outcomes with your mentor and/or professional tutor. Try to assess the activity and see what it can add to your profiling. Have you provided evidence towards the Standard for the use of ICT in subject teaching? Use the questions in the handbook to guide your discussion. Look at some of the following together:

'Is the trainee able to select and use software to support the teaching of subjects? Can the trainee access interactive on-line database content using, for example, the National Grid for Learning (NGfL) or the Teacher Resource Exchange (TRE) and select, customise and use these materials with pupils? Can the trainee provide opportunities for pupils to use ICT to find things out, try things out and make things happen? Does the trainee use ICT terminology accurately?' (see these and more on p. 51 of DfES/TTA, 2002b).

Recent research on pedagogical issues in literacy and numeracy from the University of Newcastle under David Moseley and Steve Higgins (Moseley, Higgins et al., 1999), working in collaboration with Lynn Newton and the CEM centre at Durham University, presents teacher research and case studies of ICT use in classrooms. The study is published under the title: **Ways Forward with ICT: Effective Pedagogy using Information and Communications Technology for Literacy and Numeracy in Primary Schools.** *It attempts to identify key elements for successful integration of ICT in teaching and learning by situating the work of the teachers in the context of what they themselves said and thought about the work.*

The findings of the team point clearly to the need for precise planning as well as for matching the needs of the children to the tasks themselves. This comprehensive study underlines many of the concepts about planning outlined in this and the following chapter, namely:

Clear identification of how ICT will be used to meet specific objectives within subjects of the curriculum to improve pupils' attainment...

A planned match of pedagogy with the identified purpose of ICT activities and learning by outcomes.

(Moseley, Higgins et al., 1999)

Planning primary ICT:

a summary of key points

—— **This chapter has sought to negotiate the area between the content of the National Curriculum for ICT, its aims and objectives and the curriculum specified for teacher training. It has identified a possible model for planning which takes account, amongst other things, of the curriculum content, the context of the class, the learning needs of both teachers and children, the need to differentiate and the essential requirement to evaluate the outcomes in depth.**

—— **The recent history of the curriculum for ICT was outlined and a description was provided for how the QCA Scheme of Work operates in relation to Curriculum 2000. An example plan was provided together with a suggested planning activity which would take trainee teachers through the main concepts around successful lesson planning for ICT. The correlation between good planning for ICT and good practice in planning generally was seen to be very strong.**

Further reading

Cook, D. and Finlayson, H. (1999) *Interactive Children, Communicative Teaching: ICT and Classroom Teaching*, Open University Press.

DfEE (1998a) *Teaching: High Status, High Standards – Circular Number 4/98: Requirements for Courses of Initial Teacher Training*, DfEE.

DfEE/QCA (2000) *The National Curriculum: Handbook for Primary Teachers in England*, DfEE/QCA.

Kyriacou, C. (1997) *Effective Teaching in Schools*, Stanley Thornes.

Leask, M. and Meadows, J. (eds) (2000) *Teaching and Learning with ICT in the Primary School*, Routledge.

McFarlane, A. (ed) (1997) *Information Technology and Authentic Learning: Realising the Potential of Computers in the Primary School*, Routledge.

Passey, D. *et al*. (1997) *Improve Your Use of IT in Teaching*, Folens.

QCA (1998) *Information Technology: A Scheme of Work for Key Stages 1 and 2*, DfEE/QCA.

QCA (2000a) *Information and Communications Technology: Update to the IT Scheme of Work*, DfEE/QCA.

Smith, G. (1998) *A Hundred Ideas for IT*, Collins.

Smith, H. (1999) *Opportunities for ICT in the Primary School*, Trentham Books.

Somekh, B. and Davis, N. (eds) (1997) *Using Information Technology Effectively in Teaching and Learning: Studies in Pre-service and In-service Teacher Education*, Routledge.

Trend, R., Davis, N., and Loveless, A. (1998) *Information and Communications Technology*, Letts Educational.

Wheeler, T. *et al*. (1998) *101 Easy-Peasy Things To Do With Your Computer*, Kingfisher.

This chapter is concerned with planning for the use of ICT in subject teaching, beginning from the subjects themselves rather than the QCA Scheme of Work for ICT. We have seen in the previous section that it is perfectly possible to explore cross-curricular opportunities by beginning with the QCA Scheme of Work for ICT. However, it is equally important to consider the approach which starts with the National Curriculum schemes of work and moves towards the relevant ICT applications. Curriculum 2000 for Key Stages 1 and 2 makes many explicit references to, and gives examples of, the use of ICT within the schemes of work for each subject. At the same time, the Professional Standards for QTS (TTA/DfES, 2002) and the associated Handbook (TTA/DfES, 2002b) set out the requirements for trainees to develop their knowledge of how to apply ICT in their teaching of the core curriculum and their own specific subject.

The sections which follow address the context of ICT in subject teaching, beginning with the core curriculum, taking in the national initiatives in English and mathematics and moving through to the foundation subjects. Throughout, while the emphasis is on how the ICT supports the learning in each of these subjects, there is clearly a parallel development going on of the trainees' own skills.

Planning ICT in English (literacy hour)

There is more to the teaching of English in the primary school than the literacy hour itself. Indeed, some early evidence shows that there must be more or children will not have the time in the day to develop their extended writing skills (HMI/OFSTED, 2000). However, the National Literacy Strategy (NLS) framework as it was originally issued is now established in most primary schools in the UK. Furthermore, in Curriculum 2000 it is explicitly stated that the framework 'provides a detailed basis for implementing the statutory requirements of the programmes of study for reading and writing' (QCA, 2000b). In other words, the NLS is a de facto scheme of work for some, perhaps not all, of the National Curriculum subject of English. Given that ICT should be used in every subject scheme of work, it must also have a place in the literacy hour itself. There is clearly a need to begin to address what ICT can do alongside the framework in helping to raise levels of achievement in literacy.

The framework, with which trainees will become very familiar during their training in English, outlines the activities in literacy by year group from Year 1 to Year 6, over each of the terms of the school year. There are materials for Reception which are also in use in some schools although there will be a change in emphasis as the curriculum guidance for the Foundation Stage is adopted in schools.

The issue for those attempting to work with ICT in the literacy hour is how to integrate it into the very tight timescales available. The solution to this issue will, as usual, be different in almost every setting and contingent upon the resources available in all the categories: human resources, hardware resources and software resources.

The outline of the literacy hour is as follows:

- **The first ten to fifteen minutes outline the work of the day in terms of word level or sentence level.**
- **The next fifteen minutes focus on an aspect of word level work (Key Stage 1) and sentence or word level work (Key Stage 2). Up to this point in the basic model of provision, children have been sitting on the carpet for half an hour.**
- **For the next twenty minutes, children move to their tables to undertake group activities in fives and sixes related to the overall learning objective.**
- **Finally, there is a plenary, lasting approximately ten minutes. This attempts to draw the strands from the hour together and to underline key teaching points with the children.**

The original guidance does not make explicit use of ICT to meet the objectives. There is further guidance promised but until now it has been up to the individual teachers and schools to think of ways of integrating ICT within practice. Inevitably this results in complete integration where confidence in using ICT is high and where, as we have seen repeatedly, resources are available. In schools where confidence is low and resource provision poor it is quite likely that you will see less ICT used at this time of the day.

There is, however, great potential at all the different resource levels for the use of ICT in the literacy hour and planning can take account of this.

Group activities – low resource setting

The twenty minutes of group activity lends itself best to the use of the computer. In a low resource setting, with one computer in the corner of the classroom, there will need to be some creativity with the planning. Depending on the nature of the task and the nature of the software being used, it could be possible to split a group of six into two lots of three with ten minutes each. This group would then become part of the working week in the normal way and the whole class rotated through in a week.

In some ways, this is an example of the atomised curriculum at its worst, with children not being able to develop any real ICT skills in such short bursts. It also has high planning overheads because of the need to think of something for the children to do while they are waiting for their turn. On the other hand, there are activities which lend themselves to shorter amounts of time at the computer. In tutorial software from CD there might be short activities and investigations around a particular learning objective. An onscreen exercise, for example, to identify parts of words and break them down into constituent sounds would be one. Clearly, pointing and clicking on items in a menu or a game in such software is not doing a great deal to advance the knowledge and understanding of ICT. However, the literacy hour provision itself might be enhanced by the regular presence of reinforcement of learning objectives away from worksheets.

Another idea is to use open-ended software in this situation to create your own short activities. Using a word processor, a document template could be created which allowed children to, for example, search and replace nouns with pronouns. Another could allow children to highlight all the verbs in a sentence in sentence level work and change the font in some way. At this level of resourcing, activities are going to be low level with some element of repetition and reinforcement. However, in this example with open-ended software, the ICT is being used to provide stimulus and variety and one more planning option for the hard-pressed class teacher. It can also legitimately be said to be providing variety for the children and a further opportunity to address children's learning styles.

The plenary in a low resource setting

If you have access to presentation software and the computer is accessible to the carpet area, then in a given week, children could be preparing small presentations on the learning objective for the plenary each day. This is potentially the highest order development of ICT skills, perhaps also of the literacy focus. As the class teacher, familiar with the children concerned, you would be in a position to determine which of the children would benefit from this. It need not always be the most able. In this situation, having an adult helper who is also familiar with the software would allow the children who are struggling with a given concept to reinforce their learning by having to construct a presentation for others.

For further information on human resources, see page 137, Chapter 6

The situation in this resource setting could be as described in the following table:

Activity	Software	Literacy v. ICT potential
Ten-minute onscreen reinforcement of learning objective	Tutorial CD, focused aims, revision in a games style environment	High literacy Low level ICT skills
Ten-minute onscreen search and replace, reinforcement of learning objective	word processing	High literacy Higher level ICT skills
Collaborative work on presentation for the plenary about a particular learning objective	Presentation software Word processing sofware	High literacy High level ICT skills

The literacy hour in a high resource setting

Looking at the other extreme, where a school has very rich provision for ICT, there is inevitably more room for using ICT in the literacy hour.

In the simplest example, if there are more computers in the classroom (perhaps three) then a group can go on in pairs for the whole of the twenty minutes of group activity, undertaking any of the examples illustrated above at a higher level owing to the extended time available.

If the high resource setting manifests itself in the form of a collection of handheld computers, there is very great potential. A group of six children can have access to search and replace activities on the palmtops as well as onscreen templates of various kinds. Children can also undertake guided writing with adult support if this is appropriate. This activity can become part of the cycle of activities during the week, perhaps combined with the uses of the desktop described above.

In a network room, it could be possible to run the entire literacy hour in there at regular intervals. Each child would have access to the computers, plenaries could be held using the large monitors or whiteboards (if available) or screen control software. The opening sections of the literacy hour could be presented to the children using hypermedia resources, perhaps containing scanned parts of books for the big book part of the session. These activities have a high overhead in terms of staff training and confidence. In a high resource setting where training has taken place which fully integrates ICT into the good practice of the school and where the children are using the network room confidently, ICT has much to offer the literacy hour, specifically:

- **It provides a different resource base for the literacy hour, a break from the classroom.**
- **It allows children to develop ICT skills alongside literacy skills (except in the case of tutorial software).**
- **It reinforces the message that ICT is a medium in which to carry out work of different kinds.**
- **It provides the opportunity for children to combine text, graphics, sound and video in different software packages.**

The following table summarises the literacy hour in the high resource setting:

Activity	Software and hardware	Literacy v. ICT potential
Group activity reinforcing learning objective for twenty minutes	Three computers, tutorial software or word processing	High literacy Low level ICT skills (tutorial) Higher level ICT skills (word processing)
Group activity on search and replace, guided writing	Palmtops available for groups	High literacy Higher level ICT skills
Collaborative work throughout literacy hour on learning objective	Network room Presentation software, HTML editors, etc. Word processing software	High literacy High level ICT skills

The Internet and the literacy hour

The Internet, in a high resource setting, is an area of real potential. Very large numbers of teachers and children are already online sharing ideas for lesson plans. Many of these are downloadable without charge and provide a basis for planning.

Other sites provide onscreen activities with immediate feedback, all of them directly related to the literacy hour framework.

School web pages or local authority Intranets can provide rich sources of material and opportunities for publication, including many examples of good practice in the literacy hour.

ICT and your own planning

Various companies have started to produce resources which specifically address the planning needs of teachers. CDs from the BBC provide lesson examples and CDs from such companies as the Skills Factory provide complete lesson planners and databases of activities. Downloadable updates provide a way of staying ahead of the guidance as it changes. The guidance itself, the entire literacy hour framework, is available from the DfEE standards website.

Practical task

Literacy hour planning

Look at the National Literacy Framework for a given year group and consider the learning objective in relation to the children you are working with:

- *Decide what level of activity you could aim at according to the tables above, depending on whether you are in a high resource setting or a low resource setting.*
- *Design an activity for five or six children for the twenty minutes of group activity.*
- *Remember to consider factors such as individual school variation (some schools are evolving the way they operate and may have longer for this part of the hour than in the original guidance).*
- *Remember also to discuss the levels of ability of the group with the class teacher and to target the actual content appropriately.*

For example, if we consider one of the activities supporting learning objectives from Year 3, Term 1 for sentence level work on verbs, namely:

> *... to use verb tenses with increasing accuracy in speaking and writing, e.g. catch/ caught, see/saw, go/went, etc. Use past tense consistently for narration ...*

Our context from the NLS is mapped out in the analysis to the planning. For the ICT element in a low resource setting, where there is one computer to the thirty children in the class, consider getting the children to work on a pre-prepared word template file which contains, say, ten sentences with verbs in the present tense. Have a series of regular and irregular examples differentiated for ability groups through the week. Ask the children to identify the verbs in the text and change them into the past tense using the features of the word processor.

In a high resource setting, in a network room, prepare templates for the whole class, differentiated according to ability, and ask them to search and replace. Alternatively, ask children to investigate the patterns in pre-prepared onscreen texts and prepare a presentation about them. This is going to depend on flexibility of implementation of the strategy in the school. The context is everything. Part of analysing the situation accurately is about taking into account the school, the children, the resource setting and the relevant curriculum and strategy documents as they are being applied in that setting.

Some questions to ask yourself after the activity, some of which form the usual pattern for the use of ICT, some adapted for the purpose of this activity, could be:

- *How was the activity integrated into the normal running of the classroom?*
- *What skills did I need in order for the activity to succeed?*
- *What skills did the children need?*
- *How did I ensure that all children had access to the activity?*
- *What were the learning outcomes for the children in literacy?*
- *What were the learning outcomes for the children in ICT?*
- *What assessment opportunities were there?*
- *How does this experience add to my understanding of ICT in subject teaching?*
- *What will I do next time?*

AUDITING
After the lesson, discuss the outcomes with your mentor and/or professional tutor. Try to assess the activity and see what it can add to your profiling. Have you provided evidence towards the Standard for the use of ICT in subject teaching? Use the questions in the Handbook to guide your discussion. Look at some of the following together:

'Is the trainee able to select and use software to support the teaching of subjects? Can the trainee access interactive on-line database content using, for example, the National Grid for Learning (NGfL) or the Teacher Resource Exchange (TRE) and select, customise and use these materials with pupils? Can the trainee provide opportunities for pupils to use ICT to find things out, try things out and make things happen? Does the trainee use ICT terminology accurately?'
(see these and more on p. 51 of DfES/TTA, 2002b).

Planning ICT in English (general and cross-curricular)

We have examined in the previous section how the use of ICT can have an impact on the literacy hour. It is worth spending some time considering briefly how to use ICT in the teaching of English in a wider sense. Beyond the structure of the literacy hour, children are using English in a cross-curricular way, for example:

- publishing a science write-up;
- creating a local area guidebook in geography;
- writing school web pages;
- generating a historical account;
- writing about their beliefs in RE;
- creating rules for classroom and playground behaviour in PSHE;
- generating captions to explain findings in maths data-handling;
- reading for information in any of the foundation subjects, science and maths.

The issue in planning for ICT to support these wider uses of English is, as usual, how to operate in the differing resource settings and differing cultures of ICT in UK schools.

Higher resource settings are going to allow for much greater exploration of the provisional nature of information, simply because faster, more distributed Internet access through a school means that greater numbers of teachers and children can become involved. Section A of Annex B of the Initial Teacher Training Curriculum requires that trainees develop this awareness of information sources from CD ROM or the Internet, such that text in, for example, a classroom newspaper setting can be updated rapidly.

In lower resource settings, where one computer is still shared between the class, there are still opportunities for engagement with the wider English curriculum. The TTA commentary on the subject (*Using ICT to Meet Teaching Objectives in English*, TTA, 1999b) describes examples from speaking and listening (encouraging children to defend choices made in simulations and adventure games), reading (whole class reading sessions from the screen) and writing (using the word processor as an aid to drafting materials and understanding the writing process better).

The cross-curricular opportunities for developing English outside the literacy hour are many and varied and the limit to what is feasible will be determined largely by the access children have to the software and hardware.

Practical task

Planning cross-curricular English outside the literacy hour

Consider a curriculum area in which you are expecting the children to write at the computer. It could be taken from the list above, i.e.

- *publishing a science write-up;*
- *creating a local area guidebook in geography;*
- *writing school web pages;*
- *generating a historical account;*
- *writing about their beliefs in RE;*
- *creating rules for classroom and playground behaviour in PSHE;*
- *generating captions to explain findings in maths data-handling;*
- *reading for information in any of the foundation subjects, science and mathematics.*

Create a lesson plan which focuses on the specific areas of development of the writing itself which you are developing using the ICT.

LESSON OVERVIEW
Include here the English element, the ICT element and the element from the other subject. For example, a lesson overview for 'Creating a local area guidebook in geography' for Year 4 might describe the ICT element as using desktop publishing software and digital images. The geographical element could be from the work on localities described in Curriculum 2000 (see page 185). The English element is the developing sense of audience and of how to present information in a clear and accessible manner.

SCHOOL/CLASS CONTEXT
As described previously.

LEARNING NEEDS OF THE CHILDREN
Note these in the cross-curricular context.

GROUPING/TIMING
Think about different groupings from the literacy hour if your class employs ability groups. Children should experience a range of working partnerships and not always be grouped with the same children. We know from our understanding of the ways in which children learn that they need to interact with one another and learn in the context of talk with a whole range of peers of different abilities.

RESOURCES
Make the most of information collected on local area trips, in particular, digital images, video clips and sound recordings which could be incorporated into the work on the computer. Consider working with a multimedia authoring package to produce a multimedia version of the guidebook if you are fortunate enough to be in a highly resourced setting.

THEORETICAL CONTEXT
As described previously.

NC/FOUNDATION STAGE CONTEXT
One example for ICT could be from 'Finding things out' at Key Stage 2 – children should be taught how to 'Prepare information for development using ICT...'

For geography: from the Programmes of Study for KS2 – In their study of localities and themes, children should: 'study at a range of scales – local, regional and national...'

For English: from the Programmes of Study for KS2 – The range of purposes for writing should include: 'to inform and explain, focusing on the subject matter and how to convey it in sufficient detail for the reader...'

SCHEME OF WORK CONTEXT
E.g. For ICT: QCA Unit 4a.

For English see the National Literacy Strategy Units for Y4, for geography, see the Scheme of Work...

Make notes under the following headings as described previously:

YOUR OWN LEARNING NEEDS

ORGANISATIONAL MEMORY JOGGERS

OTHER ADULTS

LEARNING OBJECTIVES

DIFFERENTIATION

LEARNING NEEDS – EAL

LEARNING NEEDS – SEN

ASSESSMENT OPPORTUNITIES

KEY QUESTIONS

LESSON FORMAT

EVALUATING THE LESSON part 1 – OPERATIONAL ISSUES

EVALUATING THE LESSON part 2 – LEARNING OUTCOMES

EVALUATING THE LESSON part 3 – NEXT TIME

AUDITING
After the lesson, discuss the outcomes with your mentor and/or professional tutor. Try to assess the activity and see what it can add to your profiling. Have you provided evidence towards the standard for the use of ICT in subject teaching? Use the questions in the Handbook to guide your discussion. Look at some of the following together:

'Is the trainee able to select and use software to support the teaching of subjects? Can the trainee access interactive on-line database content using, for example, the National Grid for Learning (NGfL) or the Teacher Resource Exchange (TRE) and select, customise and use these materials with pupils? Can the trainee provide opportunities for pupils to use ICT to find things out, try things out and make things happen? Does the trainee use ICT terminology accurately?'
(see these and more on p. 51 of DfES/TTA, 2002b).

Planning ICT in the daily mathematics lesson

The guidance for the daily mathematics lesson contained within the published National Numeracy Strategy outlines more explicit teaching opportunities for the use of ICT than the Literacy Strategy. Furthermore, there is a more flexible approach to timings within the hour which means that the different resource levels within schools can address the issues of integration more consistently.

The opening of the daily mathematics lesson concentrates on the development of mental mathematical strategies. Children are 'warmed up' with questions relating to the learning objectives which enable them to make connections between their previously gained aspects of mathematics knowledge.

The National Numeracy Strategy contains detailed guidance about what to do in the middle section of the daily mathematics lesson in which children are expected to work on what is called 'the main teaching activity'. The settings for this can vary between whole class, groups, pairs or individuals.

The final element of the daily mathematics lesson is the same as for the literacy hour. It is the plenary, in which the class has an opportunity to consolidate the knowledge gained during the lesson. The teacher can identify and correct any misconceptions about particular concepts and 'summarise key facts, make links to other work and discuss the next steps' (DfEE, 1999).

The guidance available on the use of ICT suggests that it can be incorporated into most parts of the lesson and gives suggestions which are related to the level of resource provision. The opening section on mental mathematics can be varied in its use of resources by the inclusion of a large display monitor, electronic whiteboard or projection from an overhead projector. The same applies to the plenary where the strands of the lesson can be drawn together by the use of electronic media.

Once again, however, it is the central part of the lesson which lends itself most readily to the incorporation of ICT. ICT is broadly defined in the guidance to include all of the available audio-visual aids and, of course, calculators. For the computer, several different possible uses are described for this section of the lesson, summarised as follows:

- **software to explore number patterns, including the use of spreadsheets;**
- **tutorial software for practising a particular skill, with rapid assessment;**
- **data-handling software;**
- **software for giving instructions of movement and turn in order to develop subject knowledge in, for example, measurement of distance and angle;**
- **software for transforming shapes;**
- **software for branching and sorting in order to develop logical thinking and problem-solving.**

Some of these possible uses have the potential to develop high order ICT skills. There is also a distinct overlap with items from the QCA Scheme of Work for Information Technology (QCA, 1998). Given the flexible nature of the daily mathematics lesson, it ought to be possible to plan in a cross-curricular way for some of the numeracy framework. However, it is worth remembering that the focus of the lesson has to be mathematics specifically and the lesson succeeds or fails partly by the way in which the teacher can draw the class together in a plenary at the end of the session. If the activity has moved out of the realm of the initial focus and is meeting some other planning requirement, the quality of the mathematical experience will decline.

The potential for ICT skill development and mathematics together is summarised in the following table, where, as for literacy, it is possible to see little in the way of such skill development in the use of tutorial software:

Software type in the daily mathematics lesson	ICT skills, knowledge and understanding
Software to explore number patterns (tutorial)	Low order ICT skills
Tutorial software for practising a particular skill, with rapid assessment	Very low order ICT skills
Software for transforming shapes	Middle range ICT skills (depending on the package being used – some are much more complex than others)
Data-handling software	Higher order ICT skills
Spreadsheets (e.g. to explore number patterns)	Higher order ICT skills
Software for giving instructions of movement and turn in order to develop subject knowledge in, for example, measurement of distance and angle	Higher order ICT skills (link with programming)
Software for branching and sorting in order to develop logical thinking and problem-solving	Higher order ICT skills

Types of software in the daily mathematics lesson

The impact of the low and high resource settings is felt in a reduced way because of the added flexibility of delivery of the numeracy strategy. However, in a low resource setting it is possible to become dependent on poorer quality tutorial software of a very basic drill and practice type. Where this is focused (on reinforcing a topic which is under development) and targeted (at children who need it), such software is extremely useful. As we have seen in earlier sections, where this software is used to keep certain children busy or as a reward or sanction, there is little justification for using it in pursuit of real learning objectives.

In a high resource setting, again in a network room or similar, all children could experience some daily mathematics lessons with access to the relevant software and hardware. The whole lesson could be run in the computer suite from time to time (timetabling allowing).

Practical task

Daily mathematics lesson planning

Consider the framework for Y1, 2 and 3 and look at the learning outcomes for Year 3 pupils for the Spring term – Handling Data, unit 12.

In a low resource setting, or one where the children's experience of using ICT is limited, collect simple data about the packed lunches brought to school across a given week. Ask children to enter the information and display it in data-handling software. This could be done using a simple graphing tool or a more complex data-handling package.

In a medium resource setting, where there is regular access to the computer and the Y3 children have already gained experiences of simple graphing in Y2, extend their knowledge by building a more complicated database based on the different methods which children use to come to school each day.

In either case, in your planning develop questions which exploit the ICT learning opportunities alongside the mathematical learning opportunities. The following table characterises some of these sorts of questions:

Example ICT knowledge questioning	Example mathematics knowledge questioning (adapted from the NNS)
Which graph shows the information best?	Do most children walk to school? How do we know?
What did we have to do after entering each piece of information?	How many more children walk to school than come by car?
How did we add to the file the next day?	What would happen if it was a wet day?

Questions to compare ICT and mathematics knowledge

In this way, the ICT supports the subject and the subject supports very important conceptual developments in ICT.

Questions worth asking as a result of the activity:

- *How was the activity integrated into the normal running of the classroom?*
- *What skills did I need in order for the activity to succeed?*
- *What skills did the children need?*
- *How did I ensure that all children had access to the activity?*
- *What were the learning outcomes for the children in mathematics?*
- *What were the learning outcomes for the children in ICT?*
- *What assessment opportunities were there?*
- *How does this experience add to my understanding of ICT in subject teaching?*
- *Did the ends justify the means in terms of time costs?*
- *What will I do next time?*

AUDITING

After the lesson, discuss the outcomes with your mentor and/or professional tutor. Try to assess the activity and see what it can add to your profiling. Have you provided evidence towards the standard for the use of ICT in subject teaching? Use the questions in the Handbook to guide your discussion. Look at some of the following together:

'Is the trainee able to select and use software to support the teaching of subjects? Can the trainee access interactive on-line database content using, for example, the National Grid for Learning (NGfL) or the Teacher Resource Exchange (TRE) and select, customise and use these materials with pupils? Can the trainee provide opportunities for pupils to use ICT to find things out, try things out and make things happen? Does the trainee use ICT terminology accurately?'
(see these and more on p. 51 of DfES/TTA, 2002b).

ILS software in the core curriculum
You may find yourself working in a school which uses an ILS or integrated learning system in the core curriculum, particularly in English and in mathematics. These systems present particular issues for planning ICT work. They differ from normal tutorial software in that they deliver particular units according to an individual child's need. In other words, they have a built-in management, administration and assessment facility. There is a useful discussion about the background to these systems in Fox, Montague-Smith and Wilkes (2000).

For the teacher working with them it is as well to be aware of the types of ILS and of the research that has been done on the subject. There are two main kinds – one is closed and the other is open (sometimes known as an OILS – an open integrated learning system). The first restricts teacher control over the selection of the tutorial material and makes closed choices in units delivered to the children using it. The second provides a measure of teacher control and flexibility; some of the management choices are open to the teacher. They are usually, but not exclusively, delivered over a network and, in some cases, over the Internet.

Research under the direction of Jean Underwood from Leicester University was instigated by the NCET (National Council for Educational Technology, currently known as BECTa) in the early 1990s after the UK government provided money for pilot projects in primary and secondary schools around the country. Jean Underwood's research showed a mixed picture of learning gains and was by no means a ringing endorsement of the technology or its application. Some groups, however, did show learning gains in using ILS, most notably children who used it for revision in some parts of the core curriculum. Some children exhibited enhanced self-esteem. There were also gains for children using the open systems where the teacher was able to intervene and bring the software into the world of the classroom (NCET, 1996).

It has been pointed out, however, that ILS does not sit well within the philosophy of the Numeracy Strategy with its emphasis on whole class teaching and collaboration, as well as flexible learning styles. The emphasis of ILS is on the individual (to the extent that ILSs are sometimes accidentally referred to as individual learning systems). For a fuller discussion of ILS and the issues and research around it for mathematics learning, see Fox, Montague-Smith and Wilkes (2000), pp. 71–81.

Planning ICT in science

Science, as a subject, appears to have had its curriculum time reduced by the strategies in the other two core areas and schools needing to provide curriculum coverage across the Foundation subjects. However, with a 'science hour' or equivalent poised to enter the equation and with the very wide potential of ICT to support the teaching of science, there is ample opportunity for both subjects to support each other.

Planning for science with ICT means identifying the sorts of activities where ICT can support and enhance the learning of science. The Curriculum for Initial Teacher Training insists that trainees develop a sense of when and when not to use ICT. It is important to develop an idea of where, in the science programmes of study and/or scheme of work, ICT is likely to be essential, where it is desirable and where it need not be any part of what goes on.

As with the rest of the core subject provision discussed above, some activities develop the scientific knowledge, skills and understanding of children but do not necessarily generate further ICT skill development. There are other activities which develop much higher order ICT skills alongside scientific skills of enquiry and hypothesis. To take a simplistic example, a CD ROM which is tutorial in nature and which describes and then questions the user about certain concepts does not necessarily advance the ICT skills of the user who is, as in all tutorial software, rehearsing skills of navigation over and over again. On the other hand, an activity which requires that the user set up and maintain a monitoring situation with ICT equipment and software is clearly requiring a higher order of skills in both subjects.

There is considerable guidance in Curriculum 2000 for teachers and trainees who are looking for the links between science and ICT. The marginal notes throughout the programmes of study make the connections as they do in all subjects.

At Key Stage 1, there are two examples of strong linkage between the subjects. The first is the suggestion that in learning how to recognise and compare the main external features of humans and animals, 'Pupils could use multimedia sources to make comparisons' (KS1, Sc2 Life Processes and Living Things/Humans and other animals). The second is that in examining variation and classification, 'Pupils could use data collected to compile a class database' (KS1, Sc2 Life Processes and Living Things/Variation and classification).

In the first case, quite low order ICT skills are being employed. In the second case, much higher order ICT skills are being employed and there are strong links to the ICT Scheme of Work possible, in particular, Labelling and Classifying (1D) and Finding Information (2C). The decision to make in terms of lesson planning is to focus on the appropriate activities in the whole scheme of work for the children. Is it the case that you need a context for developing their awareness of databases? Have they browsed CDs at length? Do you now need, in terms of the science, to deepen their awareness of subject knowledge in classification by asking them to work with the data they are collecting? The scientific enquiry and the ICT skills development could usefully go hand in hand with these particular units.

There are further planning opportunities described for Key Stage 1 with strong links back to the ICT Scheme of Work. For 'Materials and their properties', it is suggested that children combine words and pictures about materials and objects on the computer. This comes slightly ahead of the unit of work suggested for ICT for Year 3, Combining Text and Graphics (3A). The other opportunity described is in Physical Processes, wherein it is argued that 'Pupils could use sensors to detect and compare sounds' in their study of light and sound (KS1, Sc4 Physical Processes/Light and sound, 3c).

Throughout Key Stage 1 the breadth of study is intended to include ICT-based sources of information and data. At Key Stage 2 this strand of study is extended and developed further and becomes more closely linked to higher order ICT skills. For example, there is a higher order database activity described to support statement 2b, 'Pupils should be taught about the need for food for activity and growth, and about the importance of an adequate and varied diet for health' (KS2, Sc2 Life Processes and Living Things/Humans and other animals). It is suggested that children could 'use a database or spreadsheet to analyse data about types of food in school lunches'.

There follows a series of further suggestions all of which amplify the growing links between the two subjects, some examples of which are:

- **children could use a branching database to develop and use keys (to support KS2, Sc2 Life Processes and LivingThings/Variation and classification, 4a);**
- **children could use video or CD ROM to compare non-local habitats (to support KS2, Sc2 Life Processes and LivingThings/Adaptation, 5b);**
- **children could use simulation software to show changes in the populations of micro-organisms in different conditions (to support KS2, Sc2 Life Processes and LivingThings/Adaptation, 5f).**

If the school you are placed in is using the Scheme of Work for science, there are numerous opportunities in your planning to use ICT. Similarly, thinking about the ICT Scheme of Work from a science perspective allows you to discover contexts in which children can develop their ICT capability. The following table explores some of those links. It is a starting point for planning links between the two subjects and is not intended to be exhaustive. Reading the two schemes, you will discover many other possibilities:

Science Scheme of Work: Units with higher order ICT skills	ICT Scheme of work: Units with potential for work in science
Unit 1A Ourselves	Unit 1C The information around us
Unit 2B Plants and animals in the local environment	Unit 2C Finding information
Unit 3D Rocks and soils	Unit 3C Introduction to databases
Unit 4C Keeping warm	Unit 4D Collecting and presenting information
Unit 5D Changing state Unit 5A Keeping healthy	Unit 5F Monitoring environmental conditions and changes
Unit 6A Interdependence and adaptation	Unit 6D Using the Internet to search large databases and to interpret information

Science and ICT Scheme links

There are many ways in which ICT can support science in a more general way, with the use of templates, for example, in write-ups as a form of aide-mémoire so as to further structure scientific thought and develop skills of planning and enquiry.

Above all, the use of ICT in science should be seen as something in which the scientific learning has the upper hand; it should be a key to opening up the world of scientific development and not an end in itself. There are benefits for both subjects in close integration.

Practical task

Planning ICT in science

Choose a unit of work from the science Scheme of Work for which you have access to the appropriate software and hardware. Plan for one session within the unit to have a major input from ICT. Use the links suggested between the two schemes previously in this section to help you.

When you evaluate the session, consider the following aspects:

- *Make a judgement, in conversation with your mentor and/or tutor, about the contribution of the ICT to the subject knowledge in the sessions.*

- *Did the ends justify the means?*

- *Would you use ICT to work with this particular concept or unit again?*

- *If yes, would you do anything differently?*

- *If no, why would you prefer not to use ICT in this way again?*

If you complete the task and attach notes and samples of evidence it should go some way to meeting the following standards in the Initial Teacher Training Curriculum:

AUDITING
After the lesson, discuss the outcomes with your mentor and/or professional tutor. Try to assess the activity and see what it can add to your profiling. Have you provided evidence towards the standard for the use of ICT in subject teaching? Use the questions in the Handbook to guide your discussion. Look at some of the following together:

'Is the trainee able to select and use software to support the teaching of subjects? Can the trainee access interactive on-line database content using, for example, the National Grid for Learning (NGfL) or the Teacher Resource Exchange (TRE) and select, customise and use these materials with pupils? Can the trainee provide opportunities for pupils to use ICT to find things out, try things out and make things happen? Does the trainee use ICT terminology accurately?'
(see these and more on p. 51 of DfES/TTA, 2002b).

Planning ICT in the Foundation subjects

The situation with planning for ICT and the Foundation subjects is similar to the one for science. There is a great deal of pressure of time in the primary school day on the core curriculum subjects of mathematics and English. However, with imaginative organisational strategies and access to the appropriate hardware and software, it ought to be possible to ensure the children's entitlement both to the Foundation subjects and to ICT.

Planning for ICT in the Foundation subjects, as for the core curriculum, means identifying those activities where ICT provides an essential part of the learning experience. In other words, it means identifying the lessons in the Foundation subjects where, with ICT, the learning opportunities are enhanced in depth, range and quality. The following examples given under the relevant subject headings are by no means an exhaustive list. They are intended to be starting points for planning for ICT in the Foundation subjects.

Following this section, a table helps you to negotiate the schemes of work for the Foundation subjects in terms of ICT (see page 190).

Art and design

Some of the Foundation subjects depend on a sophisticated understanding of how ICT works and of how it uniquely contributes to the learning in that subject area. One example would be art where the understanding of what is happening in a graphics package is crucial to understanding the contribution which it makes to the subject.

Graphics packages, in spite of their onscreen appearance with virtual canvases and paintpots and virtual pencils, are a new and different medium for artists. They may look as though they are replacing the physical world of brushstrokes and charcoal marks. The fact is that they aren't. The way that they work is by arranging digital information on screen. Avril Loveless in 'Working with images, developing ideas' (in McFarlane, 1997) builds an argument about helping children and teachers to understand that they are interacting with a new medium, rich with different possibilities. She writes that 'IT has the potential to be a catalyst in the development of new ways of expressing a visual language' and goes on to define the central role that the teacher has in the process:

> It is the interaction of the facilities of IT, the children's ability to explore and extend their visual ideas and the teacher's pedagogy that can improve the quality of teaching and learning.
>
> (Loveless in McFarlane, 1997)

Opportunities for links between subject and ICT are spelled out in the margins of Curriculum 2000. For art, now known as art and design, these are given as:

- **At Key Stage I, while children are being taught about 'visual and tactile elements, including colour, pattern and texture, line and tone, shape, form and space', they could use painting software to explore some of these elements (Art and Design, Knowledge and Understanding, KSI 4a in DfEE/QCA, 2000).**
- **At Key Stage 2, the use of digital and video cameras to record observations is suggested as part of the strand on exploring and developing ideas (KS2, Ic). There is also a recommendation that children are encouraged to create material for a school art gallery on the school web page. A powerful suggestion is made about the use of the Internet as a medium for children exploring the work and styles of many different genres across the world. This will depend as always on the accessibility of reliable and fast Internet access in the various resource settings in which teachers, children and trainees find themselves. Nevertheless,**

these are possibilities which are unique to ICT and which significantly enhance the teaching of the subject. With bandwidth and distribution of the Internet around schools improving all the time, virtual art galleries represent a significant contribution to the art and design curriculum. The higher bandwidth (much faster transfer of much bigger files around the Internet) is of particular benefit in this area because the files are so much larger than with other uses of ICT – for example, word processing.

In terms of planning appropriately, the usual judgements apply about how the subject is enhanced and which ICT skills are being utilised and developed. You can find connections between art and ICT in the ICT Scheme of Work and could usefully situate your ICT content within the art curriculum. Units such as IA (An introduction to modelling), 2B (Creating pictures), 2C (Finding information), 3A (Combining text and graphics) and 6A (Multimedia presentation) are all areas which can be approached from the direction of ICT and taken into the area of art and design.

Similarly, it is possible to find examples within the QCA Scheme for art which are rich with possible links to ICT. Unit 2A, Picture this!, for example, suggests a unit of work around children recording an issue or event in their lives which 'could also link with Unit IA 'An introduction to modelling', in the ICT Scheme, when children create their own representations of real or fantasy situations' (Scheme of Work for art).

Purposeful exploration of painting packages, image recording devices and websites which bring art into the classroom in ways which were not possible before are all unique to ICT and offer something back to children's learning in art and design. The important thing to remember for your planning is the word 'purposeful' and all that implies. Of particular importance is the notion that the ICT is adding to the potential achievement and learning by the children in the given subject.

Geography

History and geography are two subjects in which ICT can make a contribution to the enhancement of the learning process. We have seen, on page 172, an example of a connection between a geographical activity and a Unit of Work in the ICT Curriculum (in the cross-curricular English planning example).

The World Wide Web brings much potential to the teaching of geography. The subject itself offers a context for developing skills of searching, emailing and publishing. Similarly, early understanding of mapping and routes is enhanced by the use of a programmable toy. Curriculum 2000 suggests this and others as examples:

- **routes and maps with a programmable toy (link to 2c);**
- **using a digital camera to record events outside classroom (link to 4a);**
- **using the Internet to obtain comparative weather information (link to 3d, 3f).**

Beyond comparative weather data comes the whole series of possibilities raised by email contact with children and teachers in other localities. Emailed questions about what you can see from your window on a given day generate vast amounts of interesting information between pupils of the same age, across the world, very quickly.

Geographical resources which were not available before – detailed maps and aerial photographs of most of the world – are now accessible on CD ROM and Internet. The skill in terms of the teaching will be to integrate the use of these resources usefully into planning. You will need to identify opportunities for learning which are uniquely offered by the technology and then allow your pupils to have access to it. As for all areas, if you are in a high resource setting with large numbers of computers and good Internet access, your problems are significantly reduced.

History

History is brought to life by many of the activities suggested in its own Scheme of Work for the primary school. The opportunities for ICT are present throughout.

The Internet brings not only art galleries into the school, but also museums and archival resources of all kinds. Many of these are also present on CD ROM. Incorporating such work into history lessons, as with all subject areas, becomes an issue depending on the resource setting in which trainees, teachers and children are working.

Curriculum 2000 makes several references to links between history and ICT. Some of these are simply to the resource capabilities of ICT as, for example, the link to finding out about significant people in the past from CD ROM (link to statement 4a on Historical Enquiry). Another example of quite low level ICT use would be in using digitised maps in local enquiry.

Higher order ICT skills are demanded by the sophisticated use of databases at Key Stage 2 to study patterns of change over time. This falls in the following area for history: '(the capability to) ask and answer questions, and to select and record information relevant to the focus of the enquiry' (Historical Enquiry, 4b).

History provides us with an example of the need to be very clear about the sort of order of skills in both a curriculum subject and ICT which are to be developed in a given lesson. This area was explored previously in the section on planning for the daily mathematics lesson (page 175) where we saw a trade-off between higher order ICT skills and content browsing.

Design and technology

ICT offers much to teachers of design and technology in the primary school. The area of most potential is probably that of control technology where children learn that they can control devices and models which will respond to instruction and inputs from outside. Children already know that such devices exist. A quick brainstorm at the start of work on this subject will bring to mind video recorder programmers, washing machine programmes, central heating timers, burglar alarms and a whole host of other devices.

Additionally when creating or developing ideas for themselves, children could be encouraged to create digital versions of their ideas. The programmes of study make explicit reference to this idea, pointing out the link back to ICT in the following statements:

'Pupils should be taught to:

a) generate ideas by drawing on their own and other people's experiences

e) communicate their ideas using a variety of methods, including drawing and making models' (From KS 1, Strand 1: Developing, planning and communicating ideas).

At Key Stage 2 there is a greater level of complexity and a more explicit statement of the need to engage with ICT in order to deliver the subject. There is a further statement about the tools of presentation and onscreen creation available through ICT (cf. again Strand 1: Developing, planning and communicating ideas). There is, however, an understanding that in developing a knowledge and understanding of materials and components children should be taught:

'c) how mechanisms can be used to make things move in different ways, using a range of equipment including an ICT control program' (From KS2, Strand 4: Knowledge and understanding of materials and components).

It is difficult to imagine being able to meet the needs of young learners in design and technology and their curriculum entitlements without significant levels of ICT use in their school career. Again, the major caveat is whether the resource base is high enough in your placement school to begin exploring this issue in your planning. Although, as we have seen in previous sections, the situation is improving, control technology is often down the list in terms of buying under educational funding arrangements.

A further issue is the availability of support in terms of expertise. Although relatively simple-to-use software is involved, there is something about the number of wires and additional interface boxes involved which deters many people from including this area in their planning. Most teachers that do take it on find that the equipment and software working together is highly motivating for children and stimulates a great deal of interest and creative learning potential.

Music

ICT has for a long time enjoyed a close relationship with music in primary schools. Tape recorders and CD players have been used in schools for many years to:

- **bring children into contact with music from different times and different cultures;**
- **record children's own compositions;**
- **provide resources for learning songs;**
- **provide accompaniment to dance (link to PE);**

- **provide a source of music for assemblies and performances;**
- **provide a resource for budding instrumentalists to record and assess their work.**

Additionally, schools with electronic keyboards have been able to extend the performance aspects of assembly songs. Keyboards with sound modules in which real instrument voices have been stored allow children to explore the different timbres and possibilities of different instruments.

In terms of computer use, there are software packages available which allow children to explore composing. The feedback which they gain from such software is immediate and the 'performing and appraising' aspects of the curriculum are therefore made similarly immediate. As for art and design there is no suggestion of the computer-based musical tools replacing hands-on experience with the whole range of instruments found in primary schools. Instead, the suggestion is that ICT be used to enhance the learning process.

Children learn that computers are capable of storing not just text and images but can be used to record and manipulate sound. To put it another way, they learn that sound itself can be represented and stored digitally, in which form it can be transformed in many different ways.

Computers and hard disk recorders are now the medium of choice in professional and home recording studios for composing and arranging music. Children will be aware of the possibilities of mixing and remixing songs as they hear different versions of their favourite songs produced. The learning curve for teachers and others who are seeking to use music composition software and keyboards at this higher level is quite steep and requires specialist INSET. However, once the basic concepts are mastered, such devices open up a whole range of possibilities for young composers in both Key Stages, but particularly the older ages in Key Stage 2 in the primary school.

The links between ICT and the programmes of study for music are many and can be found in statements such as:

'2. Pupils should be taught how to:
    (a) create musical patterns;
    (b) explore, choose and organise sounds and musical ideas' (from KS1, Creating and developing musical ideas – composing skills).

The link here is the use of software for sound exploration.

'3. Pupils should be taught how to:
    (b) make improvements to their own work' (from KS1, Responding and reviewing – appraising skills).

The link here is the use of recording equipment for reviewing work (this could be tape or computer based).

The Breadth of Study for Key Stage 2 in music requires that children use ICT to 'capture, change and combine sounds'.

The resource setting is one potential obstacle to exploiting fully these links between music and ICT. Another is teacher confidence and appropriate training, as well as access to hardware and software. However, at even the most basic level of using taping equipment, ICT enhances subject teaching in music in powerful ways.

RE, PSHE and citizenship

ICT in terms of its access to resources on the Internet is a major contributing factor to growing subject knowledge and understanding in the inter-linked areas of RE, Personal, Social and Health Education (PSHE) and citizenship. The diversity of religions over the world can be explored on the Internet and on CD ROM. Children can have a context for their writing which extends their sphere of personal expression into that of personal belief.

The RE scheme of work links with ICT in many places. Two examples would be:

- **in the unit on Belief and Practice (Unit ID, where it mentions the resourcing possibilities);**
- **in Unit 4D on 'What religions are represented in our neighbourhood?' This time, there is more to be made of the capacity of ICT for preparing and representing writing. Digital cameras and the Internet are suggested means of gathering and storing information about local faiths which are then to be represented in children's classwork.**

As for history and RE, the potential of the Internet to link to other cultures and belief systems can engender respect (when taught appropriately). ICT brings these worlds within reach (with all the caveats about connectivity and appropriate Internet use) in a unique way. For the ethical considerations of ICT use, it is a requirement of the Initial Teacher Training Curriculum that trainees develop a sense of the arguments and debates which rage around privacy and civil liberties. These can usefully be engaged with during ICT lessons with children of primary school age, particularly − but not exclusively − older children.

For the non-compulsory areas of PSHE and citizenship there are statements of usefulness of ICT in Curriculum 2000. One example is that of developing relationships through work and play (for example, communicating with children in other countries by satellite, email or letters).

ICT also has a part to play away from the machinery itself in the wider discussion about ethics. The sorts of issues in the standards with which trainees would be engaging in work of this kind include those listed in 18c − ethical issues − including:

'i.   access to illegal and/or unsuitable material through the Internet;
ii.   acknowledging sources;
iii. data confidentiality;
iv. the ways in which users of information sources can be (and are) monitored;
v.   material which may be socially or morally unacceptable.'

Children are aware that the school holds information about them from the earliest years (they quickly and routinely give information at the start of each day in the register). They can be explicitly made aware of the uses of ICT in gathering and processing this information. Later, they could discuss the confidentiality issues raised by large databases being held by companies and government agencies full of personal information.

It is as well to raise the issue of ethics in its widest sense with older children. Many will be aware of the fact that not everyone has access to computers and that the World Wide Web as a phrase refers to circumnavigation rather than connectivity in all countries. Access to websites which map cyberspace will be particularly revealing in this regard. One example would be the Institute of Cybergeography which has a fascinating collection of atlases of cyberspace (at *www.cybergeography.org*).

PE

There is a place on the PE curriculum for ICT at least in terms of devices which can help to record movement for pupils to analyse later. Some schemes of work are distributed for INSET using different storage and replay media, whether it is on videotape or videodisk.

Previously, PE was excepted from the list of subjects in the 1995 version of the National Curriculum in which children were expected to develop their ICT capability. Curriculum 2000 is altogether more enthusiastic and stated linkage with ICT includes the following:

- **For dance and gymnastic activity at Key Stage 1, 'Pupils could use videos of movements and actions to develop their ideas'.**
- **For dance, gymnastic and athletic activities at Key Stage 2, 'Pupils could use video and CD ROMs of actions, balances and body shapes to improve their performance'.**

Further cross-curriculum opportunities exist in the analysis of the effects of exercise which can be carried out using sensors. Here, the potential link to science has already been outlined above. The potential to link with mathematics in the exploration of data in spreadsheets is also clearly there. Some bespoke software exists to do this (the 'Five Star' athletics software, for example).

 For further information on using sensors, see page 180, Chapter 8

Clearly, it would be unwise to make strong claims for all day, every day pervasive links in planning between ICT and PE. However, there will be times, particularly when tackling the issue of assessment in PE, when ICT can make a vital contribution.

ICT and Foundation subject planning aid

The following table gives you locations of some example units in the various QCA schemes of work for the Foundation subjects with strong links to ICT. It also links the ICT Scheme of Work back to that subject. The list is not exhaustive. It is intended as a guide for planning from whatever scheme of work document you may have access to in order to incorporate ICT in that subject. There are certainly many other links between the various schemes of work.

Foundation subject	Subject scheme of work: example units with links to ICT	ICT scheme of work: example units with links back to the subject
Art and design	Picture This! (2A) Investigating pattern (3B) People in action (6A)	An introduction to modelling (1A) Creating pictures (2B) Multimedia presentation (6A)
Geography	Improving the environment (Unit 8) Investigating rivers (Unit 14) The mountain environment (Unit 15)	Combining text and graphics (3A) Multimedia presentation (6A) Using the Internet... (6D)
History	How did life change in our locality in Victorian times? (Unit 12) How can we find out about the Indus Valley civilisation? (Unit 16) What can we learn about recent history from studying the life of a famous person? (Unit 20)	Combining text and graphics (3A) Analysing data (5B) Using the Internet... (6D)
Design and technology	Packaging (3A) Lighting it up (4E) Alarms (4D)	Finding information (2C) Combining text and graphics (3A) Controlling devices (5E)
Music	Journey into space: exploring sound sources (Unit 18) Songwriter exploring lyrics and melody (Unit 19)	Manipulating sound (3B) Multimedia presentation (6A)
RE, PSHE and Citizenship	Beliefs and practice (1D) Celebrations (2C) What religions are represented in our neighbourhood? (4D)	Finding information (2C) Email (3E) Using the Internet... (6D)
PE	Dance activities (Unit 1) Gymnastic activities (Unit 5)	Finding Information (2C) Monitoring environmental conditions and changes (5F)

Links between ICT and Foundation subject planning aid

Practical task

Planning ICT in your specialist subject

Use your specialist subject as the basis for the following activity. Use the school scheme of work in your specialist subject to complete it. Where there is no scheme of work, use the relevant QCA documents as guidance.

Identify a unit of work. Cross-reference it to an ICT unit from the ICT Scheme. Decide on the balance between the two and plan a series of 4–6 lessons (or activities) which develop the subject knowledge of the children alongside some identified aspect of ICT capability.

At the end of the sequence, address the following issues as an overview of all the sessions:

- *Were the learning objectives achieved? How?*

- *Which aspects of ICT capability did the children develop (not rehearse, but develop)?*

- *What operational difficulties were encountered (if any) during the activity?*

- *Make a judgement, in conversation with your mentor and/or tutor, about the contribution of the ICT to the subject knowledge in the sessions.*

- *Did the ends justify the means? Once again, consider the time factor.*

- *Would you use ICT to work with this particular concept or unit again?*

- *If yes, would you do anything differently?*

- *If no, why would you prefer not to use ICT in this way again?*

AUDITING
After the lesson, discuss the outcomes with your mentor and/or professional tutor. Try to assess the activity and see what it can add to your profiling. Have you provided evidence towards the standard for the use of ICT in subject teaching? Use the questions in the Handbook to guide your discussion. Look at some of the following together:

'Is the trainee able to select and use software to support the teaching of subjects? Can the trainee access interactive on-line database content using, for example, the National Grid for Learning (NGfL) or the Teacher Resource Exchange (TRE) and select, customise and use these materials with pupils? Can the trainee provide opportunities for pupils to use ICT to find things out, try things out and make things happen? Does the trainee use ICT terminology accurately?'
(see these and more on p. 51 of DfES/TTA, 2002b).

RESEARCH SUMMARY

ICT in subjects

The work of David Moseley, Steve Higgins and others (Moseley, Higgins et al., 1999) identifies ways in which effective teaching using ICT in literacy and numeracy is underpinned by the need to develop an effective pedagogy around the use of computers in classrooms. They highlight a number of ways in which this might happen, many of which relate directly to the importance of planning appropriately. They also refer to the need for support for teachers in terms of training and professional development.

Teachers in the Newcastle study reported to the team on the barriers they felt were preventing the integration of ICT into their subject teaching. The biggest reported factor was that of time (time to learn new skills, time to learn new software, etc.). Also significant was the level of technical and adult support available to them in implementing the use of the computer. The report suggested that there was some way to go in the provision of developmental support to teachers. It is to be hoped that the training programme in the NGfL funded by NOF will address many of the concerns. There are a number of research programmes underway to look into this issue (e.g. at the Open University, researching the Learning Schools programme).

Nevertheless the overall conclusions of the report were positive and generally optimistic about the benefits of using ICT in subject teaching 'where clear subject objectives have been identified'. Detailed and consistent planning is central to effective teaching with ICT.

Planning ICT in subject teaching:

a summary of key points

This chapter provided discussion, examples and activities in all areas of the curriculum for planning for ICT from the perspective of the other subjects in the curriculum. Issues of appropriateness, models of good practice and suggestions for ideas were all provided for the core curriculum (including the literacy and numeracy strategies) and for all the Foundation subjects. The activities were focused on practical applications in subject teaching of concepts outlined in the previous section on generic planning of ICT activities.

Further reading

DfEE (2000) *Information Technology in Maintained Primary and Secondary Schools in England: 1999*, DfEE.

DfEE/QCA (2000) *The National Curriculum: Handbook for Primary Teachers in England*, DfEE/QCA.

Fox, B., Montague-Smith, A. and Wilkes, S. (2000) *Using ICT in Primary Mathematics: Practice and Possibilities*, David Fulton.

HMI/OFTSED (2000) *The Teaching of Writing: Could Do Better*, OFSTED publications.

Leask, M. and Meadows, J. (eds) 2000 *Teaching and Learning with ICT in the Primary School*, Routledge.

McFarlane, A. (ed) (1997) *Information Technology and Authentic Learning: Realising the Potential of Computers in the Primary School*, Routledge.

Passey, D. *et al*. (1997) *Improve Your Use of IT in Teaching*, Folens.

QCA (1998) *Information technology: A Scheme of Work for Key Stages 1 and 2*, DfEE/QCA.

QCA (2000a) *Information and Communications Technology: Update to the IT Scheme of Work*, DfEE/QCA.

Sefton-Green, J. and Parker, D. (2000) *Edit-Play: How Children use Edutainment Software to Tell Stories*, BFI.

Smith, G. (1998) *A Hundred Ideas for IT*, Collins.

Smith, H. (1999) *Opportunities for ICT in the Primary School*, Trentham Books.

Somekh, B. and Davis, N. (eds) (1997) *Using Information Technology Effectively in Teaching and Learning: Studies in Pre-service and In-service Teacher Education*, Routledge.

TTA (1999a) *Ways Forward with ICT: Effective Pedagogy using Information and Communications Technology in Literacy and Numeracy in Primary Schools: Summary of Findings and Illustrations of Teacher Development*, TTA.

TTA (1999b) *Using ICT to Meet Teaching Objectives in Design and Technology (Primary Initial Teacher Training)*, TTA.

TTA (1999c) *Using ICT to Meet Teaching Objectives in Art (Primary Initial Teacher Training)*, TTA.

TTA (1999d) *Using ICT to Meet Teaching Objectives in English (Primary Initial Teacher Training)*, TTA.

TTA/DfES (2002) *Qualifying to teach: Professional Standards for Qualified Teacher Status and Requirements for Initial Teacher Training*, TTA.

TTA/DfES (2002a) *Guidance on the Requirements for Initial Teacher Training*, TTA.

TTA/DfES (2002b) *Guidance on the Standards for Qualified Teacher Status*, TTA .

This section is about planning for ICT activities in the Early Years setting. Trainees in the Early Years are expected to achieve additional standards during their training. This section will give some consideration to the issues around planning in a very different environment from the mainstream primary classroom.

The Early Years setting is defined as the range of learning environments for young children from about the age of three until they enter the primary school in Year I. The QCA guidance refers to this stage as the **Foundation Stage**.

The Foundation Stage has an entirely different structure from Curriculum 2000. If you are not an Early Years specialist but find yourself in a placement which is an Early Years setting, you need to familiarise yourself with the very thorough guidance provided. In particular, you need to become attuned to a setting which looks at **key learning goals** for young children, rather than explicit programmes of study and schemes of work.

The definition of these key learning goals is informed by Early Years specialists' understanding of the ways in which young children think and learn. They are also intended as laying the foundation for the child's future engagement with the curriculum in the mainstream primary setting. The Early Learning goals are mapped out for the Foundation Stage in six developmental areas as follows:

- **personal, social and emotional development;**
- **communication, language and literacy;**
- **mathematical development;**
- **knowledge and understanding of the world;**
- **physical development;**
- **creative development.**

The key issue for practitioners who are seeking to use computers to support young children's development in these areas is how to merge the use of the computer with the philosophy and methodology of planning for young learners.

The adults who work in Early Years settings, planning for and interacting with young children, set out their environment to maximise the opportunities for learning to take place. This is not a simple template for daily use of a space with young learners, it is an environment underpinned by a knowledge of how children develop skills, explore and grow in understanding of key concepts. Early Years professionals are trained to plan from the perspectives of child development and the major theorists of children's learning. Adults concerned with designing activities and planning for young learners are cognisant of the fact that learning happens both in the opportunity for play and in the interaction between people, all people, in learning spaces.

The theories of Vygotsky are important here as a major component of the theory underpinning the mapping out of Early Years settings. He believed that children are continually refining their growing understanding through a sort of innate, inner speech. Learning potential is enhanced in settings where children verbalise their inner speech and test and re-test it in their interaction with others. This happens in what Vygotsky characterised as the 'Zone of Proximal Development'. Many texts are available which explore these concepts in some depth. One example would be the book by David Wood, *How Children Think and Learn* (1997). Early Years specialists will also be familiar with the work of Sandra Smidt in *A Guide to Early Years Practice* (Smidt, 1998).

Vygotsky's theories and others underpin the Early Years setting. As a result, such environments are rich in opportunities for play (the context for the inner speech of children) and rich in opportunities for interaction (in the zone of proximal development).

Where does the computer fit into this environment? With its associated certainties and appearance of rigidity and non-fluid thinking, the computer appears to contradict this widely held view of the way in which children learn in the zone of proximal development. Some writers (Crook, 1996; Mercer and Fisher, 1997) have, however, attempted to analyse the working of the computer in the zone of proximal development and to look at the key features of talk around children working with computers. Their work suggests that computers are particularly rich in their possibilities for collaborative learning in the zone of proximal development.

This in turn suggests that the best organisational strategies for the Early Years are the same, in many respects, as for the classroom. It means making the computer much more a part of the world of the Early Years setting. At the most basic level this means making the computer more a part of the general experience of play and dialogue alongside the writing area, the modelling, the books, the play equipment. It means making the computer accessible for use in a range of contexts both collaboratively and singly, with an adult, without an adult, in the same way as any Early Years activity might be designed to maximise learning opportunities.

Clearly, giving children and the adults around the computer the space to talk and to play is crucial. Placing the computer in, for example, a role play situation, building a small office play environment around it and running open-ended software on it could be a starting point for stimulating much of the inner dialogue and talk in the zone of proximal development.

From the planning point of view it is important to be clear about how each of the defined areas of learning can be enriched and enhanced. It means thinking about the computer in each of the six contexts listed above.

For **personal, social and emotional development** this could mean planning opportunities for any of the following to occur:

- **learning how to share the equipment and take turns (particularly with such a motivating and attractive resource) – in other words, using the computer to** allow children to establish constructive relationships with each other and with other adults;

- using the computer to encourage collaboration between children and between adults and children in problem-solving (even at the basic level of switching on, selecting an item from a menu, clicking on a name);
- using the computer to explore worlds beyond the Early Years setting through the Internet or **CD ROM**;
- using the computer as a tool to encourage collaboration between children who are experiencing difficulties and others in the Early Years setting (using alternative access devices alongside mice and keyboards).

Encouraging children's development of **communication, language and literacy** in the Early Years setting with the computer means planning opportunities for children to:

- Write messages, label pictures with their name and otherwise engage with the communicative aspects of ICT. They do not have to get it right, in the same way as a writing area doesn't exclude children who can't yet form letters. The uncritical nature of the ICT can prove extremely motivating (particularly when the computer is in a role play area and the child is experiencing an impetus to try from the imaginative play).
- Experience the notion that computers can communicate words and pictures from books. If an adult helper, parent or older child is present, much useful talk and discussion about books and print, words and sounds, computers and communication can occur.
- Communicate with friends, relatives, peers in other settings nearby and very far away if possible. Children know that the computer is one among many tools for communication over distance and time. If the computer cannot deliver the necessary experiences then other ICT equipment such as a digital camera, video camera, tape recorder may be able to.

For children's **mathematical development**, the following opportunities might be useful:

- Plan to use software which allows children to experience situations of counting and sharing and identifying numbers, e.g. in counting items for a picnic. The most enduring and widely used Early Years software appears to be amongst the most simple and involves such activities as identifying numbers and counting items.
- Use software which relates a counting song or nursery rhyme known to the children to reinforce early counting concepts and which allows the children to have some free play. If children are working with parent helpers or other adults and making conscious what they understand, much constructive dialogue can take place which takes the child forward.

For the child's developing **knowledge and understanding of the world**, ICT can develop the skills of enquiry, of building understanding of the world in the Early Years setting in many ways. Some of the following might be used to plan to address this key learning area:

- As mentioned above, set up the computer within a role play area. Consider settings with which the children are familiar such as libraries, doctors' surgeries, any kind of office. This creates a powerful context for imaginative play because the computer reinforces the 'reality' of the situation for the child. It is a powerful stimulus for the inner speech and the outer dialogue in the zone of proximal development.
- The computer provides everyone in the Early Years setting with a means of recording in writing, orally and visually (still and full motion) the children's experiences as learners. Digital cameras are highly significant tools in this context, with their capacity for immediate feedback.
- The capacity for ICT to provide access to activities for many children with Special Educational Needs (including sensory impairment, physical and behavioural problems) allows for activities which promote knowledge and understanding of the world to be planned for all.
- As mentioned in the context of personal, social and emotional development, there is plenty of scope for the Internet and CD ROMs to bring experiences of other cultures and other worlds into the Early Years setting.

Children's **physical development** can be planned for in terms of computer use with the following considerations in mind:

- The use of ICT equipment to promote and develop fine motor skills, in particular, the use of the mouse.
- For children who are experiencing difficulties in fine motor skills across the whole range of severity, access devices such as brightly coloured, larger keyboards, touch windows and trackballs can all be used. Concept keyboards which contain teacher-defined touch areas, touch screens and big switches which can be wheelchair mounted, and others all allow for inclusion and development within the Early Years setting.

For children's **creative development** ICT brings into the world of the Early Years setting experiences with new media which can be used alongside the range of traditional, hands-on experiences. For example:

- The use of graphics software is an area of great potential in the Early Years setting. The medium in which the learner operates is infinitely editable and scalable. Colours in huge areas of the onscreen canvas can be varied at the click of a mouse. Shapes can be created with and without filled areas. With support from an adult or working with a friend, the child can be encouraged to verbalise their thoughts on the image they are making. Digital cameras allow images of the child themselves to become part of the onscreen canvas.
- ICT also offers the Early Years setting the potential to be creative with sound and with video. Simple musical composition software allows young learners to see that you can do more than just paint and write at a computer. A recording studio is another imaginary scenario in which to explore and develop.

Practical task

For those in an Early Years placement or Early Years specialist trainees:

- *Choose one of the early learning goals.*
- *Identify, with the help of the Early Years team at the school, an appropriate piece of software with which the children are already familiar.*
- *Set the computer up within some kind of role play context if possible (if space allows and if it fits with the current planning in the setting).*
- *Observe the children working with the software over a period of a few days for a few minutes each day. Ask for one or other of the co-workers in the setting to do the same.*
- *Collate your observations.*

Questions

- *How has the presence of the computer assisted in generating talk around the area of learning?*
- *Have you been able to observe any interactions in which peer learning was evident?*
- *Did the children work in the ways in which you expected?*
- *Were there any surprising outcomes?*
- *Were there any overlapping areas of development from the other early learning goals?*

Keep records of your observations and any photographs or pieces of work for your ICT profiling.

RESEARCH SUMMARY

Talk and ICT

A great deal of research has been carried out into the importance of talk around the computer which is of particular interest to Early Years practitioners, in particular as they plan for contexts in which young learners express their 'inner speech' (Smidt, 1998).

In Wegerif and Scrimshaw's Computers and Talk in the Primary Classroom (1997) a number of projects are outlined which analysed talk in and around computers according to a variety of frameworks. In one example, Eunice Fisher reports on the influence of software type on the kinds of talk generated (Fisher, 1997). A pattern of talk emerges in the use of less open-ended software which is quite different from the wide-ranging exploratory talk in evidence when open-ended software is being used by children. Wegerif responds in the chapter which follows making a case for exploratory talk which is generated around closed software and which actually extends children and 'leads to the educationally valuable combination of directive teaching software with children's active peer learning' (Wegerif, 1997).

Cook and Finlayson (1999) provide a series of case studies and an overview of children learning through talk around computers from the world outside the home into the Early Years and the primary classroom. They make a series of observations contextualised by a discussion of theories of learning (Vygotsky in particular) and by reference to the research in Wegerif and Scrimshaw. Their work makes out a case for the consideration of ICT in the context of what they describe as 'sound pedagogical principles'. In other words, the professional use of ICT depends on a sound set of principles in the same way as any teaching intervention. In the case of the work of Cook and Finlayson this is grounded in socio-cultural learning theory. Their approach is summed up in the title of their book: Interactive Children, Communicative Teaching.

Planning ICT in the Early Years:

a summary of key points

This chapter has examined the different perspective on the use of ICT working in an environment which had its own curriculum and approaches to teaching and learning. In particular, in an environment which places interaction and communication at the centre of many of its organised learning activities, we looked at the possibilities afforded by talk around computers. Each of the learning goals in the Curriculum Guidance for the Foundation Stage (QCA, 2000b) was considered and a practical task was provided which was intended to aid profiling in ICT for trainees working in the Early Years.

Further reading

Cook, D. and Finlayson, H. (1999) *Interactive Children, Communicative Teaching: ICT and Classroom Teaching*, Open University Press.

QCA (2000b) *Curriculum Guidance for the Foundation Stage*, QCA.

Smidt, S. (1998) *A Guide to Early Years Practice*, Routledge.

Wegerif, R. and Scrimshaw, P. (eds) (1997) *Computers and Talk in the Primary Classroom*, Multilingual Matters.

Wood, D. (1997) *How Children Think and Learn*, Blackwell.

10 ASSESSMENT AND RECORDING IN PRIMARY ICT

The scheme of work is intended to provide progression and a possible map of the learning of a child in a given subject. Assessment is a vital part of the process because it allows teachers to track progress and plan appropriately for children to achieve. Without proper assessment and recording in a given subject, there is no real evidence or knowledge of where the children are up to and planning becomes empty and meaningless. In the worst cases, it leads to the same activities being given out year on year to children who will underachieve because of it. In ICT this means seeing the same basic word processing activities going on at Year 6 as happened at Year 2. The planning and assessment cycle is incomplete in a school where this occurs and the children make no real progress in the subject (or in its use in other subjects).

The principles which underpin good practice in assessment apply equally to ICT and ICT in subject teaching. As teachers, we are looking for ways to measure achievement which, at the same time, allow us to identify a child's learning needs. These methods of assessment, in turn, will allow us to plan efficiently and appropriately. Ways of assessing children in ICT, as in other subjects, include some or all of the following:

- **observing how the child goes about a piece of work;**
- **diagnosing difficulties which become apparent over a series of lessons;**
- **observing which planning strategies appear to work and allow the child to succeed in a given area;**
- **collecting significant pieces of work in a portfolio of development;**
- **noting the context of the work and any factors which were significant: the grouping, the time taken, the level of concentration, and so on;**
- **noting the views of the child about the piece of work and asking her or him what made the activity so successful/significant;**
- **feeding the information back into the planning process;**
- **when appropriate, making a judgement about the child's level in terms of the level descriptions in the attainment targets for ICT in Curriculum 2000 (at the end of the Key Stages in the primary school);**
- **at all times a clear focus on the objective is very important as well as a general awareness of other learning taking place.**

Nevertheless, assessment and record keeping in ICT is a complex process. Meaningful work samples are harder to come by in ICT than in most other subjects, with the possible exception of PE and RE. Print-outs of work by themselves are not useful. ICT is often used as a tool to present work in its best possible light. Any revealing errors and misconceptions are often lost along the way. The finished product is only the final element of a much longer, more complex process. The process itself is what provides the real assessment opportunities. To borrow an example from another subject, English, a writing sample which contains only the finished ('best') copy is similarly without any real use. Teachers need to go back through the draft book to understand the process the child went through. The child also needs to see and understand this in order to move forward.

Some ICT tools do allow for processes to be explored. Some word processors, for example, allow changes to be tracked and printed out. Others record how many times the child accessed the online help in a particular software package. Browser software tracks the user through the various sites and links they follow. This might provide useful assessment information. In some more forward-looking local authorities, there are systems which allow children to select pieces of work and store them in an electronic portfolio. Taken together, in context, these are useful tools for the teacher assessing a child's achievement and identifying their learning needs. If we add connectivity to the home computer into the equation we have a powerful, fluid record of achievement which is also accessible to parents and to children out of school hours. (Of course, the issue of inequality in computer and network connectivity provision in different areas becomes even more obvious in this context and will need addressing by those in positions of power.)

Tutorial software, including software produced as part of an integrated learning system (ILS), can record the units of work which the child has covered and can produce tables, graphs and collections of statistics. These relate to the software itself and closely to the subject being taught. They are of very limited use in assessing the child's ICT capability, however, and should not usually be presented as evidence of attainment in ICT. They record particular progress through an onscreen worksheet or tutorial. As we have seen in the planning chapters above, the ability to use tutorial software only demonstrates the ability to use tutorial software. True ICT capability is much more than the ability to follow onscreen instructions and click on the button which says 'NEXT' or 'CONTINUE'.

For further information on tutorial software, see page 168, Chapter 8

The most useful tool in assessment in ICT is the teacher's own observation of the child in all contexts and their interaction with them about their work. In all the resource settings we have discussed in this section, this presents real logistical difficulties and requires systematic planning and the use of other adults in order that it is carried out usefully. Many schools, for example, operate an assessment week with samples being collected across the curriculum at the same time, in each class, in each half term. Extra adults are sometimes drafted in to support the class teacher in this work. Collection of ICT evidence and observation could also be planned for in this way.

However, on teaching practice with all the course demands being placed on trainee teachers and their mentors and tutors, any assessment activity has to be focused and manageable as well as useful. The course requirements which follow the prescribed curriculum for Initial Teacher Training will spell out the number of assessments to be made of children and at what particular level in each curriculum area.

It is important to bear in mind that a further difficulty is the collaborative nature of ICT. It is sometimes hard to separate out the individual contributions to a joint project. There will be times when this is irrelevant and unnecessary. However, while collaboration itself is usually to be encouraged, there comes a time, at the end of the year and, more formally, at the end of the relevant Key Stages, when a level of operating within the National Curriculum must be ascribed to an individual. It becomes important therefore to develop skilled observations of individual contributions to partner work in ICT. Developing skills in monitoring the situation in this way protects quieter, less dominant children from being overlooked.

The examples which follow detail two very different forms of assessment. The first, individual profiling, provides a means of systematically tracking an individual child in some detail. The second, whole class snapshot, provides a means of measuring ICT capability at a very basic level in order to gain a picture of where each child in the class is at a given moment in time. They need to be employed together in order to gain the maximum benefit in terms of the assessment and planning cycle.

It is worth stating at this stage that the level descriptions of capability for a child are intended to be applied at the end of a Key Stage using a judgement of 'best fit'. That is to say, the teacher reads the descriptions and decides on a numerical level on the basis of observations and knowledge of the children in the class. The level descriptions for all subjects can be located at the back of the Curriculum 2000 handbook. If, all year, there has been a sound, formative assessment process which informs the planning, backed by samples and observations, these end of Key Stage judgements will be relatively easy to make and have a higher level of accuracy. In other words, they will be more meaningful to the child and her or his teachers and parents.

Individual profiling

Individual profiling of children in curriculum subjects provides a means of mapping their progress through the various work samples collected and observations made. It makes a link to the child's own view of their developing capabilities and a link back to planning, completing the planning and assessment cycle.

The proforma on page 204 is intended to be completed two or three times in a term and should take no longer than five or ten minutes, once it becomes familiar. Ideally, it should be completed with the child in discussion about a particular work sample. The number of these completed in a teaching practice would need to be negotiated in terms of the overall course requirements for assessment (which in turn depends on a negotiation with the standards themselves!). The questions next to each of the cells provide an aide-mémoire of how to complete the form. As you can see, the areas covered include the child's individual progress alongside notes about the school context and an opportunity to record the child's own response to the piece of work. It is intended that the same sheet is used for each child and that the columns are completed for each observation so that it is possible to check progress across the two or three observations made. The form on page 204 is a blank copy for photocopying.

Whole class snapshots

To gain a picture of the whole class over a shorter period of time, in order to map out their skills, knowledge and understanding of ICT, it would be useful to complete a very basic skills matrix. This is in no way a substitute for the detailed profiling and sampling

Date			
Name of child			
IT context (computer in class/network room, etc.)	Was the child working in the network room or on one machine? What was it?		
Software/web	Using software standalone or on the Internet?		
Type (tutorial CD, office tools etc.)	If the child was using software, write the type here.		
QCA or school unit if appropriate	Which QCA or school study units if any was the child using?		
Working with partner? Who?	Was the child working alone, with a peer, with the teacher, parent or other adult?		
Length of time	For how long?		
Confidence with hardware, mouse, keyboard	Rate the child's confidence with the hardware listed and/or with printers or other devices. Very, fairly, not very, needing support, etc.		
Software navigation (use of menus)	As above but for navigation within the particular piece of software.		
File management... saving, opening, renaming work, etc.	As above but for working with files, re-opening them, knowing where to find work, etc.		
Curriculum context. Using computer to support work in English, science, mathematics	How was the child operating within the curriculum context? Did the computer support the subject? Were there particular difficulties? Did the use of ICT help to improve the outcome?		
Child's view of their ICT	Ask the child about their view of themselves as a user of ICT. Were there significant things about this piece of work that pleased them?		
Give best fit level if appropriate	Using the level descriptors, if appropriate, make a best fit judgement of the child.		
Where next?	What activities with ICT would move the child forward?		

Example of assessment notes proforma

Date			
Name of child			
IT context (computer in class/network room, etc.)			
Software/web			
Type (tutorial CD, office tools etc.)			
QCA or school unit if appropriate			
Working with partner? Who?			
Length of time			
Confidence with hardware, mouse, keyboard			
Software navigation (use of menus)			
File management... saving, opening, renaming work, etc.			
Curriculum context. Using computer to support work in English, science, mathematics			
Child's view of their ICT			
Give best fit level if appropriate			
Where next?			

Assessment notes proforma

suggested in the previous section. It gives you an overview very rapidly upon which you can build some basic planning. The more detailed observations of individual children will be needed to gauge more accurately the effectiveness of the planning in raising the achievement of the class.

Name	Date	Mouse	Keyboard skills	Switch on or log on	Switch off or log off	Open	Save	Cut/ paste	Graphics	Indep- endence	General comment

Make best guess judgements on a consistent value scale in order to provide a snapshot of the children in the class. Remember that this is merely an aide-mémoire to help you write a short comment on the form for the rest of the class. The best practice in assessment is the longer form where curriculum contexts are taken into account alongside technical skill development. Use the longer format for the five identified children.

Use a 1–4 scale for, e.g. mouse skills and keyboard skills, switching on/off, opening and saving, cutting/pasting, inserting graphics:
1 (not at all confident)   2 (developing confidence and accuracy)
3 (accurate and confident) 4 (very accurate and confident)

Quick snapshot of skills, knowledge and understanding

Assessing Early Years ICT

We saw in the separate planning section on Early Years settings that children are working in a different context, that of the Foundation Stage. The different areas for planning were mapped out.

For further information on planning ICT in the Early Years, see page 194, Chapter 9

The same applies to differentiating assessment for children learning with computers in the Early Years. The criteria will be the early learning goals and the observations you make will be referenced to the six main areas:

- **personal, social and emotional development;**
- **communication, language and literacy;**
- **mathematical development;**
- **knowledge and understanding of the world;**
- **physical development;**
- **creative development.**

The activities which they undertake at the computer are drawn from these contexts. It follows that assessment should also be grounded in that experience.

The individual profiling sheet described in the section above is of potentially greater use in the Early Years setting than the whole class snapshot. With the more detailed observation sheet, the background to the activity and the grouping become the more significant fields in which to enter any observations. If you are working in this context, you may even find it easier than in the mainstream school since so much assessment and recording in Early Years settings depends on collating team observations of children across a period of time in different situations.

Practical task

At Key Stages 1 and 2 or in the Foundation Stage, use the proforma for individual observations to look in detail at the work of three children of varying levels of ability.

Complete the proforma during a unit of work from the ICT scheme or from a subject scheme with heavy ICT content (see table on page 203 for ideas). Carry out three observations on each child.

Collect the samples and cross-reference your observations with them.

• Did the assessment reveal any strengths and/or areas for development?

• How helpful was the assessment?

• Were there questions which you wished to see answered which were not on the form? If yes, what were they?

• Were you able to track development through the lessons?

• How did you differentiate your questioning for those children?

Discuss these issues in assessment with you mentor and/or professional tutor. See where you may be able to use these activities as evidence in your profiling. You may find that you have generic evidence which can be ascribed to wider professional standards such as those contained in section 3.2 on Monitoring and Assessment (TTA/DfES, 2002).

RESEARCH SUMMARY

Cook and Finlayson (1999) argue for the involvement of the child in recording progress in ICT. Tunstall and Gipps (1996) place great importance on the need to feed back to young children, identifying it as a 'prime requirement for progress in learning'. Both of these statements imply interaction and active involvement in the assessment process on the part of the child and we have tried to reflect this in the processes described in the preceding arguments about ICT assessment and record-keeping.

Assessment and recording in primary ICT:
a summary of key points

This chapter attempted to map out the issues and provide some potential solutions to the challenge of evaluating children's learning in ICT and ICT in subjects. We have considered the importance of involving the child in the process, alongside some suggestions how to go about it. We have provided some additional input on Early Years assessments, plus an activity in assessment and record-keeping which invites trainees to respond critically to the suggested methods. We have also explored the connection between planning and assessment.

Further reading

Cook, D. and Finlayson, H. (1999) *Interactive Children, Communicative Teaching: ICT and Classroom Teaching*, Open University Press.

DfEE (1998a) *Teaching: High Status, High Standards – Circular Number 4/98: Requirements for Courses of Initial Teacher Training*, DfEE.

DfEE (1998b) *The National Literacy Strategy*, DfEE.

DfEE (1999) *The National Numeracy Strategy*, DfEE.

DfEE (2000) *Information Technology in Maintained Primary and Secondary Schools in England: 1999*, DfEE.

DfEE/QCA (2000) *The National Curriculum: Handbook for Primary Teachers in England*, DfEE/QCA.

QCA (1998) *Information Technology: A Scheme of Work for Key Stages 1 and 2*, DfEE/QCA.

QCA (2000a) *Information and Communications Technology: Update to the IT Scheme of Work*, DfEE/QCA.

Trend, R., Davis, N. and Loveless, A. (1998) *Information and Communications Technology*, Letts Educational.

If you are training as an ICT specialist in primary schools or are one day hoping to lead ICT in a primary school, it is worth knowing about the various ways in which ICT is monitored. That is to say, at the various levels, from the DfES to the local level and the school level, it is useful to know how ICT is measured and why and with what results.

This first section looks at government monitoring of ICT provision by the DfES. The following section looks at how OFSTED reports on ICT in primary schools. The final two sections look at local structures and, finally, school-level structures.

Government monitoring

For further information on the NGfL, see page 129, Chapter 6

At the government level we have seen in earlier sections how the various strategies, such as the National Grid for Learning (NGfL) and the New Opportunities Fund (NOF) for Training have come into being. The government publishes an annual survey through the DfES which tracks the trends of computer use and computer buying in schools. The spend on educational ICT has been huge in recent years and the various initiatives associated with it have to be accountable and measurable.

The DfES collects statistics on ICT in schools every year and you can obtain this information annually, every October. The table below compares the most recent available statistics on computers in primary schools with the figures for 1998. As you will see, great changes have been taking place:

Table showing changes in computer numbers in primary schools between 1998 and 2001

Item	Figures for 1998	Figures for 2001
Average number of computers per school	13.3	20.7
Average number of pupils per computer	17.6	11.8
Percentage of schools connected to the Internet	17.0	96.0

Source: DfES (2001) Statistics of Education: Survey of Information and Communications Technology in Schools 2001 (Issue no. 09/01) p. 8

Perhaps the figure that will surprise you most is the number of schools with Internet connections. Ninety-six per cent of primary schools as of October 2001 were connected to the Internet. Many activities in this book reflect the sea change that this has brought about. However, not all connections at the moment are fast, cheap, distributed across the school or providing the revolution in curriculum delivery which has been envisaged by the government (see the original paper which launched the NGFL - DfEE (1997) *Connecting the Learning Society*).

The role of OFSTED in the context of ICT

The Office for Standards in Education (OFSTED) has a statutory duty to report on standards in education and teacher education across phases and across the curriculum.

Every year, Her Majesty's Chief Inspector of Schools produces a summary report and commentary on inspection findings in the previous year which attempts to draw together trends and developments into a picture of education in England and Wales.

Each year in the Annual Report the Chief Inspector reports on different areas of the curriculum. The early reports, from 1996 and 1997, are quite critical of the implementation of teaching and learning with ICT in primary schools. The most recent report notes that there have been significant changes but that, at Key Stage 2 in particular, there are still weaknesses. Chris Woodhead, the then Chief Inspector for Schools, writes that:

> Despite some improvement this year, particularly in primary schools, pupils' progress in information technology is unsatisfactory in over one third of schools at Key Stage 2 and over four in ten at Key Stage 4. The overall quality of teaching in both primary and secondary schools remains significantly weaker than that of other subjects. Teachers often expect too little of pupils and too much time is spent practising low-level skills.
>
> (OFSTED, 2000)

We have seen the importance of a scheme of work as a map of the teaching and learning. Where schools do not have such a scheme in place, the same low-level activities and skills are being rehearsed and OFTSED is reporting that fact.

However, the situation is changing and improving over time. Schools have had to construct development plans for ICT in order to access the NOF training money. Similarly, their LEAs have had to do the same to access NGfL funding for their schools. Structures and support are coming into play in many areas which were not there before. There is still a long way to go and trainees will notice that there are significant differences between schools in which they are placed during their training, particularly if you move from one LEA to another. OFSTED has, however, noted some positive changes taking place. The most recent OFSTED reoprts on ICT initiatives in schools, along with the most recent general, anuual reoprts, are all available on the OFSTED website (www. ofsted.gov.uk).

School-level monitoring – senior managers, ICT co-ordinators

Senior managers have a role in leading and monitoring the curriculum. In most schools this is delegated to the subject co-ordinators. ICT co-ordinators may be given additional time during the week to monitor the curriculum for ICT. We have seen, however, in earlier chapters that there are as many different kinds of ICT co-ordinator as there are kinds of school organisation for ICT itself.

 For further information on ICT co-ordinators, see page 131, Chapter 6

You need to develop an awareness of current classroom practice and inspection evidence where it relates to your specialist subject. It might be useful to carry out the following practical task and it would be advisable to do so if you are an ICT specialist in the primary phase:

Practical task

This task focuses on the people who impact on the organisation and use of ICT in the school. Find out who they are in your particular school situation. Interview them and discover more about their influence on the whole school development for ICT.

You could ask them, sensitively, if they are:

- *unpaid co-ordinators, or*
- *given one responsibility point, or*
- *given two responsibility points.*

Try to find out whether they are working solely on developing ICT or combining ICT with one or more of science, mathematics, technology or, less usually, English or a creative arts subject.

For ICT co-ordinators or senior managers in charge of ICT, try to discover the following information about them:

- *their training;*
- *how they got the job;*
- *what contact they have with their LEA advisory team;*
- *their role in the management structure of the school;*
- *their budget;*
- *how they pass on their expertise;*
- *what sort of role they take in troubleshooting (do they take on minor repairs themselves, or do they encourage others to learn more about the ICT in their school?);*
- *whether they report faults or have a system for doing so;*
- *whether there is a service contract.*

Crucially, is there a development plan for ICT and how was it constructed?

How do they involve parents and carers, classroom assistants, governors and others in ICT in the school?

Have they been or are they about to become involved in a whole-staff training programme for ICT (such as the one funded by the NOF)?

What was the outcome of the most recent inspection in terms of ICT and how is the school addressing the issues?

Relate the findings to the development of ICT in your specialist subject if it is not ICT. Are there policy statements or schemes of work which outline how ICT can be developed in the subject? Is there evidence to suggest that it is happening in the school?

Practical task

If the above research into ICT co-ordination proves too difficult in terms of the school situation, try the following task instead:

Browse the OFSTED and DfES websites. Find out about the latest inspection evidence on schools' ICT. Try the main sites for the national picture using a search string such as 'Survey of Information Technology in UK schools'. Visit your LEA inspection report (if it exists) and discover what information there is about ICT support in the area. Then visit your placement school's OFSTED report and see how the school fits into the pattern of inspection evidence. Answer the following questions:

- *What is the ratio of computers to children in primary schools as measured by the most recent inspection evidence?*
- *What is the trend in English schools' ICT inspection reports by OFSTED? Towards higher or lower standards?*
- *How does your placement school perform in its most recent OFSTED report? Does the report match up with the current state of provision?*
- *Find out about your specialist subject in relation to the ICT (if ICT is not your specialist subject). What does the national and local picture appear to be on the teaching of your subject with ICT?*

Relevant texts: theory and practice and research into ICT in the classroom

Remembering that making a judgement about the uses or not of ICT in a given situation is one of the required areas of development for trainees, it is important to have a look at some relevant readings on ICT. You should also, particularly, if you are an ICT subject specialist, be aware of some of the recently produced research and literature on ICT in the classroom.

The research summaries provided throughout this book provide starting points for identifying relevant critical literature. Your college will almost certainly supply you with a list of texts which give you a critical dimension to your understanding of ICT in the curriculum. Some of these will be books and periodicals. In other cases there are good sources of material on the Internet. The subject has a shorter history than others in the curriculum but has a growing, rich and diverse body of literature.

The reading list which follows each chapter in the book is not exhaustive, neither is it something that you could reasonably expect to work through in a PGCE year or even a full degree programme. There are, however, some reports of case studies in classroom practice which would be very useful to look at (see Practical task below). There are also studies in schools which have become regular sources of reference material, such as the PALM and INTENT projects (referred to extensively in Somekh and Davis, 1997). Many of these are easily accessible over the Internet from sources such as the Telematics Centre at the University of Exeter (visit *http://telematics3.ex.ac.uk/ERF/*).

Models of good practice exist in many LEAs and are being disseminated through the NGfL and through BECTa in particular. OFSTED finds year on year that the use of ICT in subject teaching is improving (although ICT itself is still the poorest taught subject, of which more later). You can research this in more depth on the OFSTED website at http://www.ofsted.gov.uk

As far as the use of ICT in subject teaching is concerned, BECTa, in partnership with the University of Nottingham, is managing one of the largest evaluations of learning gains with ICT ever carried out. The IMPACT2 project, due to report in the summer of 2002, has already produced interim findings that suggest that the use of ICT has a positive effect on pupil attainment. You can find this and other documents, such as the 'Primary Schools ICT and Standards' report along with the final IMPACT2 report on the research part of the BECTa website at http://www.becta.org.uk/research

A recent research project referred to in a number of chapters is the Newcastle University project under David Moseley and Steve Higgins which was published at the end of 1999 (Moseley, Higgins *et al.*, 1999). This built arguments about effective pedagogy in the teaching of literacy and numeracy on case studies and observations of teachers working in primary classrooms throughout the Key Stages. There is a substantial literature review in the original report which covers many of the major themes to have emerged from research into effective teaching methods with computers in classrooms. The case studies and a general overview of the findings are available as a separate publication from the Teacher Training Agency (TTA, 1999). The areas covered include:

- **presenting texts and supporting writing in Y2;**
- **improving reading and spelling in Y2;**
- **developing writing skills in Y3 and Y4;**
- **developing counting skills in Reception;**
- **supporting number skills in the Y4/Y5 classroom.**

The Teacher Training Agency website (*http://www.canteach.gov.uk/*) has further information on the report and it is also in the virtual library at the Telematics Centre listed above. The task below is based on a reading of the case studies it contains.

Practical task

This task might be appropriate for you if you are an ICT subject specialist wanting to look at recent research into pedagogy with ICT in the primary school.

An example of classroom-based research into the teaching of ICT in schools is Ways Forward with ICT: Effective Pedagogy Using Information and Communications Technology in Literacy and Numeracy in Primary Schools *(Summary of findings, TTA, 1999a). It is a series of eleven reports of case studies from primary schools in the north east which allows you to read accounts by teachers working to introduce ICT against the backdrop of the curriculum strategies in literacy and numeracy.*

- *Choose one of the accounts.*
- *What did the teachers need to know to carry out the activities successfully?*
- *How was their professional development enhanced by the appropriate use of ICT in subject teaching?*
- *In what ways do you think the ICT was helpful to the teaching of literacy or numeracy?*
- *What can you learn about planning and organisation from this account?*
- *What would you change to make it fit with your situation?*
- *Attach a plan and write-up of a similar or related area from the English or mathematics curriculum and evaluate it. Compare your experience with that of the teacher in the study.*

RESEARCH SUMMARY

A number of recent research projects have looked into the area of teacher training and teacher motivation to use technology in their practice.

Teachers in role as innovators is the focus of the study by Margaret Cox, Christina Preston and Kate Cox. This study focused on teachers who were already using ICT confidently and attempted to identify motivational factors which led to the successful integration of new technologies into classrooms (Cox, Preston and Cox, 2000). As with the Newcastle study (Moseley, Higgins et al., 1999) and work by Potter and Mellar (2000), Cox, Preston and Cox found that there was a high correlation between teachers' personal and professional use of ICT. Teachers who were already competent and motivated users of ICT for emailing, desktop publishing and so on at home were more motivated to include it in their practice.

Again, as with the Newcastle study, there was concern expressed over the level of technical support available and time to work on integrating resources adequately into practice. There was concern that not all ICT resources were adequate. Nevertheless, 'In spite of such disadvantages all the teachers in our sample were managing to use ICT in their teaching' (Cox, Preston and Cox, 2000).

Meadows (1999), surveying teachers working in schools in partnership with Southbank University teacher education, found that greater levels of support were needed to make the innovation work at a time of conflicting priorities and stresses in the classrooms.

Potter and Mellar (2000), in their survey of teachers using the Internet in a group of East London schools, found that training for teachers needed to address their needs holistically, including much greater integration with patterns of use at home. They also found that curriculum integration of the Internet depended to a great extent on finding proactive uses for the technology in web publishing and emailing.

Teachers in the Newcastle study were motivated to continue development work with ICT because of the impact on the teaching and learning in their classrooms:

> *They (the teachers in the study) acknowledged that ICT offered them a wider range of strategies from which an effective teacher could choose in deciding how to meet teaching and learning objectives in literacy and numeracy.*
>
> *(Moseley, Higgins et al., 1999)*

Monitoring and researching:

a summary of key points

This chapter is concerned with providing information about the sort of monitoring that goes on at all the different levels (government, LEA and school) of ICT in teaching and learning. We have considered the role of OFSTED and that of the DfEE followed by school-level monitoring by senior managers. The chapter closed with some comments about the availability of recent research into ICT in classrooms and a suggested practical task of use to ICT specialists in particular.

The area of ICT in education is changing all the time and many publications and websites reflect these changes. The time lag between research and publication in education is too wide for the pace of change in ICT and it is important to look at as wide a range of resources as possible when building arguments and undertaking further study in the area of ICT in teaching and learning.

Further reading

Cox, M., Preston, C. and Cox, K. (2000) *Teachers as Innovators: An Evaluation of the Motivation of Teachers to Use Information and Communications Technologies*, Mirandanet/TTA.

Crook, C. (1996) *Computers and the Collaborative Experience of Learning*, Routledge.

DfEE (1995) *Information Technology in the National Curriculum*, HMSO.

DfEE (1997) *Connecting the Learning Society*, DfEE.

Harrison, M. (1998) *Co-ordinating Information and Communications Technology across the Primary School*, Falmer Press.

HMI/OFTSED (2000) *The Teaching of Writing: Could Do Better*, OFSTED publications.

Leask, M. and Meadows, J. (eds) (2000) *Teaching and Learning with ICT in the Primary School*, Routledge.

McFarlane, A. (ed) (1997) *Information Technology and Authentic Learning: Realising the Potential of Computers in the Primary School*, Routledge.

Moseley, D., Higgins, S. *et al.* (1999) *Ways Forward with ICT: Effective Pedagogy using Information and Communications Technology in Literacy and Numeracy in Primary Schools*, Newcastle University.

OFSTED (2000) *Annual Report Of Her Majesty's Chief Inspector of Schools – Standards and Quality In Education 1998/99*, OFSTED publications.

Sefton-Green, J. and Parker, D. (2000) *Edit-Play: How Children use Edutainment Software to Tell Stories*, BFI.

Somekh, B. and Davis, N. (eds) (1997) *Using Information Technology Effectively in Teaching and Learning: Studies in Pre-service and In-service Teacher Education*, Routledge.

Stevenson, D. *et al.* (1997) *Information and Communications Technology in UK Schools: An Independent Enquiry*, ICT in Schools Commission.

Wegerif, R. and Scrimshaw, P. (eds) (1997) *Computers and Talk in the Primary Classroom*, Multilingual Matters.

SECTION C: ICT IN THE CLASSROOM – AN INTRODUCTION

The rapid development of ICT brings in its wake a series of challenges to which teachers must respond. In this third section we provide an overview of four aspects of teachers' involvement with ICT which are not directly curriculum-related but which are nevertheless critical for effective and positive use of ICT in the classroom. These are:

- **professional use of ICT;**
- **computers in your classroom;**
- **ethical and legal issues;**
- **choosing software.**

Introducing paragraph 2.5 of the Standards for QTS, the Handbook of Guidance identifies 'two aspects of ICT competence which trainees can be expected to develop and demonstrate: how best to use ICT to teach the subject(s) they are trained to teach, and their own ICT skills, which will allow them, for example, to complete pupils' records of progress, prepare resources for pupils and keep to a minimum their administrative tasks' (TTA/DfES, 2002). In Chapter 12 on the professional use of ICT we offer some ideas as starting points for both improved personal capability and continuing professional development.

Teachers have a clear duty of care for the children in their classroom (outlined in paragraphs 3.1.3 and 3.3.8) and it is obvious that computers, and associated peripherals, bring a particular burden of responsibility for safe operation. Primary age children may have little or no previous experience as users of electrical equipment, while typically computers in schools are being sited in locations that were not originally designed for this purpose. It would be impractical to provide an exhaustive list of 'dos and don'ts' in respect of health and safety, but Chapter 13 in this section includes guidelines on how to make your classroom as free from risk as possible, as well as referring the reader to appropriate interpretations of the relevant legislation. The practical theme of this chapter is continued with help to demystify the assembly of hardware.

The new ways of communication that ICT offers have raised a range of ethical and legal issues with which we, as a society, are grappling to come to terms. Many of these are not completely new problems; for example, there have always been opportunities for plagiarism, or for the dissemination of undesirable material. However, the need to take a moral stand and deal with potential threats has been markedly accentuated by the speed and ease with which information can now be transmitted. The earlier chapter on the Internet has discussed some of the questions involved. Chapter 14 on ethical and legal issues turns our attention to two other significant areas for ICT in education, copyright and data protection, contributing to the promotion of positive values and attitudes (covered by paragraph 1.3), but also in a pragmatic way aiming to avoid unnecessary pitfalls.

 For more information on safety issues concerning the Internet, see page 111, Chapter 5

Chapter 15, which again relates to paragraphs 3.1.3 and 3.3.8, puts forward ideas that might be engaged when choosing software. While certain criteria are proposed, the intention is not to be dogmatic; different circumstances, such as the significance of budgetary constraints, will alter the relevance and weighting of different criteria. However, the key suggestion is that criteria, determined by the teacher, do need to be in place. It is not adequate to make a judgement on software arbitrarily.

It is a requirement of the Professional Standards for QTS that teachers know how to use ICT effectively to support their wider professional role (DfES, 2002). In this chapter we shall consider this demand from two angles, personal capability and the use of ICT to source relevant information.

Personal capability

The requirement to use ICT to improve efficiency sounds obvious, but in reality a teacher might question the need to adopt ICT as a tool for her professional practice when manual alternatives appear to be quicker. The short answer to this objection is that *selective* use of ICT will repay the investment of time made to gain proficiency with the keyboard and appropriate software. In this sense, acquisition of keyboard skills is in some ways analogous to learning to drive – and takes about the same amount of time. For those who want to develop typing skills an electronic tutor such as *Mavis Beacon* or *Accutype* is invaluable. The course need not necessarily be followed to its conclusion but to a point when you are using most of your fingers and moving around the keyboard with some fluency. This will only improve with further practice.

In a similar way, cumulative benefit is derived from learning software. Modern word processors, desktop publishing packages and spreadsheets have wide-ranging functionality. To a novice they may seem daunting, treacherous and unwieldy, but in time it will prove quicker to use them than relying on 'traditional' pen and paper approaches. Time-saving possibilities include:

- **using a template in your word processor so that a lesson plan can be called up repeatedly;**
- **using a spreadsheet to keep pupils' records (for example, marks) that can readily be sorted into order and converted into graphical representations to demonstrate progress;**
- **using desktop publishing to produce professional-looking worksheets; although clip art should be used judiciously, it is nevertheless a tremendous time-saver!**

Further ideas are available on a number of websites, including Terry Freedman's useful *IT and ICT in Educational Administration Home Page*.

Professional development using ICT

In their work in the classroom, teachers will be supporting children in the use of ICT to source information. This is a key skill; the capability to access information is now critical. While reference is often made to a 'knowledge-based' society, there is an argument that it is not holding knowledge personally that is now important so much as knowing how to reach it when it is needed. Does it matter whether you retain the fact that the Battle of Bosworth was in 1485 if you can find it out in a few mouse-clicks?

Teachers can help themselves professionally to keep up to date by using ICT in a variety of ways, the most important of which is accessing information via the Internet. There are a number of key sites with which all teachers should be familiar. A useful starting point is provided by the Department for Education and Skills site (*http://www.dfes.gov.uk*), not just for its own content – which includes news and discussion of current issues in education – but for links it offers (*http://www.dfes.gov.uk/links.shtml*) to other key national bodies.

As a next stop, the National Grid for Learning website (*http://www.ngfl.gov.uk*) is recommended. This site, launched in January 1998 in conjunction with the government's drive to make all schools 'connected' by 2002, was conceived as a huge resource base for teachers, providing them with materials, support, advice and links to other vetted sites. The NGfL site is still being developed – indeed the hope must be that it will remain dynamic, responding to the changing needs of the profession. It includes the Virtual Teacher Centre (VTC), which amongst other features houses an area in which teachers have the opportunity to exchange views on matters of specific concern. There are two mechanisms by which this process is managed, conferences and mailing lists. Conferences are more sophisticated; they allow you to follow discussions by 'threading' the messages, organising them on the page so that you can see who has responded to a previous comment. However, you do need to visit the site in order to see what has been posted. Mailing lists are easier to establish, and easier to be involved in, as once you have subscribed they deliver messages to your inbox directly.

The National Grid for Learning site receives considerable input in its design and organisation from the British Educational Communications and Technology agency (BECTa) which has its own site at *http://www.becta.org.uk*. BECTa offers a substantial range of materials, specifically on the use of ICT, to support teachers. Information sheets are constructed logically, with non-specialist teachers in mind, and make clear both technical and pedagogical aspects of their themes.

A Uniform Resource Locator (URL, or address) that offers an immediate impact on efficiency is the National Curriculum site, *http://www.nc.uk.net*, from where all the current National Curriculum documents may be downloaded. They are offered in alternative forms, as Acrobat files (.pdf) or as text files (.doc). The Acrobat files (for which you will need Acrobat Reader, which can be downloaded from the Internet free of charge) are presented in the same style as the print edition.* Perhaps more useful, however, are the text versions which can be edited in a word processor and so incorporated in planning documents and for other aspects of administration. Similarly, schemes of work can be obtained from the QCA at *http://www.qca.org.uk*, again in either format.

It is important that teachers should have access to inspection evidence, and foremost among sources for this is the OFSTED site at *http://www.ofsted.gov.uk*. The site provides access to all the inspection reports carried out on schools (and other educational institutions such as LEAs and teacher training providers). This is a huge repository of information. It would be difficult to conceive how it might be made so readily available other than by the Internet. It is also worth remembering that OFSTED produces, and posts on the Internet, reports on subject and curriculum issues aggregated from its findings in individual schools. This is authoritative research that complements material that teachers might glean from other sources.

There are many further governmental and quasi-governmental sites that hold helpful information for teachers. The Standards site (*http://www.standards.dfes.gov.uk*), the General Teaching Council of England (*http://www.gtce.org.uk*) and the Teacher Training Agency (*http://www.canteach.gov.uk*) are three further locations that repay a visit. Most of these are very effective technically; they have been designed carefully and offer an interface that is attractive and intuitive. Not surprisingly, privately produced sites, which tend to offer curriculum resources rather than statutory and administrative support, are of less consistently high quality, in terms of both content and presentation. They reflect forcefully the somewhat anarchic nature of the Internet, and it is worth being circumspect about material when the provenance is uncertain. One option here is to route your search for resources through an organisation that has already vetted them. Commercial organisations such as Living Library (*http://livlib.eduweb.co.uk*) provide a substantial service, but on subscription.

Sites referred to in the text were current in July 2002.

Professional use of ICT:

a summary of key points

— *Using ICT appropriately as a tool for professional practice can improve your efficiency as a teacher as well as save you time!*

— *There are various ways in which you can use ICT to make sure that you keep yourself up to date professionally; however, you have access to a substantial range of useful material by researching current information via the Internet.*

Further reading

Freedman, T. (1998) IT and ICT in Educational Administration home page at *http://www. easyweb.easynet.co.uk/~etfreedman/tfcv.htm*. Last modified 26 April 2002, accessed 30 June 2002.

DfEE (2000) Cutting Burdens on Teachers at *http://www.dfes.gov.uk/cuttingburdens/*, accessed 30 June 2002.

In this chapter we shall examine some of the pragmatic consequences of having computers in your classroom.

Health and safety

Foremost among these practical implications is the consideration of health and safety that must apply to the use of computers and other aspects of ICT in schools. The Professional Standards for QTS (DfES 2002) demand that those qualifying to teach 'select and prepare resources, and plan for their safe and effective organisation' (3.1.3) and 'organise and manage the physical teaching space, tools, materials, texts and other resources safely and effectively' (3.1.8). The current health and safety legislation resides primarily in documents issued by the Health and Safety Executive (see Further Reading) but teachers need to think beyond the strictly legal to consider what constitutes good practice.

Room layout

Very few primary schools were designed from the outset to accommodate computers, and so in many cases the siting of equipment is at best a compromise with the overall physical arrangements of the classroom. The convention in the primary school until recently has been for computers to be dispersed around the school, usually one, two or possibly three to each classroom. Where they are positioned amongst the desks, tables, chairs, bookshelves and cupboards will to some extent be dictated by circumstances, but even so there are guidelines worth following. None of these is more than common sense, but they bear summarising.

It is important that the computer is positioned so that the monitor is **not subject to reflection**, either from artificial light or from sunshine. Not only is glare distracting, but it may also cause headaches and strain if users are subjected to it for long. The other area of the classroom to be **avoided**, for reasons of electrical safety, is a site near a **sink or other water supply**.

The computer should be as close to a **power supply** as possible. This will minimise confusion if anything goes wrong and the power has to be turned off quickly. More prosaically, but just as important, keeping the length of electrical flex to a minimum reduces proportionately the risk of someone tripping over it. If the cable supplied is too long, and an alternative of more appropriate length is unavailable, it is preferable to loop and tape or tie the surplus together (to minimise the build-up of a magnetic field the loop should not be too tight, and should not be close to the equipment for the same reason).

For convenience many schools have bought **trolleys** so that computers can be moved easily from room to room. These are fine, so long as they are designed well and have sufficient area for the 'footprint' of your equipment. The dimensions do merit checking, as trolleys may not have convenient workspace for overflow, especially if the expectation is for more than one child to be using the computer at any time. Again, attention must be paid to ensure that cable is not flapping loosely around the system.

The question of space often becomes even more acute in those schools that have decided to dedicate a room to an **ICT suite**. The challenge is to accommodate children and computers in a room that was in all likelihood only designed with children in mind. The result can be rows of computers arranged around the wall, with little space for writing or source materials – or a co-worker! Additionally, turning to face the teacher is hard for the children.

Possibly associated with a lack of space may be problems caused by **excessive heat and humidity**. Computers give off a significant amount of heat and fumes; especially if grouped together, consideration of improved ventilation may become important. Air conditioning would be ideal, but of course is very expensive. However, the whole process of designing and equipping a computer room is not a job for amateurs, and most schools now decide to bring in external contractors when contemplating this development.

Setting up the computer

Linking the components that make up a single computer system, one that is either new or has been dismantled for a move, is not difficult and there is no reason for a teacher to be disconcerted by this task. However, as with all electrical equipment, there is a potential hazard if care is not taken, and the obvious precaution is to ensure that the equipment is disconnected at the mains before making any adjustments to the cables that make up the system.

Computers in operation are not drawing much power from the mains, which means that a single computer, monitor and peripherals can share just one socket without problem. However, a gang, rather than a splitter (which is more likely to become dislodged if leads are accidentally bumped), should provide this access. Also, one gang per socket is the rule, and gangs should not be daisy-chained. In a room in which several stations are planned, professional advice should be sought. Both tidiness and safety will dictate that mains leads, and any data cables for networking, should be concealed in trunking, with as little flex as possible lying on the work surface.

The **mains lead** to the computer usually provides a kettle-type connection. This is usually effective and safe, as long as the lead has been pushed firmly home onto the projecting pins. Some monitors are provided with a lead with similar connections so that they can draw power from the computer. However, it is preferable for the monitor to have its own, separate, earthed plug into the gang or wall socket.

Data from the computer to the monitor is run through an **RGB cable**, RGB representing red, green and blue – the colours used to make up the picture on the screen.

RGB cables should come equipped with two retaining screws on each connector, which provide a secure link between the computer and monitor. Usually the cable has fifteen pin D-shaped connectors at either end, with the direction of the cable made obvious by the configuration of the pins.

The same is true for the connection of other **peripherals**. Computer manufacturers over the last few years have gone out of their way to make clear which device goes into which socket, often using colour coding to assist. The keyboard and mouse, which are standard input devices, usually have reserved sockets. However, these are essentially specialised versions of the serial port, discussed below, which is one of three types of socket by which a range of peripherals may be attached.

Printers used to be connected to the computer via the **parallel port** – sometimes called the printer port – which is a relatively large, D-shaped socket on the computer which takes 25 pins. Again, the two ends of the printer cable are distinctive and are unlikely to be confused. As with the monitor, manual screws usually secure the end with the pins to the computer. However, clips are used to hold the connection with the printer.

Equipment such as an external modem may be attached via a serial port, a smaller socket, again D-shaped but with only nine pins. Because of its use for modems, this port is often alternatively referred to as the COM (or communication) port. As always with the computer, connections to the serial port should be made or broken only when the power is off at the mains socket. The serial port itself may be damaged if connection or disconnection is made while the computer is switched on.

You will probably be using serial and parallel ports if your equipment is more than three or four years old. However, a third general type of socket was introduced a few years ago. Known as the **USB** (**Universal Serial Bus**) **port**, it is a more efficient alternative to the older ports and has largely replaced them for the connection of modems, printers, scanners and even the keyboard and mouse. One advantage of the USB port is that in contrast to the COM and parallel ports there is no risk of damage if a connection is made or broken even while the computer is running.

Other equipment may require its own hardware (as well as software) to be installed in the computer before it can work. Audio facilities such as amplified speakers or a microphone serve as examples. They are connected through a sound card that is usually located at the rear of the computer in what is known as a PCI (Peripheral Component Interconnect) slot. Although the likelihood is that a **sound card** has already been installed in a new computer, it represents just one instance of printed circuit boards you may wish to add to the computer to give it additional functionality. Another common case is when computers are networked and require the installation of a **NIC** (Network Interface Card) so that the links with other computers may be effected.

Occasionally the **installation of a new card** may demand specific links to be established or adjusted inside the computer in which case the manufacturer should provide appropriate instructions. The essential process, however, is as follows: the computer should be physically disconnected from the mains and the case opened. This should be a moment's work, sometimes not even requiring a screwdriver, but it is instructive to see the variety of case designs provided by different manufacturers. Blank plates at the back of the computer will cover spare PCI slots, and one of these should be removed. The card can then be pushed into place. On reconnecting and booting the computer, the operating systems from Windows 95 onwards should recognise that new hardware has been added and launch a series of instructions to help you install the software that will run it.

At its best, the process of installing new cards should be straightforward. However, as well as ensuring that the computer is disconnected from the mains when attempting this sort of work, it is also necessary to take care when handling cards as there is a risk of **static electricity** damaging the components. The risk can be minimised by using an earthed wristband, available quite cheaply from computer dealers. As an alternative, touch a central heating radiator before starting work, and regularly during it, in order to earth any charge. When handling the card, avoid touching the mounted components. It should be possible to install the card by holding it at the edges of the board and by the end plate.

All of the above makes the assumption that the equipment is sound and in good working order. Old or frayed leads must be replaced, and the teacher must be vigilant in watching for any accidental damage, such as cuts to plastic insulation or wear to plugs, that may have been sustained. If **repairs**, rather than connecting and setting up ICT equipment, are involved, then professional help should be sought.

Danger, children at work

Teachers must be clear that, while ultimate legal duty for health and safety in the classroom lies with employers, in practice they are responsible for the safe operation of computers in their classrooms. A cable that has not been correctly attached is a potential hazard and on a daily basis only the teacher is in a position to check this. For the same reason, none of the setting up discussed in the previous section should be delegated to primary age children. Apart from electrical safety, computer equipment is often heavy and should only be moved by an adult.

Yet children are going to be the main computer users in your classroom, and so need to know how to work efficiently and safely at the computer themselves. For older Key Stage 2 children this may extend to switching the computer on themselves, and perhaps even to switching on at the mains too. However, the teacher must be on hand to supervise either of these tasks.

If power to the monitor is organised from a separate socket then it is preferable to switch on the monitor (and other peripherals) before the computer to protect the latter from surge. Likewise, on finishing work, the computer should ideally be switched off before the peripherals. If work on the computer is to be resumed after a short while it is preferable not to switch it off, in order to minimise the cooling and reheating of components.

Good posture should be encouraged at the computer. Slouching, while generally unattractive and unhealthy, will also be detrimental to the relationship of the user's wrists with the keyboard. The lower arms should be held off the desk and be about horizontal. Children in the classroom are unlikely to be using a computer continuously long enough to be susceptible to repetitive strain injury, but if they can be encouraged to sit properly at the computer from early on it will stand them in good stead for the future. The relationship of the dimensions of the chair to the bench (or trolley) is clearly important here, but since even within a class there will be a considerable range of heights, an ergonomic chair with adjustable height and backrest is recommended. This will enable children to sit with their feet on the floor (or on a rest) and with their thighs parallel to the ground.

Computers in your classroom:

a summary of key points

There are many practical consequences of having computers in a classroom, some of which have been discussed briefly here.

As a teacher, you are responsible for the safe operation of computers in your classroom, and as such should be able to identify potential hazards in order to minimise risks. You may find it useful to read the excellent leaflet published by the Health and Safety Executive before making decisions about how to set up and use computers with your class.

Further reading

BECTa (2001a) *Health and safety: planning the safe installation of ICT in schools* information sheet. *http://www.becta.org.uk/technology/infosheets/html/safeinstall. html* (downloadable in text or pdf format), accessed 30 June 2002.

BECTa (2001a) *Health and safety: the safe use of ICT in schools* information sheet. *http:// www.becta.org.uk/technology/infosheets/html/safeuse.html* (downloadable in text or pdf format), accessed 30 June 2002.

Health and Safety Executive (1992) *Display Screen Equipment Work – Health and Safety (Display Screen Equipment) Regulations 1992*, HSE Books, PO Box 1999, Sudbury, Suffolk CO10 6FS (tel 01787 881165, fax 01787 313995).

Health and Safety Executive (1992) *The Manual Handling Operations Regulations 1992*, HSE Books, PO Box 1999, Sudbury, Suffolk CO10 6FS (tel 01787 881165, fax 01787 313995).

Health and Safety Executive (1998) *Working with VDUs*, downloadable leaflet from the Health and Safety Executive website *http://www.hse.gov.uk/pubns/vduindex.htm*, accessed 30 June 2002.

The rapid development of information and communications technology over the last few years has presented a range of new social and legal challenges. Some of the ethical questions that are raised have already been considered in the chapter on the Internet. However, the innovatory opportunities for learning, working and leisure presented by ICT have further consequences for the legal framework in which they operate, and the rapid pace of change has added an additional layer of complexity to these tangled arrangements.

 For further information on Internet safety and copyright, see pages 105, 111 and 119, Chapter 5

This chapter intends to provide an awareness of some of the issues involved. However, it is not intended to be a comprehensive guide, and if you have a concern over a particular circumstance in which the legitimacy of an action might be debated, it would be sensible for you to seek further advice, perhaps from the LEA or an appropriate professional body.

Copyright

Even before the advent of computers, the question of copyright was a vexed one for schools. The current legislation in the United Kingdom is, though, unequivocal and thorough. It applies to anything published (including text and artistic production, which might itself be literary, musical, graphic or dramatic in nature). It extends, too, to other technological media apart from computers such as films, audio and televised pro-grammes. In short, the likelihood is that anything you might want to copy is covered by the legislation. As a teacher you will want to ensure that your own position with regard to copyright is sound, and recognise that, in this area of moral behaviour as in others, you are a role model for the children in your class.

Some of the confusion over copyright for schools may originate in the concept of 'fair dealing' which is embodied in the Copyright, Designs and Patents Act 1988 (this Act still forms the basis of legislation in this country, though its impact has been modified by EU harmonisation). BECTa's helpful paper (BECTa, 2001b) summarises this idea suc-cinctly:

'Fair dealing permits certain acts without requiring the permission of the copyright holder. These include what is reasonable for private study and research. Making multiple copies for classroom use has been established as being outside these definitions.'

The inference is clear. Educational institutions are not in any way exempt from copy-right legislation. However, many schools and colleges have paid a fee to the Copyright Licensing Agency (CLA). This provides limited rights to make copies of some copyright material. Copying is restricted to works published by organisations that have joined the scheme, but this in fact covers most British publishers (a major exception, however, is printed music). More restrictive, however, is the scope of the CLA scheme in applying only to printed material. The exact allowance for copying (usually photocopying) differs between institutions and has been varied in recent years; it would be sensible to check your school's current agreement to ascertain precisely what is permitted.

If we switch our focus more particularly to ICT the same principles apply. In practice, a computer program should be regarded as a literary work, with its authors and distributors enjoying the same rights and privileges as if they had produced a book. Software publishers are usually very careful to stipulate what the purchaser has bought. In general, buying software only gains title to a licence to install and use the software, not to the software itself. The text of the licence will give details about how many copies of the software may be made. The starting point is that only one will be allowed, in order that data may be transferred to a computer's hard disk. However, it is often possible to buy at economic rates licences to cover a whole site, or multiple stations within a purchasing institution.

Teachers have an obligation to ensure that software-licensing conditions are not breached in their school. In some circles the conditions under which software has been purchased are broken with the excuse that additional, illegal copies are not hurting anyone because the transmission is electronic; no physical material is appropriated. However, the disk and packaging are negligible elements of the software bundle. What is at stake is the author's intellectual property, and an unauthorised copy represents its theft. Apart from the ethical argument against software theft, there is also the highly pragmatic consideration that, especially amongst smaller educational publishers, loss of revenue will jeopardise future development of material.

Several organisations are involved in monitoring the use of software to ensure that breaches of copyright are avoided. Foremost of these in the United Kingdom is the Federation Against Software Theft (FAST), which has its website at *http://www.fast.org.uk*. FAST do not simply act to police software use – they are a valuable source of advice and support to computer users.

The Internet poses considerable challenges to the enforcement of copyright law, not least in the difficulty of monitoring all the material that is held, and is available for download. Nevertheless, copyright laws do apply. Even if copyright ownership is not declared, it should be reckoned as applicable, unless its rightful owner has explicitly placed the material in the public domain.

Teachers will need to determine how best to introduce children to the concept of copyright. While this is a more urgent question in secondary schools, the increase in computer use, particularly at home, by primary age children means that plagiarism from the Internet or CD ROM may well arise in your classroom. While it is unlikely to be appropriate to introduce a formal system of referencing to young children, spending time to explain why sources should be acknowledged will only be to their long-term benefit.

Data protection

Teachers and schools need to know of their obligations regarding data confidentiality. These duties are enshrined in data protection legislation. In essence this dates back to the Data Protection Act of 1984, which was introduced in response to growing concern about the impact of advancing computer technology on personal privacy. Considering its vintage, it was far-sighted, providing both rights for individuals and a demand on organisations (or individuals) who held and used personal information to adopt responsible practices, even for data such as names and addresses, which might not be considered to be particularly sensitive.

Ironically the Act was limited to information held on computer, which exempted data records held by 'traditional' methods on hard copy. Another difficulty with the 1984 Act, which perhaps could not be foreseen, was that the growing internationalisation of computer use through the Internet would facilitate unscrupulous transfer of data to locations outside UK jurisdiction. Partly to improve the regulations in these areas, but also partly in response to an EU directive issued in September 1990 aimed at harmonising legislation across the member states, the 1984 Act has recently been replaced by a revision. Formulated in 1998, the new Act took effect in March 2000.

Like the original Act, the current legislation is based on eight principles. The detail of these have been rearranged from the earlier requirements, primarily to accommodate the new eighth principle. The list has been summarised by the Data Protection Commissioner as follows:

Anyone processing personal data must comply with the eight enforceable principles of good practice. They say that data must be:

- **fairly and lawfully processed;**
- **processed for limited purposes;**
- **adequate, relevant and not excessive;**
- **accurate;**
- **not kept longer than necessary;**
- **processed in accordance with the data subject's rights;**
- **secure;**
- **not transferred to countries without adequate protection.**

(DPC, 2000)

There remain exemptions to the Act. These include personal data held in connection with domestic or recreational matters and personal data that the law requires the user to make public, such as the electoral register. On the other hand, the principles provide for individuals to be able to access data held about themselves, and to insist on the data being corrected if it is erroneous.

Ethical and legal issues:

a summary of key points

There are ethical and legal issues involved when using ICT in your teaching. As a teacher, you will want to ensure that you have a firm grasp of the legal framework governing these issues so that you feel confident of your and your school's obligations with regard to them.

Even if you are not the school's ICT co-ordinator the likelihood is that at some point you will be involved in decisions to purchase software. You may be responsible for another subject area, or for a year group or Key Stage, and will have expertise to offer in determining the sort of material that will enable you and colleagues to meet the objectives that you have set out in schemes of work. Choosing the right software has significant budgetary implications, particularly if your school has a computer suite for which you will need to buy a site or multiple-user licence. It is important, then, that the conclusion you reach is based on sound criteria that you have established in advance. In this chapter we will review some of the considerations that will inform your judgement.

Thinking about purpose

A useful broad distinction may be made between 'generic' and 'content-rich' software. Generic software is 'general purpose', and includes applications such as word processors, desktop publishing packages, and software for graphics and data-handling. These applications share the attribute of being void of content at the outset. It is for the user to prepare something from a blank page, and so involvement may be considered essentially creative in nature. The software is open-ended in terms of the achievable outcomes, and process represents a major aspect of its use (which, incidentally, should sound a warning against assessing children's capability solely by outcome). The packages are free of context, and in consequence have wide relevance across the curriculum. Nor, in the school environment, are generic applications bound closely to an age range. While across the full primary Key Stages there is a strong argument for introducing technically more challenging software to older children, a well-chosen generic application will provide interest and motivation across several year groups. As they gain confidence and capability with the software, the children will become progressively more demanding and explorative of the functions that are offered.

Content-rich software, by contrast, will be tied much more closely both to an age range and to a subject. Typical examples are CD ROMs for, say, history (such as Granada's *How We Used to Live* series) or for general use, including multimedia encyclopaedias. These serve two very important purposes: they should be the source of exciting, interesting and relevant knowledge in a range of multimedia formats and they should support the development of children's research skills. However, there are limitations. If a school buys the *How We Used to Live* 'Late Victorians' title, for example, it will have an excellent resource available, but one which only has sustained use for one class in one subject during the year.

There is, though, no rigid polarity between these two broad categories. Many educational CD ROMs now incorporate programs that enable children actively to construct their own notebooks or research records. Furthermore, some software falls between the two definitions that we have suggested. There are music applications (RM's *Compose World* is an example) and some graphics and design packages (*Spex+* and some of the *My World* screens are illustrations) which are linked closely to specific subjects but which are nevertheless characterised by the creative nature of their use. The empty stave of a music composition application is filled with notes. Symbols populate the *My World* screen. We have here instances in which the open-ended spirit of generic software has been successfully channelled to meet the specialist demands of a subject area.

Setting criteria

With an understanding of the general types of software that we might buy for school, we now need to look at some specific criteria. The key point here is not, particularly, to accept anyone else's view of what it is important to look for – and that includes the comments that follow – but to ensure that you have established clearly what factors will be critical in making *your* choice.

The following pointers may be helpful, but they clearly will not apply universally to all software purchasing decisions and will have to be tailored accordingly.

Purpose

- **Does the rationale for the software coincide with your learning objectives?**

Where content is involved this should be relatively easy to decide, and in all likelihood is embodied in the title, as in the history example given above. The task will be to assess the quality of the content, which we will consider in the next section.

The answer in the case of generic software, which you will be using in a variety of curriculum areas but also to develop children's ICT skills, is subtler. Data-handling packages, in particular, vary considerably in sophistication. A helpful response to this need for a range of functionality in generic software has been provided by RM in their *Window Box* solutions in which the user sets a level of functionality according to capability and need.

The popular titles of generic software, some of which have been noted elsewhere in this book, have generally deserved their success through meeting classroom needs. Colleagues in your school and cluster, and the advisory staff at your LEA, are a valuable source of judgement on the effectiveness of particular titles that you may be considering.

Authenticity and provenance

When choosing software essentially for its content some assessment of that subject matter must be made.

- **Is the material valuable in the context of your classroom?**
- **Are you able to rely on the accuracy of the information it contains?**
- **Has the publisher already a reputation for producing high quality educational titles?**

As with books, be wary of inappropriate bias. For example, some multimedia encyclo-paedias have been prepared with primarily the American market in view, and their content reflects this interest. Potentially more serious is the risk of buying a CD ROM in which there is an attempt to convey an overt or subliminal message of intolerance of alternative beliefs and values.

Relevance to the curriculum

While the declared purpose of content-rich software may appear appropriate, you will need to dig a little deeper to establish whether it really meets your needs. There are a number of considerations to bear in mind.

- **Has the software been designed for school use?**

The high resource demands involved in the production of multimedia software are making it progressively more difficult for publishers to offer titles just for school use. Home purchase by parents may also be important to the positioning of the product, which in turn may mean that links to the National Curriculum are not paramount.

- **Is the right quantity of information provided?**

While you may judge that the contents of a CD ROM appear to match your require-ments, it is worth checking that the quantity of information provided is appropriate. Some multimedia encyclopaedias, for example, have scant information on many topics that are important in the National Curriculum. There is also a judgement to be made on the balance of multimedia elements involved. In some cases, though the text may not be quite right for your class in terms of reading age, there may nevertheless be a benefit from the graphics, audio and video clips – and you may find the text useful for your lesson planning!

- **What was the date of publication?**

The 2000 introduction of a revised National Curriculum, and changes made in the last few years to the teaching of literacy and numeracy, have rendered some software obsolete. Equally, a number of software houses have a history of responding inventively to such developments and have produced titles that genuinely support the introduction of new initiatives.

This is not to say that older software should be discounted. Many practitioners with long experience in ICT in education will point to earlier material that is still the best available for the specific learning objectives that it serves. Everyone will have their own favourites; *Podd* and 4Mation's *Granny's Garden* come to mind. At the same time, children are growing up in a world of increasing technological sophistication, in which – for better or worse – the quality of presentation is valued. It is futile to hope that they will not be deprecating about poor graphics or sound support even if the teaching point is well made.

Interface and navigation

A great deal has been learned and developed in the sphere of software design in the last twenty years, and we should expect the interface and navigation of educational material to reflect this progress. There are a number of points to assess:

• **Is the interface intuitive?**

Buttons and menus usually initiate operations in software. Even for adult users these should be made as obvious as possible, but for children it is essential that their meaning is clear and that confidence and independence in the use of the software should be possible. Usually buttons (and sometimes menus) are signified by icons as well as by text, and it is helpful that standard symbols are being used for common operations such as saving and cut, copy and paste.

• **How is the information organised?**

While generic software generally uses just a handful of windows, effective navigation through a content-rich CD ROM demands that the material be structured effectively. There may be alternative pathways through the available topics, and alternative ways of organising them on screen. This is fine, as long as they are not confusing. A clear contents page, and an index too, should be expected.

If the software is a resource for incorporation into the children's work, then facilities for retrieval, including printing, copying and pasting, should be available.

Teacher support

Teachers are busy people, and need to be able to understand and see how to utilise software as quickly as possible. The best publishers of educational material recognise this pressure and provide support to ensure that their product can be used efficiently.

• **Is the manual helpful?**

Computer manuals formerly were a source of derision, but enlightened publishers have worked to make them accessible to the lay reader. If they are less than readable it may be that there has been a disregard for the needs of the user which is more pervasive through the package than in the manual alone.

• **Is on-screen help built into the software?**

Children are often loath to use a help menu, but it can be an invaluable ready reference to their teacher! Some applications now have context-sensitive help, whereby different areas of the screen are hot-linked to relevant comments in the help index.

• **Does the software have a teacher's page?**

While requirements will vary according to the software, it is reassuring to find a teacher's page provided. This may allow for modification of the configuration of the software (e.g. turning the sound on or off) or for recording children's access to different aspects of the software and their achievement in its use. Some integrated learning systems, such as RM's *Success Maker*, have developed the teacher's page concept to an art form, providing highly detailed feedback about a child's progress.

• **What other support is provided?**

Apart from providing the technical details necessary for installation and use of the software, the manual, or supplementary material, should also provide curriculum support. This may range from links to the National Curriculum and suggestions for contexts in which to use the software to worksheets providing activities in conjunction with what the children see on screen.

Choosing software:

a summary of key points

The list above is by no means exhaustive and it is likely that you have thought of other factors that will be relevant and important to you – such as your budget! However, the message of this chapter is that there are many considerations involved in software evaluation; your decision will be sound if you have identified them in advance.

As a final thought, you may be able to preview software prior to purchase. A number of educational software suppliers are prepared to let schools have an inspection copy for evaluation for a limited period prior to purchase. This is sound marketing on their part – depending to some extent on inertia in order to make a sale. However, if the material doesn't stand up to scrutiny you will be able to return it. Most of the leading suppliers are represented at venues such as BETT and the Education Show which provide you with the opportunity to quiz them about their products.

Please note that every care has been taken in the listing of website addresses. The addresses included in this book are current at the time of going to press, although the dynamic nature of the World Wide Web means that inevitably some of these will move and change.

Abbott, C. (1998) New writers, new audiences, new responses, in Monteith, M. (ed.) *IT for Learning Enhancement*, Intellect Books.

Aldrich, F., Rogers, Y. and Scaife, M. (1998) Getting to grips with 'interactivity': helping teachers assess the educational value of CD ROMs, *British Journal of Educational Technology*, September.

BECTa (2001a) *Health and Safety: the Safe use of ICT in Schools* advice sheet, *http://www.becta.org. uk/technology/infosheets/general.html*.

BECTa (2001b) *Copyright Involving Electronic Materials: Advice and Issues for Schools* advice sheet, *http://www.becta.org.uk/technology/infosheets/html/copyright. html*

Cook, D. and Finlayson, H. (1999) *Interactive Children, Communicative Teaching: ICT and Classroom Teaching*, Open University Press.

Cooper, P. and McIntyre, D. (1996) *Effective Teaching and Learning: Teachers' and Students' Perspectives*, Open University Press.

Cox, M., Preston, C. and Cox, K. (2000) *Teachers as Innovators: An Evaluation of the Motivation of Teachers to Use Information and Communications Technologies*, Mirandanet/TTA.

Crook, C. (1996) *Computers and the Collaborative Experience of Learning*, Routledge.

DfEE (1995) *Information Technology in the National Curriculum*, HMSO.

DfEE (1997) *Connecting the Learning Society*, DfEE.

DfEE (1998b) *The National Literacy Strategy*, DfEE.

DfEE (1999) *The National Numeracy Strategy*, DfEE.

DfEE (2000) *Information Technology in Maintained Primary and Secondary Schools in England: 1999*, DfEE.

DfEE/QCA (1999) *The National Curriculum: Handbook for Primary Teachers in England*, DfEE/QCA.

DPC (Data Protection Commissioner) (2000) *Data Protection Principles*, *http://www.dataprotection.gov.uk/principl.htm* dated 26th June 2000. Details of the principles may be downloaded in text or pdf format from this site.

Fisher, E. (1997) Children's talk and computer software, in Wegerif, R. and Scrimshaw, P. (eds) (1997) *Computers and Talk in the Primary Classroom*, Multilingual Matters.

Fox, B., Montague-Smith, A. and Wilkes, S. (2000) *Using ICT in Primary Mathematics: Practice and Possibilities*, David Fulton.

Goldstein, G. (2000) ICT – Where have we got to, where are we going? Talk given to 'Educating for the Third Millennium' conference, Cheltenham, July 2000.

HMI/OFTSED (2000) *The Teaching of Writing: Could Do Better*, OFSTED publications.

Kyriacou, C. (1997) *Effective Teaching in Schools*, Stanley Thornes.

Leask, M. and Meadows, J. (eds) (2000) *Teaching and Learning with ICT in the Primary School*, Routledge.

Lie, K., O'Hare, A. and Denwood, S. (2000) Multidisciplinary support and the management of children with specific writing difficulties, *British Journal of Special Education*, 27(2) June.

Lopuck, L. (1996) *Designing Multimedia*, Peackpit Press.

Loveless, A. (1997) Working with images, developing ideas, in A. McFarlane (ed.) (1997) *Information Technology and Authentic Learning*, Routledge.

McFarlane, A. (ed.) (1997) *Information Technology and Authentic Learning: Realising the Potential of Computers in the Primary School*, Routledge.

Meadows, J. (1999) Primary schools and the National Grid for Learning. Paper presented at British Education Research Association Conference, August.

Mercer, N. and Fisher, E. (1997) The importance of talk, in Wegerif, R. and Scrimshaw, P. (eds) *Computers and Talk in the Primary Classroom*, Multilingual Matters.

Moseley, D., Higgins, S. *et al.* (1999) *Ways Forward with ICT: Effective Pedagogy using Information and Communications Technology in Literacy and Numeracy in Primary Schools*, Newcastle University.

NCET (1996) *A Report on Phase II of the Pilot Evaluation of ILS in the UK*, NCET.

OFSTED (2000) *Annual Report Of Her Majesty's Chief Inspector of Schools – Standards and Quality In Education 1998/99*, OFSTED publications.

Phillips, R. J. (1997) Can juniors read graphs? A review and analysis of some computer-based activities, *Journal of Information Technology for Teacher Education*, 6(1), 49-58.

Potter J. and Mellar, H. (2000) Identifying teachers' Internet training needs, *Journal of Information Technology for Teacher Education*, 9(1).

QCA (1998) *Information Technology: A Scheme of Work for Key Stages 1 and 2*, DfEE/QCA

QCA (2000a) *Information and Communications Technology: Update to the IT Scheme of Work*, DfEE/QCA.

QCA (2000b) *Curriculum Guidance for the Foundation Stage*, QCA.

Rogers, Y. and Aldrich, F. (1996) In search of clickable Dons: learning about HCI through interacting with Norman's CD ROM, *SigCHI Bulletin*, 28(3), 44–7.

Rogers, Y. and Scaife, M. (1998) How can Interactive Multimedia facilitate learning, at *http://www.cogs.susx.ac.uk/users/yvonner/ecolihome/IMMI.html*

Sharp, P. (1995) *Computer Assisted Learning to Develop Literacy Skills: a Manual for Learning Support Assistants*, Hampshire CC/Hampshire Educational Psychology Service.

Smidt, S. (1998) *A Guide to Early Years Practice*, Routledge.

Smith, H. (1999) *Opportunities for ICT in the Primary School*, Trentham Books.

Somekh, B. and Davis, N. (eds) (1997) *Using Information Technology Effectively in Teaching and Learning: Studies in Pre-service and In-service Teacher Education*, Routledge.

Steadman, S., Nash, C. and Erault, M. (1992) *CD ROM in Schools Scheme: Evaluation Report*, NCET.

Stevenson, D. *et al.* (1997) *Information and Communications Technology in UK Schools: An Independent Enquiry*, ICT in Schools Commission.

TTA (1999a) *Ways Forward with ICT: Effective Pedagogy using Information and Communications Technology in Literacy and Numeracy in Primary Schools: Summary of Findings and Illustrations of Teacher Development*, TTA.

TTA (1999d) *Using ICT to Meet Teaching Objectives in English*, TTA.

TTA/DfES (2002) *Qualifying to Teach: Professional Standards for Qualified Teacher Status and Requirements for Initial Teacher Training*, TTA.

TTA/DfES (2002a) *Guidance on the Requirements for Initial Teacher Training*, TTA.

TTA/DfES (2002b) *Guidance on the Standards for Qualified Teacher Status*, TTA.

Tunstall, P. and Gipps, C. (1996) Teacher feedback to young children in formative assessment, *British Educational Research Journal*, 22(4).

Wegerif, R. (1997) Children's talk and computer software: a response to Fisher, in Wegerif, R. and Scrimshaw, P. (eds) (1997) *Computers and Talk in the Primary Classroom*, Multilingual Matters.

Wood, D. (1997) *How Children Think and Learn*, Blackwell.

Clicker
Crick Software Ltd
35 Charter Gate, Quarry Park Close, Moulton Park, Northampton NN3 6QB
01604 671691
http://www.cricksoft.com

Counting Pictures, Counter, CounterPlus
BlackCat Educational Software
Granada Learning, Granada Television, Quay Street, Manchester M60 9EA
0161 827 2927
http://www.blackcatsoftware.com

Dazzle
Granada Learning, Granada Television, Quay Street, Manchester M60 9EA
0161 827 2927
http://www.granada-learning.com

Excel
Microsoft
http://www.microsoft.com

FlexiTREE
Flexible Software
PO Box 100
Abingdon
OX13 6PQ
http://www.flexible.co.uk

Frontpage Express
Microsoft
http://www.microsoft.com

Internet Explorer
Microsoft
http://www.microsoft.com

Junior Insight
Longman Logotron
124 Science Park, Milton Road, Cambridge CB4 4ZS
01223 425558
http://www.logo.com

Junior PinPoint
Longman Logotron
124 Science Park, Milton Road, Cambridge CB4 4ZS
01223 425558
http://www.logo.com

Musical Instruments
Microsoft
http://www.microsoft.com

My First Amazing Incredible Dictionary; My Ultimate Human Body
Dorling Kindersley
9 Henrietta Street, Covent Garden, London WC2E 8PS
020 7836 5411
http://www.dk.com

Netscape
http://www.netscape.com

NumberMagic
RM plc
New Mill House, Milton Park, Abingdon OX14 4SE
01235 826000
http://www.rm.com

PickaPicture
BlackCat Educational Software
Granada Learning, Granada Television, Quay Street, Manchester M60 9EA
0161 827 2927
http://www.blackcatsoftware.com

Sherston's Primary Clipart
Sherston Software
Angel House, Sherston, Malmesbury SN16 0LH
01666 840433
http://www.sherston.com

Pictogram and DataPlot
Kudlian Soft
Nunhold Business Centre, Dark Lane, Hatton, Warwickshre CV35 8XB
01926 842544
http://www.kudlian.demon.co.uk

Splosh
Kudlian Soft
Nunhold Business Centre, Dark Lane, Hatton, Warwickshre CV35 8XB
01926 842544
http://www.kudlian.demon.co.uk

Talking First Word
RM plc
New Mill House, Milton Park, Abingdon OX14 4SE
01235 826000
http://www.rm.com

Talking Write Away
BlackCat Educational Software
Granada Learning, Granada Television, Quay Street, Manchester M60 9EA
0161 827 2927
http://www.blackcatsoftware.com

Textease
Softease Ltd
Market Place, Ashbourne, Derbyshire DE6 1ES
01335 34342
http://www.textease.com

Word
Microsoft
http://www.microsoft.com

Achieving QTS

The Achieving QTS series now includes over 20 titles, encompassing *Audit and Test*, *Knowledge and Understanding*, *Teaching Theory and Practice* and *Skills Tests* titles. The series also has two sub-series – the *Reflective Readers* and the *Practical Handbooks*. As well as covering the core primary subject areas, the series addresses issues of teaching and learning, and of theory and practice, across both primary curriculum and secondary phases. You can find more information on each of these titles on our website: www.learningmatters.co.uk

Assessment for Learning and Teaching in Primary Schools
Mary Briggs, Peter Swatton, Cynthia Martin and Angela Woodfield
176pp   ISBN: 1 903300 74 6

Primary English
Audit and Test (second edition)
Doreen Challen
64pp   ISBN: 1 903300 86 X

Primary Mathematics
Audit and Test (second edition)
Claire Mooney and Mike Fletcher
52pp   ISBN: 1 903300 87 8

Primary Science
Audit and Test (second edition)
John Sharp and Jenny Byrne
80pp   ISBN: 1 903300 88 6

Learning and Teaching in Secondary Schools (second edition)
Edited by Viv Ellis
176pp   ISBN: 1 84445 004 X

Passing the ICT Skills Test (second edition)
Clive Ferrigan
80pp   ISBN: 1 84445 028 7

Passing the Literacy Skills Test
Jim Johnson
80pp   ISBN: 1 903300 12 6

Passing the Numeracy Skills Test (third edition)
Mark Patmore
64pp   ISBN: 1 903300 94 0

Primary English: Knowledge and Understanding (second edition)
David Wray, Jane Medwell, George Moore and Vivienne Griffiths
224pp   ISBN: 1 903300 53 3

Primary English: Teaching Theory and Practice (second edition)
David Wray, Jane Medwell, Hilary Minns, Elizabeth Coates and Vivienne Griffiths
192pp   ISBN: 1 903300 54 1

Primary ICT: Knowledge, Understanding and Practice (second edition)
Jane Sharp, Avril Loveless, John Potter and Jonathan Allen
256pp   ISBN: 1 903300 59 2

Primary Mathematics: Knowledge and Understanding (second edition)
Claire Mooney, Lindsey Ferrie, Sue Fox, Alice Hansen and Reg Wrathmell
176pp   ISBN: 1 903300 55 X

Primary Mathematics: Teaching Theory and Practice (second edition)
Claire Mooney, Mike Fletcher, Mary Briggs and Judith McCullouch
192pp   ISBN: 1 903300 56 8

Primary Science: Knowledge and Understanding (second edition)
Rob Johnsey, John Sharp, Graham Peacock and Debbie Wright
232pp   ISBN: 1 903300 57 6

Primary Science: Teaching Theory and Practice (second edition)
John Sharp, Graham Peacock, Rob Johnsey, Shirley Simon and Robin Smith
140pp   ISBN: 1 903300 58 4

Professional Studies: Primary Phase (second edition)
Kate Jacques and Rob Hyland
224pp   ISBN: 1 903300 60 6

Teaching Arts in Primary Schools
Stephanie Penny, Susan Young, Raywen Ford and Lawry Price
192pp   ISBN: 1 903300 35 5

Teaching Citizenship in Primary Schools
Hilary Claire
160pp   ISBN: 1 84445 010 4

Teaching Foundation Stage
Edited by Iris Keating
200pp   ISBN: 1 903300 33 9

Teaching Humanities in Primary Schools
Pat Hoodless, Sue Bermingham, Elaine McCreery and Paul Bowen
192pp   ISBN: 1 903300 36 3

ACHIEVING QTS: REFLECTIVE READERS

Reflective Reader: Primary Professional Studies
Sue Kendall-Seatter
160pp   ISBN: 1 84445 033 3

Reflective Reader: Secondary Professional Studies
Simon Hoult
160pp   ISBN: 1 84445 034 1

Reflective Reader: Primary English
Andrew Lambirth
128pp   ISBN: 1 84445 035 X

Reflective Reader: Primary Mathematics
Louise O'Sullivan, Andrew Harris, Margaret Sangster, Jon Wild, Gina Donaldson and Gill Bottle
128pp   ISBN: 1 84445 036 8

Reflective Reader: Primary Science
Judith Roden
128pp   ISBN: 1 84445 037 6

Reflective Reader: Primary Special Educational Needs
Sue Soan
128pp   ISBN: 1 84445 038 4

ACHIEVING QTS: PRACTICAL HANDBOOKS

Successful Teaching Placement: Primary and Early Years
Jane Medwell
128pp   ISBN: 1 903300 92 4

To order please phone our order line 0845 230 9000 or send an official order or cheque to
BEBC, **Albion Close, Parkstone, Poole, BH12 3LL**
Order online at www.learningmatters.co.uk